I0816100

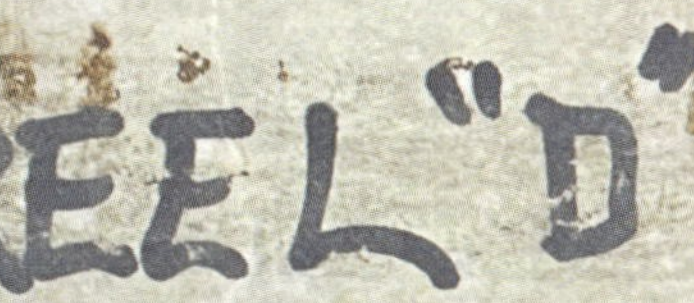
DOORS
XFER
TO
GTRK
W/ O.D.s
UNKNOWN
REEL "D"
SAFE PLACE
6-1-92-26

the
DOORS
SPARES
OUT-TAKES
&
ALTERNATE
VERSIONS
4th L.P.
DOLBY 301 STRETCHED
BONDED ARCHIVES
1297818
75005
DOO-
887
-152-

QUEEN OF THE HIGHWAY
A SAFE PLACE
Loc. #

DOORS
JANUARY
1970
MONEY
Roadhouse
MASTER

BEKINS
ACCOUNT #
BEKINS #
MASTERS
3
74024

Night Divides the Day

By The Doors

DO NOT DROP
FRAGILE
HANDLE CAREFULLY
CONTINENTAL AIRLINES
FRAGILE
THE DOORS
CASE
THE DOORS
FRAGILE

Night Divides the Day

By The Doors

GENESIS PUBLICATIONS SINCE 1974

ISBN: 978-1-905662-89-0
Printed in Malaysia

Genesis Publications Ltd
Genesis House
2 Jenner Road, Guildford
Surrey, England, GU1 3PL

www.genesis-publications.com

Friendly strangers came
To town
Every body put them down
But the women loved
Their ways
Come again some other
day
like the gentle rain
Like the gentle rain
That falls
& we all fall down (3)

FOREWORD
Krist Novoselic

In 1979, I was 14 years old and discovering a lot of music. Eight years after The Doors effectively ended, I was part of a new generation of fans.

In 1980, my parents sent me to live with relatives in Croatia, which was then part of Yugoslavia. Zadar is an ancient city on the Adriatic Sea. While I was there, I continued to discover new music – Yugo-Rock bands and a lot of sounds coming from London at the time.

There was an older cohort in town, fanatically into The Doors. I did not associate with these people, mostly because they smoked hash, and that was out of my league. These were the kind of dedicated people who could make the pilgrimage to Paris and visit the grave of Jim Morrison. In fact, for many years there was a Morrison bust on the trashed grave that had been sculpted by a Yugoslavian fan. Just as it all of a sudden appeared, the tribute bust eventually vanished.

I too am dedicated to The Doors. I love the way their music synthesises rock with the esoteric. The band grooves, but in a way that hangs in the ancient gallery. There is gravitas, magic, but also grit. It's the Hollywood bungalow with that freeway soot which seems to cover everyplace in LA. It's like hanging out at the beach at the evening golden hour. Not to swim or get a tan, but fully clothed, with your shoes on in the sand, taking the last gulp from a can of beer, before walking east to a Venice dive bar. Because if we do not find that next whisky bar ...

Let it roll, baby roll, at the bar counter. We then step outside into the late night, feel and smell the ocean air to catch the full moon above us. Let's swim to the moon as traffic moves on the boulevard in the city tonight. The night progresses, and we get to the end of our elaborate plans, the end, my friend.

However ... eternity has no end. The scream of the butterfly is the chrysalis, the transformation. The Doors are not just a band, or rock music – we find an apotheosis. I witnessed this as a teenager.

I know about this phenomenon. Nirvana has also captured the collective imagination in such a way. It must be about intense lead singers who left us at the age of 27. There is a lot more too, and this book offers insight into the music Jim Morrison, Robby Krieger, John Densmore and Ray Manzarek created together.

New generations of fans connect with the music. I know. I have been listening to The Doors for almost my whole life.

Who knows the guys in a group better than their manager? He works with them, knows their secrets and their worries and often practically lives with them. With this in mind, we asked the Doors' manager, Bill Siddons, to give us a glimpse of what the Doors are really like. Here's his rushed reply as he was just bounding out the door with the Doors to catch a plane for England.

SPEAKING OUT, THEIR MANAGER, BILL SIDDONS...

OPENS THE DOORS!

JOHN DENSMORE — "John's the leprechaun of the group. He really is, as a matter of fact. He plays the most consistently of anyone — I've never heard him play a bad set. A good person, bright, laughing all the time, and a very serious meditator like Robby, which they've both been for a couple of years now. Which of course Jim has told me not to tell anyone 'cause it destroys our image. That's basically John. He went and bought a VW camper 'cause he likes to go back to nature, and it's better than the little sports car which he got too many tickets in. John and Robby both just returned from a meditation retreat in the hills of the high Sierras."

ROBBY KRIEGER—"Robby's the mysterious one of the group, believe it or not, and musically he's the most inconsistant. Sometimes, like at the Hollywood Bowl, he's terrible, other times he's just the best I've ever heard. On the records he always manages to come out right though. His soul is just unbelievable sometimes. He's a hardnosed businessman—his background comes out real strong—he's a pretty good dealer. And he seems to manage to have a few girl friends."

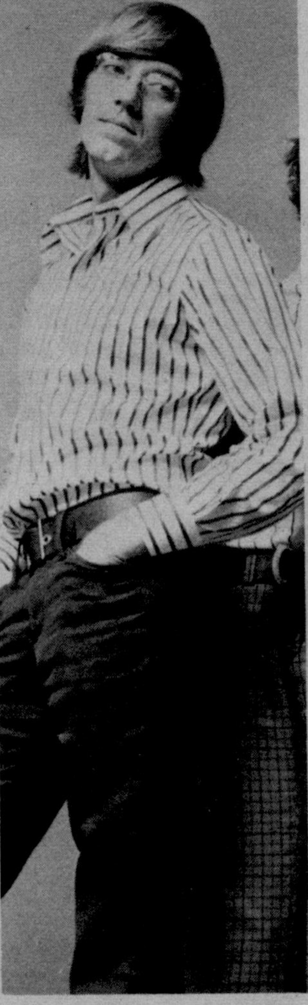

RAY MANZAREK — "Raymond is the married man of the group. He likes being married and does all that kind of stuff. He fits his image perfectly, wears his clothes correctly, his little suits that are just a little far out. He has a lovely Japanese wife and a little house in Hollywood which he's been spending months and months fixing up. He's having great fun being a homey person. Ray's really relaxed and at peace with himself, I think. He always has been. He's been the one that never had any real conflicts. He seems to know what's happening pretty much."

JIM MORRISON — "One of the better people I know, believe it or not. I don't want to ruin his image but he's really a good person. As much as I'd like to say he's a snake in the grass and all that, he only is sometimes. Most of the time Jim's the most human of the group. He has both the good and bad sides of it, in the sense that he has feelings and he also has a lot of the human frailties. The funny things about Jim is that his performance as a performance is toning down generally and his singing is getting better all the time. Jim goes through a lot of stages, though. He does a lot of developing and a lot of figuring out what he's doing. He used to have a lot of little demons inside him and he'd go up on stage and work 'em out, but I don't think he has so many any more. He's still the performer of the group, of course. He's the one that gets up there and works, really works. He's the hardest to get to, a very inner person. He's not really shy, just very hard to make contact with. Jim will always be a mystery."

INTRODUCTION

The Doors. Two simple words that bring forth a flurry of emotion in millions of us. If you know, you know. If you don't, we'll get you there.

It all starts with the music. That's the bait that hooks us. The instant we hear it, it activates a part of our brains that we didn't know existed until that moment. It changes our lives from that point on. At that moment, some move on with their lives like nothing happened. But not us!

After our newly rewired brains settle down, we eventually realise there is so much more to The Doors than just the music. There are a thousand different tributaries you can travel from there. Most start with Jim Morrison, the misunderstood poet; the Lizard King; the psychedelic Shaman, Dionysus; Jimbo, the raging alcoholic. And once you get yourself past the Jim obsession, you realise there are three other sides of the diamond: Ray Manzarek, the stoic keyboardist from Chicago who could split his brain in two, playing piano bass with his left hand and organ with his right. Robby Krieger, the surfer from Pacific Palisades whose flamenco guitar background, slide guitar playing, and prolific hit-writing were an irreplaceable piece of the puzzle. And John Densmore, the jazz-drumming student of the Maharishi, who, with a flurry of drumbeats, could take Jim Morrison to a different plane while performing on stage.

It turns into a lifetime of exploration, contemplation, and sometimes imitation.

And back to the music, starting with the hits: 'Light My Fire', 'Hello, I Love You', 'Touch Me', 'Love Her Madly', the epic deep cuts like 'When the Music's Over', 'The End', 'Celebration of the Lizard', and the driving road songs like 'Roadhouse Blues' and 'L.A. Woman'. Wherever you want to go, Doors music can take you there, activating that secret switch in your brain. For some of us, the music does something we can't describe: a cross between a psychedelic trance and a religious experience with a dose of the best sex you've ever had. It's drugs without the drugs.

That's what two words can do. The Doors.

Now, throw on a Doors LP, close your eyes, and teleport to your favourite timeline. Maybe it's 1966, and you're walking through the front door of the Whisky a Go Go; perhaps it's 1968, and you're in the front row at the Roundhouse in London; or if you're in a heavy mood, you're in Miami, Florida on 1 March, 1969, about to participate in Jim's version of the Living Theatre. But regardless of where you travel, be sure to look around while you're there because odds are I'll be right there with you!

Now you know.

Ladies and gentlemen ... *Night Divides the Day*.

David Dutkowski, Doors Archivist

GUITAR
Robby Krieger

ROBBY I talked my dad into buying me my first guitar. The guy who made it was related to Ramirez who makes the really good flamenco guitars in Spain, and he knew what he was doing. For $150 it was great. They didn't have winders, they had pegs, so that's what gave it a distinctive sound.

I traded in that guitar to get my Gibson. At first I was playing flamenco and folk music but I started playing electric guitar about a year before I joined The Doors. I wanted to get a Gibson 335 like Chuck Berry had, but they were too expensive so the pawnshop guy offered me the entry-level Gibson SG Special instead. I didn't want to leave empty-handed. At least it was a Gibson. And at least it was red.

After that it was always by my side. It's the guitar I used in my very first band, the guitar that got me into The Doors, the guitar I used at all our early live shows, the guitar that helped me write 'Light My Fire' and the guitar I played most of the songs on for the first two Doors albums. It helped set me on the course my life was meant to take.

I wish it had never been stolen. Whoever has my guitar, please call the Doors office in LA. I'll pay double.

This page: One of Robby Krieger's first guitars, a Ramirez flamenco
Opposite right: Robby's replacement Gibson SG
Opposite, top left: A 1967 bio, used by Elektra for profile material
Opposite, middle left: Robby, front right, at about age ten, with his twin brother, Ron, and parents, Stu and Marilyn, at their family home in Pacific Palisades, CA
Opposite, bottom left: Robby, far right, as a member of the publicity committee at Menlo School in Atherton, CA, circa 1964

ROBBY KRIEGER - GUITARIST - THE DOORS

FULL REAL NAME: ROBERT ALAN KRIEGER

BIRTHDATE & PLACE: JANUARY 8, 1946- LOS ANGELES

PERSONAL DATA: 5'9", 135 LBS., BROWN HAIR, GREEN EYES

FAMILY INFO: FATHER, STU; MOTHER, MARYLIN; BROTHER, RON

HOME: LAUREL CANYON, LOS ANGELES

SCHOOLS ATTENDED: UNIVERSITY HIGH SCHOOL, L.A., MENLO J.C.
UCLA, UNIVERSITY OF CALIF. AT SANTA BARBARA

MARITAL STATUS: SINGLE

INSTRUMENTS PLAYED/PART SUNG: GUITAR

FAVORITES:
SINGING GROUPS:
INDIVIDUAL SINGERS: VAN MORRISON, JIMMY REED AND JAMES BROWN
ACTORS: MARLON BRANDO & W.C. FIELDS
TV SHOWS:
COLORS: ALL
FOODS: PEANUTS

HOBBIES: MUSIC

SPORTS: SURFING

WHAT LOOKED FOR IN A GIRL: SOUL

WHAT DO YOU LIKE TO DO ON A DATE?: AS MUCH AS POSSIBLE

PLANS/AMBITIONS: PRODUCE

ADDRESS: 6725 SUNSET BLVD.
HOLLYWOOD, CALIFORNIA

DRUMS

John Densmore

JOHN I wasn't in love with any subject in school but music. My grades had been average in all my classes other than music and sports, and no major universities were seeking a snare drum player for their marching bands. So, in 1963 I was off to Santa Monica City College, where I majored in apathy and changing majors. First it was music, but I thought I could never make a living at it. Therefore, I switched to business. After getting a D in accounting (the second time around), I thought someone was trying to tell me something. Maybe college wasn't for me.

But music was in my blood. Some kids went to the movies for escape. I found it in jazz. Coltrane and Miles seemed to be the culmination of 20 years of jazz. This is where I got religion. It was a kind of raw spiritual anarchy.

JOHN DENSMORE - DRUMMER - THE DOORS

FULL REAL NAME: JOHN PAUL DENSMORE

BIRTHDATE & PLACE: DECEMBER 1, 1944- SANTA MONICA, CALIF.

PERSONAL DATA: 5'9½", 135 LBS., BROWN HAIR, BROWN EYES

FAMILY INFO: FATHER, RAY; MOTHER, MARGARET; SISTER, ANN, BROTHER, JIM

HOME: LOS ANGELES

SCHOOLS ATTENDED: UNIVERSITY HIGH, SANTA MONICA CITY COLLEGE, L.A. CITY COLLEGE, SAN FERNANDO VALLEY STATE

MARITAL STATUS: SINGLE

INSTRUMENTS PLAYED/ PART SUNG: DRUMS, PIANO, TYMPANI, VIBES

FAVORITES:
SINGING GROUPS: BEATLES
INDIVIDUAL SINGERS: VAN MORRISON, JIMMY REED
ACTORS & ACTRESS: CHARLES BRONSON, PETER SELLERS & CLAUDIA CARDINALE
TV SHOWS: OLD MOVIES, ROCK & ROLL SHOWS
COLORS: BLUE
FOODS: VEGETABLES, CHINESE, ZEN MACROBIOTICS, MEAT

HOBBIES: LISTENING TO ALL KINDS OF MUSIC

SPORTS: TENNIS, BASKETBALL

WHAT LOOKED FOR IN A GIRL: SENSITIVE

WHAT DO YOU LIKE TO DO ON A DATE?: COMMUNICATE IN ONE WAY OR ANOTHER

PLANS/AMBITIONS: MUSICAL PRODUCTION OR ENGINEERING (MUSICAL) OR MANAGEMENT

ADDRESS: 8455 BRIER DRIVE HOLLYWOOD, CALIFORNIA

Above: John's 1967 bio for Elektra
Right: A floor tom from John's primary drum kit, a 1968 Ludwig Mod Orange (further information and specs can be found on p.286)
Opposite, top left: John pictured with his first drum set
Opposite, top and bottom right: John's high school yearbook
Opposite, bottom left: John Coltrane's Giant Steps *and Miles Davis's* Kind of Blue*, two of John's early influences*

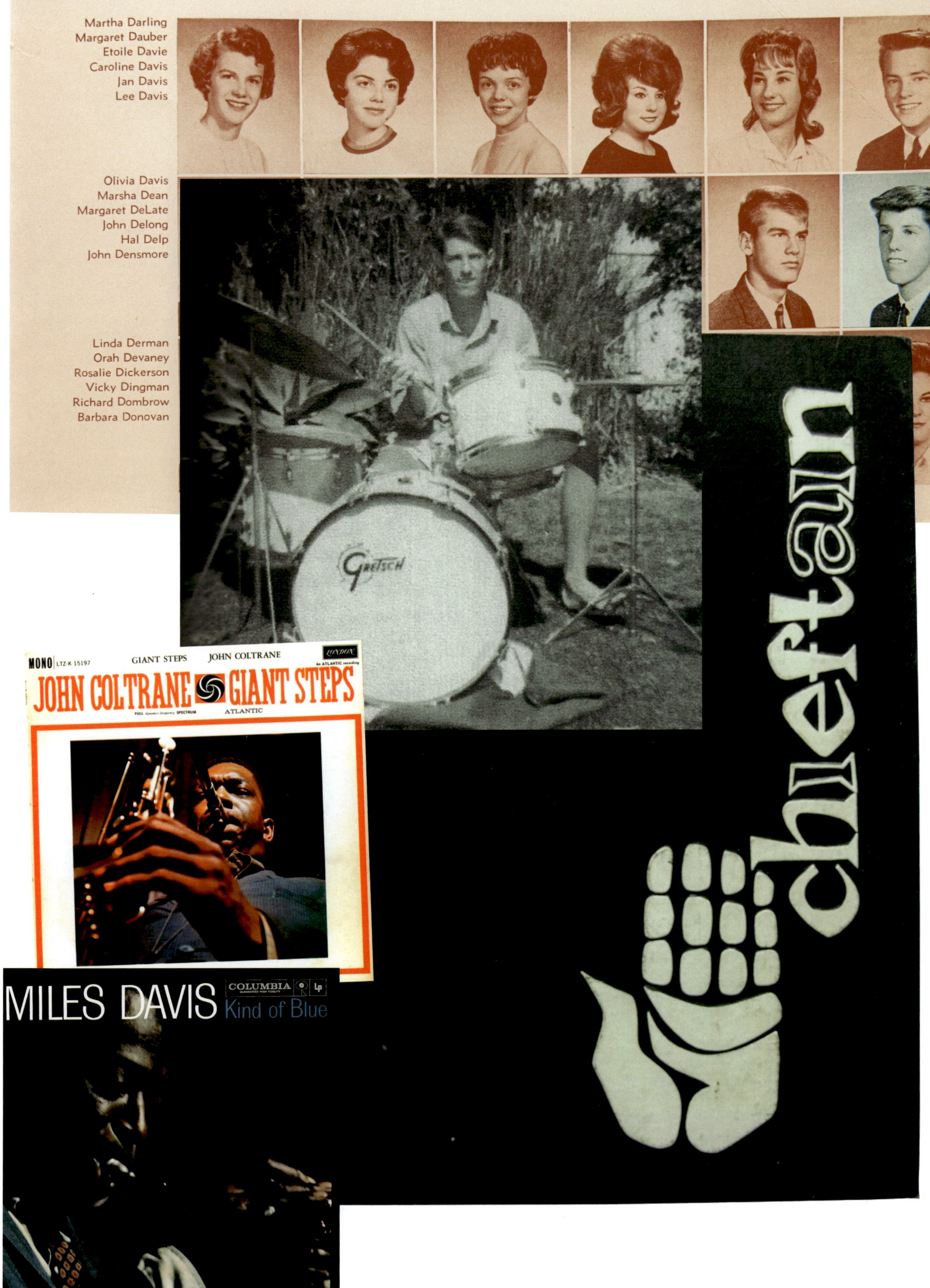
Martha Darling
Margaret Dauber
Etoile Davie
Caroline Davis
Jan Davis
Lee Davis
Olivia Davis
Marsha Dean
Margaret DeLate
John Delong
Hal Delp
John Densmore
Linda Derman
Orah Devaney
Rosalie Dickerson
Vicky Dingman
Richard Dombrow
Barbara Donovan
Gretsch
MONO LTZ-K 15197
GIANT STEPS
JOHN COLTRANE
LONDON
An ATLANTIC recording
JOHN COLTRANE GIANT STEPS
ATLANTIC
MILES DAVIS
COLUMBIA
Kind of Blue
chieftain

KEYBOARD & PIANO BASS
Ray Manzarek

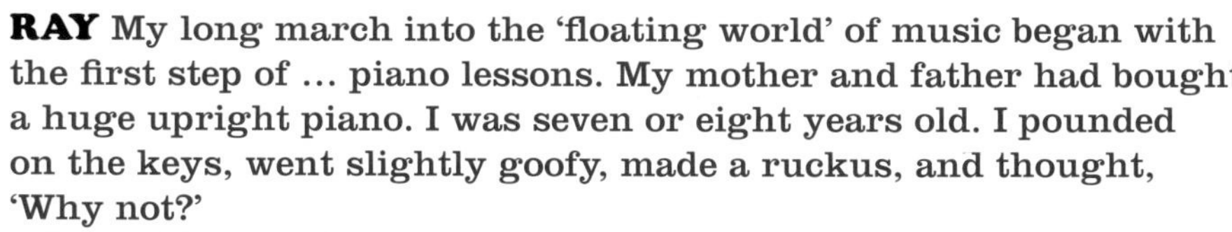

RAY My long march into the 'floating world' of music began with the first step of … piano lessons. My mother and father had bought a huge upright piano. I was seven or eight years old. I pounded on the keys, went slightly goofy, made a ruckus, and thought, 'Why not?'

Lots of kids in Chicago had to learn how to play the accordion. In the post-World War II Midwest, the accordion was a very popular instrument. Large masses of children played 'Lady of Spain' together on stages all over the city. It was not a pretty sight.

My parents told me many years later about their record collection of 78s that melted in a fire just before I was born. Blues records. Bessie Smith and other singers from musical groups they couldn't remember. South Side of Chicago music. My mother told me the two of them would go record hunting together. 'We used to go to Maxwell Street and we'd go into these record stores,' she said. 'But they weren't even stores. People lived in them and sold records too. And people were poor in those days. They would have a rug hanging in the doorway to keep the cold out and you'd go in behind the rug and they would have records for sale. You could hear the music from the street as you'd walk by. They would have the greatest music playing. I tell you, Raymond, those black people … they've got it!' Man, would I love to have that record collection today.

RAY THANK GOD MY MOM AND DAD WERE HIP AND DIDN'T BRING HOME AN ACCORDION.

1956

Manczarek, Raymond D.
Everett
Forum 3,4; Glee Club 4; Bantamweight Basketball 2; Intramural Football 1,2,3,4; Intramural Basketball 1,2,3,4; Frosh-Soph Baseball 2; Lawyer

Maringer, Fred A.
St. Clare of Montefalco
Electrical Engineering

1956 CASCIAN

Above: Ray Manzarek and his younger brother, Richard (Rick) Manczarek (Ray dropped the 'c' from his birth name around the time that he formed The Doors)
Top right: Ray's 1956 yearbook
Bottom right: Ray's army passport, February 1963. After enrolling in the UCLA School of Law, Ray realised being a lawyer wasn't for him. Following a bad breakup, Ray joined the army, where he played in an army band and also discovered Thai stick marijuana
Below: Ray's 1967 Elektra bio, which has incorrectly stated his year of birth (he was actually born in 1939)
Opposite, top left: At the piano, 1958
Opposite, bottom left: Ray at his first piano recital, 1949
Opposite, bottom right: Ray at Santa Monica beach during his first summer in Los Angeles, 1961

RAY MANZAREK - ORGANIST - THE DOORS

FULL REAL NAME: RAYMOND DANIEL MANZAREK

BIRTHDATE & PLACE: FEBRUARY 12, 1942 - CHICAGO

PERSONAL DATA: 6', 160 LBS., BLONDE HAIR, BLUE EYES

FAMILY INFO: FATHER, RAYMOND; MOTHER, HELEN; BROTHERS, RICK AND JIM

HOME: HOLLYWOOD, CALIFORNIA

SCHOOLS ATTENDED: UCLA

MARITAL STATUS: SINGLE

INSTRUMENTS PLAYED/ PART SUNG: ORGAN, PIANO, BASS

FAVORITES:
SINGING GROUPS: NO GOOD NEW GROUPS AT THIS DATE
INDIVIDUAL SINGERS: MUDDY WATERS, JACQUES BREL
ACTOR & ACTRESS: ORSON WELLS & MARLENE DIETRICH
TV SHOWS: DOCUMENTARY, NEWS & SPORTS
COLOR: BLUE
FOODS: OYSTERS, SNAILS & PRIME RIB

HOBBIES: PROJECTING THE FEEL OF THE FUTURE

SPORTS: TENNIS AND SWIMMING

WHAT LOOKED FOR IN A GIRL: COMPATABILITY, REALITY

WHAT DO YOU LIKE TO DO ON A DATE?: DINNER, MOVIES, WALK, ICE CREAM, DRIVE TO THE BEACH

PLANS/AMBITIONS: FILMS

ADDRESS: 1764 N. SYCAMORE
LOS ANGELES, CALIFORNIA

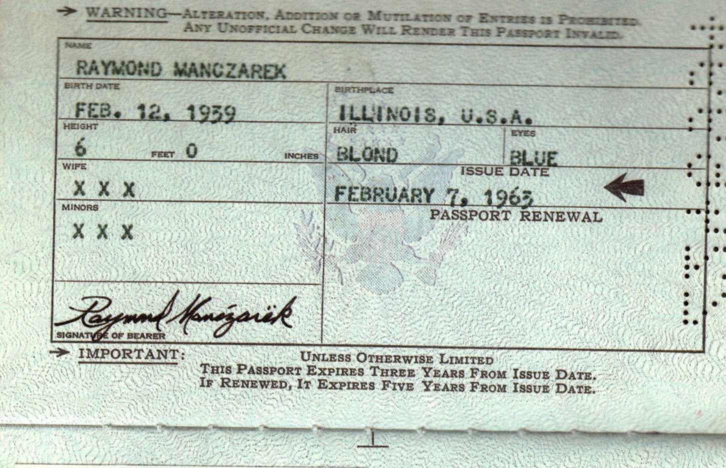

VOCALS & LYRICS
Jim Morrison

JIM I thought I was going to be a writer or a sociologist, maybe write plays. I never went to concerts – one or two at most. I saw a few things on TV, but I'd never been a part of it all. But I heard in my head a whole concert situation, with a band and singing and an audience – a large audience. Those first five or six songs I wrote, I was just taking notes at a fantastic rock concert that was going on inside my head. And once I had written the songs, I had to sing them.

I came along when the old rock and roll was a big thing and then I discovered blues in college. I liked that. If I ever listen to anything I listen to jazz, but there's so much music. It's like swimming in a sea of marshmallows.

I rebelled against church after phases of fervor

I curried favor in school & attacked the teachers

History of Rock coinciding w/ my adolescence

JIM MORRISON - LEAD SINGER - THE DOORS

FULL REAL NAME: JAMES DOUGLAS MORRISON

BIRTHDATE & PLACE: DECEMBER 8, 1943 - MELBOURNE, FLORIDA

PERSONAL DATA: 5'11", 145 LBS., BROWN HAIR, BLUE-GREY EYES

FAMILY INFO: PARENTS DECEASED

HOME: LAUREL CANYON, LOS ANGELES, CALIF.

SCHOOLS ATTENDED: ST. PETERSBURG J.C., FLORIDA STATE U., UCLA

MARITAL STATUS: SINGLE

INSTRUMENTS PLAYED/ PART SUNG: LEAD VOICE

FAVORITES:

SINGING GROUPS: BEACHBOYS, KINKS, LOVE
INDIVIDUAL SINGERS: FRANK SINATRA, ELVIS PRESLEY
ACTOR & ACTRESS: JACK PALANCE, SARAH MILES
TV SHOWS: NEWS
COLORS: TURQUOISE
FOODS: MEAT

HOBBIES: HORSE RACES

SPORTS: SWIMMING

WHAT LOOKED FOR IN A GIRL: HAIR, EYES, VOICE, WALK

WHAT DO YOU LIKE TO DO ON A DATE?: TALK

PLANS/AMBITIONS: MAKE FILMS

ADDRESS: 8021 ROTHDELL TRAIL
LOS ANGELES, CALIFORNIA

I was given a
desk in the corner

I was a fool
&
The smartest kid
in class

Top right: Jim's high school yearbook, 1961
Middle left: Jim pictured in a red shirt at his cousin's house, 1955
Bottom left: Jim at the beach with his mother, Clara Virginia, and his father, George Stephen Morrison, circa 1944
Opposite, bottom right: Jim's 1967 bio sheet for Elektra

UNIVERSITY OF CALIFORNIA
245 Charles E Young Dr E, LA

RAY It all begins at UCLA. Jim Morrison went to the film school at UCLA and so did I. We had enrolled in the Department of Cinematography, seeking to study the art of the cinema.

JIM I travelled around a lot as a child and I went to so many schools. Every year and a half I'd go to a different one. I finished up at UCLA. The only reason I did it was because I didn't want to go into the army and I didn't want to work. School was fairly easy for me so I just kept doing it. They have a good library, that's about it.

RAY One of the teachers at the film school was none other than the fabled French director Jean Renoir, who had done *La Règle du Jeu* (*The Rules of the Game*). He was only there for a year and I had signed up for the directing class in the fall but he was gone by the end of the summer. However, they brought in a substitute for Jean Renoir ... and it changed my whole life. He changed my outlook on art. He was the one who took me into that world of dark, brooding film noir, of haunted German expressionism and I loved it. He opened my mind to the possibility of making movies that were deeply passionate, mysterious and psychological. I know he had a profound effect on The Doors' music. A music that was slightly kinky and slightly Germanic. After all, The Doors did do Brecht and Weill's 'Alabama Song', or 'The Whisky Bar' as it has come to be known.

The next semester Jim Morrison took the very same class. An interesting coincidence: the two guys who would eventually, inevitably create The Doors were worshipping at the feet of the same teacher, the great man himself, Josef von Sternberg. The creator of Marlene Dietrich. And maybe that's why The Doors are what they are today.

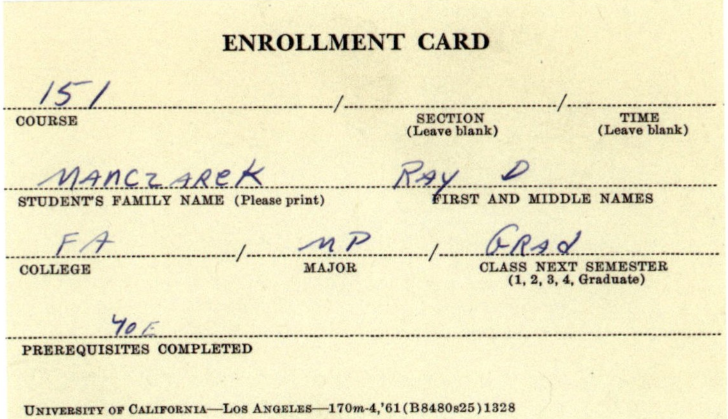

ENROLLMENT CARD

151 / /
COURSE — SECTION (Leave blank) — TIME (Leave blank)

MANCZAREK — RAY D
STUDENT'S FAMILY NAME (Please print) — FIRST AND MIDDLE NAMES

FA / MP / GRAD
COLLEGE — MAJOR — CLASS NEXT SEMESTER (1, 2, 3, 4, Graduate)

70E
PREREQUISITES COMPLETED

UNIVERSITY OF CALIFORNIA—LOS ANGELES—170m-4,'61(B8480s25)1328

Came to LA to Film school

PAUL FERRARA *When I first met Jim at UCLA in the film department, he was rather ordinary looking. Like so many of us, he was changing with the times. We all let our hair get long. The hippie generation was born. Music worshippers. Drug experimenters. Jim was no exception.*

JIM The only film I made at UCLA was a film that was questioning the film process itself. So it was a film about film. A few people liked it and most people were indifferent to it. You see, you shoot the film and the soundtrack is separate. It costs more money to have the two tracks together so that you can show it in the theatre and it wasn't deemed worthy of being married together so I never got a copy of it.

PAUL FERRARA *The visuals of Jim's film are vivid in my mind. He turned the camera on his own crew. He was being free, letting the situation develop and capturing moments on film. It was so pure. His editing was not so good, but his eye and his creativity made up for it.*

Ray Manzarek was in the same class and his film Evergreen *and my film* End of Summer *were chosen for the showing in Royce Hall, the university auditorium.*

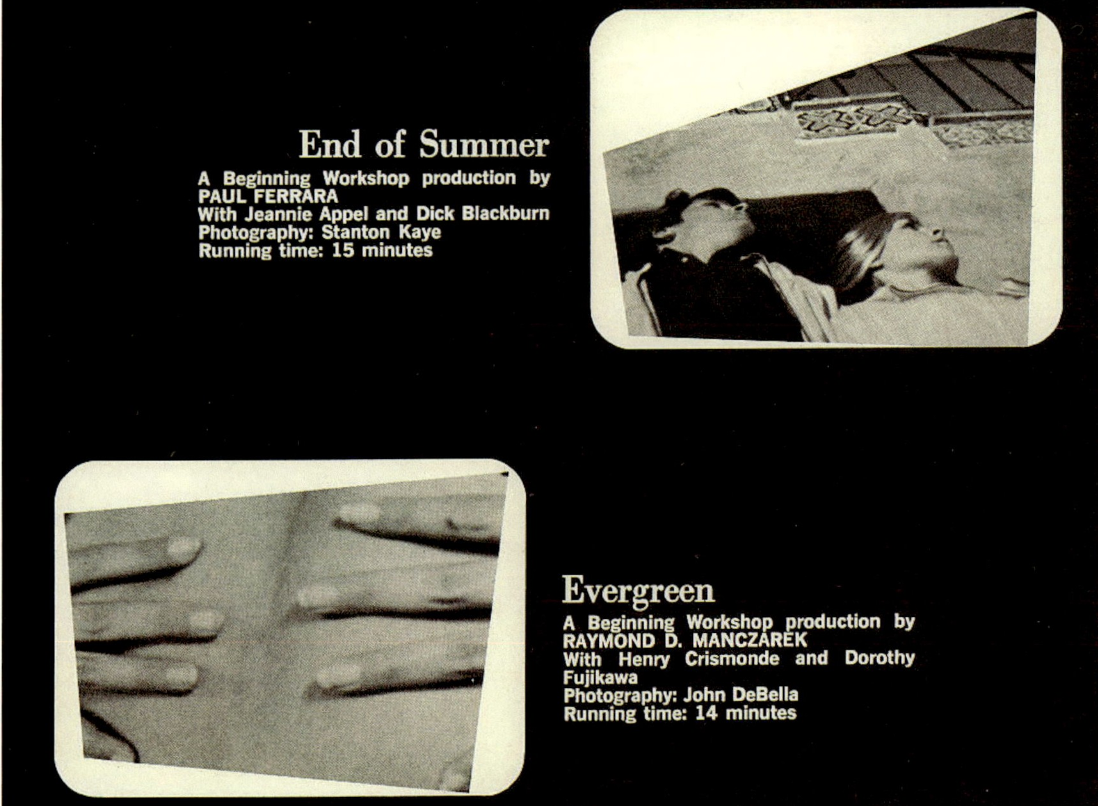

End of Summer

A Beginning Workshop production by PAUL FERRARA
With Jeannie Appel and Dick Blackburn
Photography: Stanton Kaye
Running time: 15 minutes

Evergreen

A Beginning Workshop production by RAYMOND D. MANCZAREK
With Henry Crismonde and Dorothy Fujikawa
Photography: John DeBella
Running time: 14 minutes

Above: Tapes of Ray's student film Evergreen
Left: A cutting from a Royce Hall showings programme giving details of Ray's film Evergreen *and Paul Ferrara's film* End of Summer. *Paul went on to be The Doors' photographer between 1967 and 1969*
Opposite, top right: Ray (middle) and Jim (right) seen together for the first time in Induction, *another of Ray's student films*
Opposite, bottom left: Ray's UCLA enrolment card

INDUCTION

BY RAY MANCZAREK

Induction

An Advanced Workshop production
by *Raymond D. Manczarek*
With Kathy Zeller, Paul Ferrara, Dorothy Fujikawa
and Ray Manczarek
Cinematography: John De Bella
Camera: Chris Gray
Sound: Steve Wax, Carl Schultz and
Stephanie Hughes
Assistant Director: Norman Sher
Sixteen minutes

Top: Stills from two of Ray's student films, Evergreen *(top) and* Induction *(bottom)*
Right: Ray and his mother at his graduation from DePaul University in Chicago. He got a degree in economics at DePaul before enrolling at UCLA
Opposite, top: Ray and Jim's 'degree conferred' sheets
Opposite, middle: Rick and the Ravens business card
Opposite, bottom: Venice Beach, CA

RAY In *Evergreen* you can see the actual Venice Beach apartment that we lived in. Me, [my girlfriend] Dorothy and Jim. And you can see me and Jim together on screen in *Induction* before The Doors were even conceived of. A party is taking place and Jim and I exchange a conspiratorial moment together. It's brief, but there we are, young pups together.

PAUL FERRARA *Ray and his brothers had a cover band named Rick and the Ravens. Ray played a mean keyboard even then. One night at the Turkey Joint West in downtown Santa Monica they were playing late into the night. The club was about to close and most of the patrons had left. There were a handful of us from the film department, sitting around drunk as skunks. Ray invited us up on stage to join in on the final song. Some of us did: Jim Morrison and a few others gathered around and snorted into the mic. Jim grabbed the microphone and wouldn't let go. He was improvising. This was a glimpse into the future.*

DEGREES CONFERRED

James Rudolph Mallek .... Political Science
Raymond Daniel Manczarek .... Theater Arts
John Tracy Mansfield .... Psychology
Genevieve Marcus .... Music
Umberto Marsella .... French
Adolfo Caridade Mascarenhas .... Geography
Carolyn B. Mason .... Mathematics
Kahombo Christophe Mateene .... African Area Studies
Lawrence Eugene Maxwell .... Geography
John Daniels McCully, Jr. .... Mathematics

DEGREES CONFERRED

August 13, 1965

COLLEGE OF FINE ARTS

The Degree of Bachelor of Arts

Richard Kimball Harsh
Harald Oleg Hoeffding
Ronald Lee Jamison
Dennis John Jennings
Corrine Laurel Joseph
Nickolaus Konstantein Kopp
Antonieta Sosa Laufer
Patricia Lee Meyer
James Douglas Morrison
Michael Ephraim Porter
Norman Ross Sher
James Dale Snodgrass, Jr.
Sharon Dale Streeter
Margaret Joanne Tepper
Felix Strickland Venable
Evan Glyndwr Williams
Diane Phyllis Yates
D. Gail Ziferstein

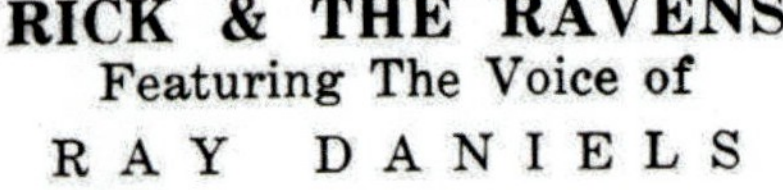

RAY We graduated from UCLA and Jim was going to New York and I was going to stay in Los Angeles. I'd just got there a couple of years ago after Chicago. Jim had come from Florida. Jim said he was going to go to New York to make his fortune and make avant-garde films.

JIM Films have always fascinated me.

RAY About two months later in July 1965, I was on the beach not knowing what to do with myself and who comes down the beach but James Douglas Morrison. He was totally transformed. He was lean, his hair had grown, he was like a young Adonis, like Michelangelo's *David*. I thought he had gone to New York! He told me that he'd decided to stay in LA and that he'd been writing some poetry, writing some songs. I told him to sit down and sing me a song and he sang 'Moonlight Drive'.

Easy to love you as I watch you glide / Falling through wet forests on our ... moonlight drive.

JIM For no reason at all I just started writing some songs. They just kind of popped into my head. I never did any singing. I never even conceived it. I wasn't in a group or anything. I just got out of college and I went down to the beach. I wasn't doing much of anything. I was free for the first time. I had been going to school, constantly, for 15 years. It was a beautiful hot summer and I just started hearing songs.

I ran into Ray and he'd been working in bands. He grew up in Chicago and he'd been doing it a long time and he said that we should get a band together, and we did. The person that writes the songs ought to sing them because he'll feel it more than anyone else. So since I was writing the songs I just gradually became a singer.

Moonlight Drive

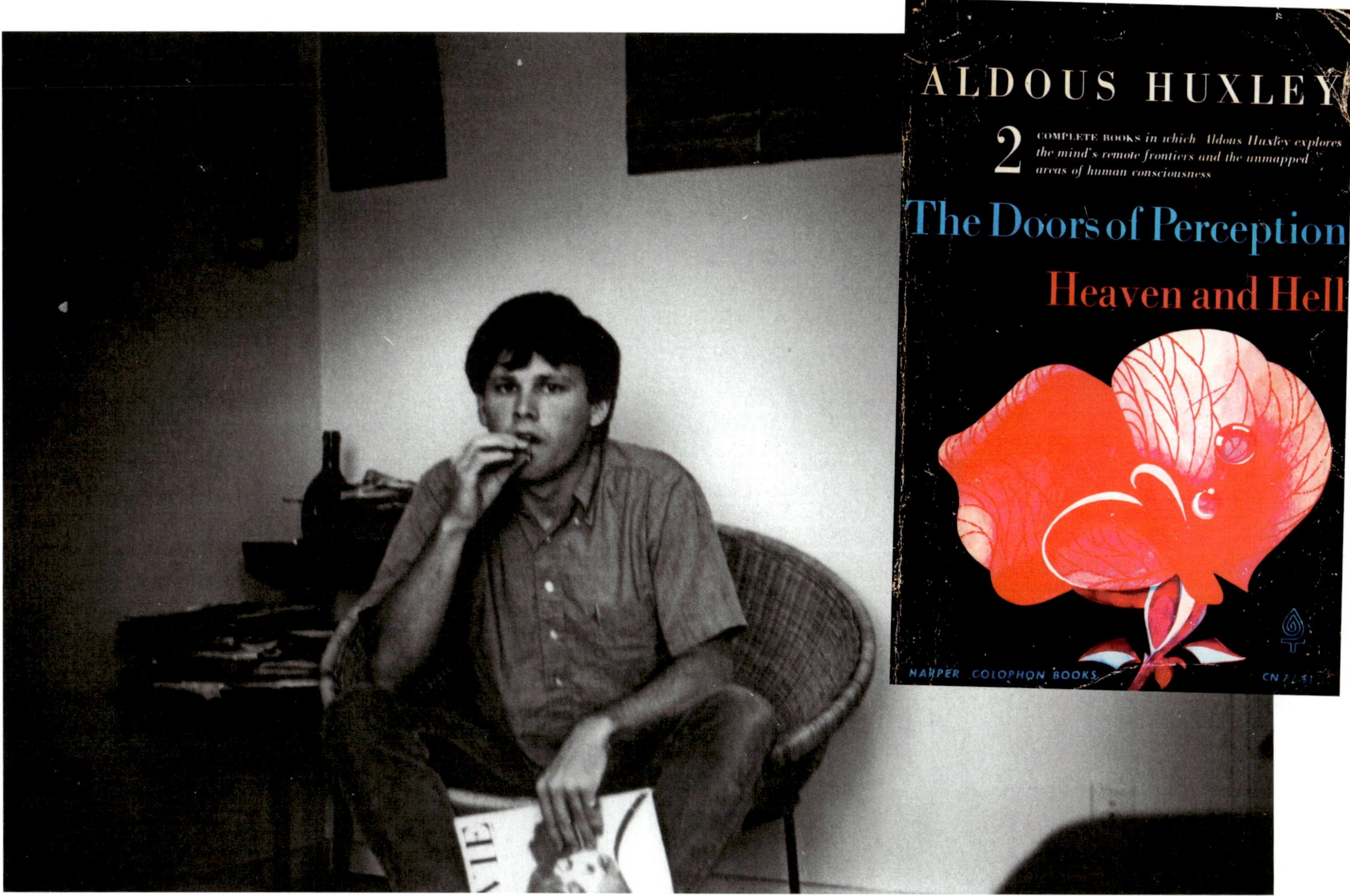

RAY I had chills. He sang three or four more songs and I told him those were some of the best lyrics I'd heard for rock and roll. I said we should get a rock and roll band together, and Jim said, 'That's exactly what I want to do.'

We needed a name for the band. We weren't going to call it Morrison and Manzarek, like a folk duo. Jim said, 'We'll call it The Doors.' I said, 'The what? That's the most ridic-' and then stopped mid-word. I flashed on the logic of it. It made perfect sense. 'Like the doors in your mind? Like opening the doors of perception? Like Aldous Huxley?' 'Exactly,' Jim said. 'Cool huh?'

ROBBY Aldous Huxley took the phrase 'the doors of perception' from a book by William Blake called *The Marriage of Heaven and Hell,* which Morrison had also read.

JIM KERR *From the youngest age Jim developed a profound interest in poetry, devouring the works of William Blake and contemporary Beat poets like Jack Kerouac and Allen Ginsberg.*

JOHN In the summer of 1964 something amazing started happening to the music scene in LA. New clubs were opening up and down the Sunset Strip: Fred C. Dobbs, the Trip, Bido Lito's and the Brave New World. The bands that played there weren't into Top 40 music. They played their own stuff, at deafening volume. Every night I could, I would go to Hollywood with a high school friend, Grant, and hang out at the clubs until two or three in the morning. There was no age limit because they didn't serve alcohol. My parents were sure I was going to end up in the gutter.

WILLIAM BLAKE **IF THE DOORS OF PERCEPTION WERE CLEANSED, EVERY THING WOULD APPEAR TO MAN AS IT IS, INFINITE.**

Name came 1st
Doors of Perception

ROBBY I played the guitar in high school and when I was in college at UCSB I gave flamenco lessons to the kids. I played folk and flamenco and I played some coffee houses with the harmonica on the top as well.

JOHN One of the first times I met Robby, back in high school, he was recklessly driving his parents' fancy Plymouth and using a credit card to buy gas. This was a bit much for me, living south of the railroad tracks that ran along Olympic Boulevard. I thought he was a rich kid with attitude. He was also very quiet. It didn't take me long to realise that Robby's demeanour was due to shyness and gentleness, not snobbery. As I got to know him better I also realised that in his solitude, ideas were always spinning in his head. While everyone else was listening to the Top 40, Robby was digging Paul Butterfield, Robert Johnson and Jimmy Reed. Plus playing flamenco guitar.

ROBBY Ray was classically trained and grew up in Chicago so he loved the blues – Muddy Waters and all that. John was a jazz drummer and his friends were mostly jazz guys. Jim liked all kinds of stuff, although he'd never really sung before The Doors – he became a singer in a very short period of time. I hadn't played electric guitar much before The Doors. I think that's why my playing was different to everyone else's.

Robby pictured, second from left, playing his Ramirez Spanish guitar in The Back Bay Chamberpot Terriers, a jug band he formed while attending Menlo School in Atherton, CA
Opposite: Jim smoking a joint in his apartment, located behind the Veteran's Cemetery in Los Angeles, 1965

JOHN That spring Robby got me interested in taking a meditation course. I liked the 'separate reality' perspective that acid had given me, but I knew I couldn't take it all the time. Meditation sounded like a less shattering route.

RAY I found out about a class starting up in Los Angeles in which the Maharishi's type of mantra yoga would be passed on to novitiates and seekers of the way. A class in meditation. Transcendental Meditation. It was what I needed. Guess who is also in attendance. Doors guitarist-to-be, Robert Alan Krieger, and Doors drummer-to-be, John Paul Densmore. But they don't know it. They don't know about a rock band called The Doors and a keyboard player named Ray Manzarek and a poet-singer named Jim Morrison. All they knew was that they were looking for something to change their lives. They wanted something else, something different.

JOHN After one of the meetings this blond guy came up to me and said, 'I hear you're a drummer. Want to put a band together?' I was already in a couple of other bands, so why not? I wouldn't pass up the chance to play. Jamming was a natural high and I was hooked. He told me that he was in a band with his brothers and wanted to try something new, but the time wasn't quite right yet so he would give me a call.

RAY Somebody pointed John out and told me he was a drummer. I went up to John and told him we were starting a rock and roll band, that I was a keyboard player, we had a singer and we needed a drummer. He said, 'Well, I'd be interested in what you've got.'

Ray on stage with Rick and the Ravens, Turkey Joint West, CA, 1965
Opposite: Jim at the Self-Realization Fellowship Meditation Gardens, Encinitas, CA, 1965

JOHN The time's not quite right yet? What is this guy? Is he into astrology or something? Interesting dude. Definitely off the wall. His name was Ray Manzarek. A few months later he called me and said, 'I've got this guy and he's got these great lyrics.'

ROBBY I was at the meditation class too but at that time they only needed a drummer, so John got into the band and then later they got me in after Ray's brothers left.

JOHN In the spring of '65 Ray called me and invited me down to his parents' place in Manhattan Beach to play. He introduced me to his two brothers, Rick, the guitarist, and Jim, the harmonica player. Their band was called Rick and the Ravens.

Ray played some nice blues licks, coming from his Chicago roots, but I thought they needed a good lead guitar player. Lurking in the corner of the garage, meanwhile, was this guy wearing standard collegiate brown cords and a brown T-shirt and he had bare feet. Ray introduced him as 'Jim, the singer'.

JIM I didn't start out to be a member of a band. I wanted to make films and write plays and books. So when I found myself in a band I wanted to bring some of those ideas into it.

RAY If Jim and I were going to realise the dream of The Doors, we needed two guys of exceptional abilities. If we were going to create this Doors something out of nothing but our collective will and imagination, we needed a pair of psychedelic warriors. A brace of fevered, maniacal souls who could plug their spinal column electrical cords into our collective *kundalini* and not feel they were being strapped into the electric chair at Sing Sing University with Manzarek and Morrison flipping psychic overload switches to full fry! We needed two men of courage and vision. Two adventurers in the void. Two brave and hearty sailors of the psychological sea of dread to accompany us on our mad journey into the unknown.

JOHN Ray and I broke the ice when we started talking about our mutual love of jazz. I told him that I had seen all the greats at the Manne Hole in Hollywood: Miles Davis, John Coltrane, Art Blakey, Cannonball Adderley, Bill Evans and so on. The first song we played was a Miles tune that had an interesting tempo, like a waltz. You had to really know what you were doing and we hooked right away. Then we started playing the blues with Jim, and Jim was pretty shy. I didn't think he was the next Mick Jagger at that point. He started giving us lyrics and we started doing Doors stuff. I always knew what to play just hearing the lyric.

JIM Rick and the Ravens had a contract with World Pacific. They'd tried to get a couple singles out and nothing happened. They still had their contract to do a few more sides and we'd gotten together by then and so we went in and cut six sides in about three hours. At that time, Robby wasn't with the group. John was the drummer, Ray was on piano, I was singing, one brother played harp, one played guitar, and there was a girl bass player. We got an acetate demo and we had three copies pressed. I took them around everywhere I could possibly think of. I hit most of the record companies just going in the door and telling the secretary what I wanted. Sometimes they'd say leave your number and sometimes they'd let you in to talk to someone else. The reception game.

At Columbia they were interested. They liked it. A girl named Joan Wilson was the secretary. She called me a few days later and said they'd like to talk to us. We got a contract with Columbia for six months, during which they were going to produce so many sides. Having that contract was kind of an incentive for us to stay together. It turned out that no one was interested in producing us at that time, though, so we asked to get out of the contract. We knew we were on to something and we didn't want to get held to some kind of contract at the last moment.

JOHN Jim wrote the words for 'Hello, I Love You' when we were still in Rick and the Ravens. 'Sidewalk crouches at her feet / Like a dog that begs for something sweet.' That's a crazy great lyric! He couldn't play an instrument but he'd come up with melodies in order to remember his incredible words. We recorded a raw demo with Ray Manzarek on keyboards and his two brothers playing guitars. But the brothers were worried about Jim. He was crazy and had never sung before.

When Ray's brothers quit, I invited Robby Krieger to rehearsals. He played bottleneck guitar and the next thing I knew we'd become The Doors.

Venice Beach, CA, circa 1969
Above: The six-song acetate demo recorded by Jim, Ray, John, bass player Patty Sullivan and Rick and Jim Manczarek at World Pacific Studios, Los Angeles, CA, September 1965
Opposite, top left: Rick and the Ravens
Opposite, top right: Venice Canals, CA, 1967
Opposite, right: Stills from the Ford Motor Company training film Love Thy Customer, *for which The Doors provided an instrumental score, 1965*

TURKEY JOINT WEST
PRESENTS
Soul Music (Blues - Rock - Soul)
Shindig Stars RICK and THE RAVEN'S
Plus "The Man" RAY DANIELS
FRIDAY AND SATURDAY NITES
DANCING
2nd - Broadway
Santa Monica
Hens - 18
Gobblers - 21

PRODUCTION MANAGER SAM FARNSWORTH
ASSISTANT DIRECTOR LARRY SULLIVAN
ORIGINAL MUSIC BY THE DOORS

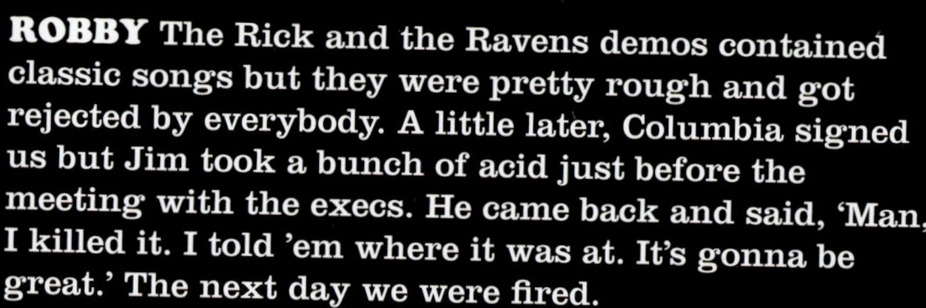

ROBBY The Rick and the Ravens demos contained classic songs but they were pretty rough and got rejected by everybody. A little later, Columbia signed us but Jim took a bunch of acid just before the meeting with the execs. He came back and said, 'Man, I killed it. I told 'em where it was at. It's gonna be great.' The next day we were fired.

Like any band, we took whatever gigs we could get in those days. We had a friend who had a connection with the Ford Motor Company and they hired us to provide an improvised instrumental track for one of their sales training films, which had the sublime title *Love Thy Customer*.

JIM I love movies as much as anybody else but the spectacle of millions and millions of people sitting in movie theatres and in front of television sets every night, watching a second or third-hand reproduction of reality when the real world is right there in their living room or right outside in the street or down the block somewhere, I think it's a tool to hypnotise people into a kind of waking sleep.

Love Thy Customer *was created in 1965 after The Doors were released from their contract with Columbia Records, but before they were signed by Elektra. The Doors were out of work and in need of cash. A friend of theirs approached them with an idea to make some money quickly: to provide the instrumental score for a customer service training film that would be sent to Ford dealerships. The band was to get paid $200 for a day's work in the studio.*

Ray, Robby and John provided the instrumental soundtrack, while Jim contributed some sound effects and additional percussion. The music itself has The Doors' distinctive sound, as you can pick out Ray's Vox Continental and Robby's guitar style almost instantly. Much of it is mixed into the background, so as not to distract viewers from the film's dialogue and message. The Doors do get a chance to jam during the end credits, adding in an instrumental that some have compared to the future Doors song 'I Looked at You'.

Until the film was unearthed from the UCLA vaults in 2002, it was considered something of a 'holy grail' and there was quite a bit of mystery around what this film really was. When Ray discussed it, he had always said that the band played the soundtrack live as the film was played, but after seeing it agreed that there was some editing involved. He then surmised that they played live to each scene a few times and things were edited together later.

ROBBY My friend Bill Wolff and I both auditioned for The Doors. Wolff tried out a few days before I did and I was surprised he didn't get picked. He was a much more experienced and technical player than I was. We had taken flamenco guitar classes together, we had formed a jug band together, we had played as part of a folk trio together, and we had jammed in an acid rock band with John Densmore. Wolff should have been The Doors' first choice. But my hair looked better (I had had it relaxed a week before), and my bottleneck made all the difference. Originally, I was a purist and exclusively played acoustic, but just before my audition for The Doors I had become enamoured with the sound of a bottleneck slide on an electric guitar.

RAY I didn't want anybody who wanted to be in a rock band or some egomaniacal nut-butters who wanted to be 'rock stars'. I wanted that same passion and commitment to art that Jim and I were bringing to the table.

ROBBY I had previously met everyone in the band, so there was no need for introductions, and John had already given me a copy of their six-song demo, so I came prepared. The first song we ever played together was my favourite of their six tracks, 'Moonlight Drive'. The demo version was much more bouncy and bluesy than the one we'd later record together, and Jim sang in a fluttering high register that Doors fans would hardly recognise today.

RAY We got together to do poetry and rock and roll. Kind of an extension of poetry and jazz like the Beats in the Fifties. Kerouac and Ginsberg, McClure and Ferlinghetti, they were all Jim's influences. John and Robby and I were into jazz.

ROBBY At first Ray wasn't sure if he liked my playing because he was thinking they needed a Mike Bloomfield type, but my trip at the time was to stay as far away from a Chuck Berry type of blues trip as possible.

Then I asked if I could try something. I slipped on my bottleneck and we ran through the song again as I wove in a warbling, spaced-out slide riff. Between my flamenco fingerpicking and my Muddy Waters bottlenecking I guess I stood out from the other candidates. Jim went crazy for the sound of the bottleneck and said The Doors should use it on every song. And that's why I ended up getting the gig over Wolff. All it took was one song to know it felt right.

JOHN If you combine my jazz, Robby's flamenco and folk, Ray's blues from Chicago and classical, and then Jim, the word man, you have this sort of melting pot. American gumbo, that's pretty tasty!

RAY That first time was like 'boom'. The greatest musical experience I'd had in my whole life up to that point. It was the first time I'd ever really played music. With John and Robby and Jim.

Top: Ray on Venice Beach, circa 1969
Opposite, left: The Doors at their beach house, which became The Doors' rehearsal space, Venice Beach, CA 1966
Opposite, right: Ray's mother, Helena Kolenda, Ray's girlfriend and future wife, Dorothy Fujikawa, and Jim on Venice Beach, circa 1965

ROBBY We had all lived down in Venice at one time or another. First Ray found this place on Fraser Avenue. When they moved out they moved to the house we had rehearsals in. It had a huge, long living room where we had all the gear set up. I don't know how they suckered us into that one but we all ended up paying for it.

JIM The group began practising in Venice in Los Angeles. It's a beach town with the atmosphere of a dying arcade.

RAY Our goal at the time was to be like The Beatles or The Rolling Stones. The Stones were playing blues and I thought they were really good, and growing up in Chicago with the Chicago blues I thought we could do that.

RAY My girlfriend and I had a nice little place above the garage of a bungalow, overlooking the rooftops of Venice, looking out to the beach, the Pacific Ocean, the setting sun, and, ultimately, Asia. An idyllic student apartment. Great times were had there.

There would be no Doors if it wasn't for Dorothy Fujikawa. Dorothy was right there with us. Dorothy actually worked and supported me and Jim. When I ran into Jim on the beach and we decided to start the band, I asked him where he was living, and he was living with a mutual friend of ours, Dennis Jakob. I said, 'You're living with Dennis? And you sleep in there?' He said, 'No, I sleep up on the rooftop of the apartment building.' Dennis was on the fourth floor of the apartment building and Jim slept upstairs – slept out on the roof. I said, 'You can't be sleeping on the roof! Man, you've gotta come live with us.' We started working on the songs and Dorothy supported us. Jim had the bedroom and then Dorothy and I took the living room, with the mattress, because it had a heater and we could stay warm at night. We would take Dorothy to work, drop her off, and go to the UCLA music school where they had pianos. We would go down into the little practice rooms and practise. Jim would work on his singing. We worked on his song structure, and I would play the piano, figuring out chord changes. Boy, that was fun. We had no money, but it was a lot of fun.

ROBBY I think our very first rehearsal was a sign of the things to come. At the end of the rehearsal this guy walked in the room and Jim just jumped on him for no apparent reason. No matter what the guy had done I didn't think he deserved what he was getting. The guys had told me that Jim was crazy but I couldn't believe it. We rehearsed for around a month and then we started getting gigs. We played at little parties here and there.

JIM THE WEST IS THE BEST.

ROBBY One of my first gigs with The Doors was at a Hughes Aircraft warehouse. One of Ray's parents worked at Hughes Aircraft and they needed a band for some sort of occasion. So, we got together, along with a bass player who only had one string on his bass. Ray was on acid and totally freaked out. I don't know how he even played. It was pretty weird. Jim tried to sing a couple of things but we didn't really have any songs worked out yet. We'd get gigs wherever we could. We used to go around to all the clubs and beg them to let us play.

JOHN We'd go to these bars on Hollywood Boulevard and beg to play. We just wanted to do something. It was a 24-hour, seven-days-a-week campaign.

ROBBY We hit all the clubs. The Sea Witch, an underground kind of place. Pandora's Box, the Unicorn, the Trip, the Galaxy next to the Whisky a Go Go, Brave New World, Bido Lito's and Gazzarri's. Gazzarri's was a place right down from the Whisky and on Sunday afternoons they had B.B. King playing. People didn't really know about him at the time. So we'd go in there and it was pretty amazing. The four of us watching B.B. King playing to no audience but us.

Ed Ruscha, Sunset Strip (Gazzarri's Supper Club), 1966/95. Silver gelatin photograph mounted on museum board, 23 × 30 inches (58.4 × 76.2 cm)
Opposite: Contact sheet of photo shoot at The Doors' beach house, 1966

→1A →2 →2A →3 →3A →4 →4A →5 →5A →6 →6A →7
KODAK TRI X PAN FILM
KODAK SAFETY FILM
→7A →8 →8A →9 →9A →10 →10A →11 →11A →12 →12A →13
KODAK TRI X PAN FILM
KODAK SAFETY FILM
KODAK TRI X PAN FILM
→13A →14 →14A →15 →15A →16 →16A →17 →17A →18 →18A →19
KODAK SAFETY FILM
KODAK TRI X PAN FILM
KODAK
→19A →20 →20A →21 →21A →22 →22A →23 →23A →24 H J J →25
SAFETY FILM
KODAK TRI X PAN FILM
KODAK SAFETY FILM

RAY 1966 was right between the hippies and the beatniks. The hippies were just getting started in '66. There were random, scattered groups of 'freaks' as they were called at the time and they had long hair and let their beards grow. They started to wear soft garments, rather than tight, binding clothes. You'd see them occasionally and they would flash the peace sign to each other.

JIM The hippie lifestyle is really a middle-class phenomenon. It could not exist in any other society except ours where there's such an incredible surplus of goods, products, leisure and time. I think that's the reason for it: because the generations immediately preceding ours had world wars and depressions to contend with and for the last 10 or 15 years in this country there's time enough and money enough to live a flagrant, outrageous lifestyle which was impossible before.

RAY We would stand and watch the sunset and it would put you in the perspective of realising this is a planet, a globe that we are living on, we've come as far as we can with western civilisation and there had to be some other way of living on this planet. That realisation came to an entire generation of young people whose motto was 'make love not war'.

JIM Look at how other cultures live – peacefully, in harmony with the earth, the forest, the animals. They don't build war machines and invest millions of dollars in attacking other countries whose political ideals don't happen to agree with their own.

Take a Journey w/ me to the West!

Previous pages, above and overleaf: The Doors at their beach house, Venice Beach, CA, 1966
Opposite: Venice canals, Venice Beach, CA, 1967

ROBBY When I joined The Doors, Jim was writing all the songs but we didn't have enough originals so he suggested I write some. I asked him what I should write about and he said, 'Write about something universal that won't go out of style.' So I said to myself, OK, I'll write about earth, air, fire or water. I picked fire because I liked the Stones song 'Play with Fire'. That was how I came to write 'Light My Fire'. Jim added the second verse, which included the line about the funeral pyre. I never liked the line and I still don't think it was necessary. 'No time to wallow in the mire' – what the hell is that? Jim put it there to rhyme with 'funeral pyre'. Looking back I wish we had spent some time and found something else to rhyme with that.

RAY We had this beach house and Robby came by and said that he had a new song called 'Light My Fire'. He started to play the song and it had a folk-rock kind of feel to it and I thought they were great chord changes – A minor to F sharp minor. Densmore didn't like the beat and wanted to give it a Latin feel, which he started to put in, and then when it got to the chorus it went into the hard rock. We had two choruses and two verses. I thought it would be great if we added some solos in there to stretch it out so I said to John that we should do an Elvin Jones/John Coltrane 'My Favorite Things'. So we did the solo, two more choruses and out. At the beginning of the song we had no introduction and so after telling everybody to leave, I managed to put together the intro.

ROBBY It took months of playing it over and over every night and Ray would add a little bit here and there until we got it. It actually evolved from playing it every night at places like the London Fog and the Whisky. It became longer and longer, like a lot of our songs did.

JIM Our first job was a Christmas party at the house of a relative of Robby's. After that we were at the London Fog on Sunset Strip, a small club that no longer exists.

JESSE JAMES'
LONDON FOG
Most Unique Club
on The Strip
Entertainment
Dancing Nitely
SHOWS • CELEBRITIES
"watch the actual fog roll in"
8919 SUNSET STRIP
652-9480

LONDON FOG

8919 Sunset Blvd, LA

RAY We started auditioning and got turned down at a lot of places. We finally went to the London Fog on the Strip and auditioned there. There was nobody in there, but it was a hip place. We got the gig at the London Fog before I got the piano bass. I played the organ and no bass at all. We had a light, airy sound.

JOHN By the beginning of 1966, the marquee of the London Fog read 'The Doors'. We had made it to the Sunset Strip. Having hit all the clubs along the Strip, we talked the owner of the Fog into booking us for a month, after we packed the house with friends.

JIM The most it could hold would be about 50 people. There was a bartender named George, a doorman named Sam, or sometimes Joey would be at the door, a waitress named Susie and a dancer named Rhonda, who danced in a roped cage across from the bandstand. Jesse James was the owner. He was a young man but he was dying of cancer and it was kind of a struggle to keep the place going.

ROBBY The London Fog was a small place but the good thing about it was that it was near the Whisky, so the people that were at the Whisky would come down to see what was going on.

JOHN Underneath our name we had them add 'Band from Venice'. The place was a dump and a hangout for misfits, but it was on the same block as the Whisky a Go Go, so we were game. We were hired to perform Thursday through Sunday, from 9 p.m. until 2 a.m. Five hours of hardcore lounge music, for ten dollars apiece – way below union scale.

JIM The songs developed over a period of time. Night after night in the clubs we'd start off with a pretty basic song, the music would settle into a kind of hypnotic river of sound which would leave me free to make up anything that came out of my head at the time. That's the part of the performance I enjoy the most – picking up vibrations from the music and the audience and just kind of following it wherever it goes.

JOHN We had about 25 originals – including 'Light My Fire', 'The End' and 'Break On Through' – about five covers, including 'Gloria', 'Back Door Man' and 'Little Red Rooster', which meant repeating a couple. If we played them early in the evening around 9 p.m. and then again at 1 a.m., the audience would have either turned over or gotten too drunk to remember that they'd already heard the songs. Night after night of drunken sailors, perverts in raincoats, and lounge lizards. Hour after cramped hour in a funky club stuck on a crow's-nest-sized stage.

Opposite and this page: The Doors performing at the London Fog, Los Angeles, CA, May 1966
Opposite, top right: Advertisement for the London Fog, November 1965
Above right: UCLA programme for Nettie Peña's 1966 student film, Call It Collage, *which featured photos and music of The Doors live at the London Fog*
Right: Released in 2016 on Rhino Records, London Fog 1966 *contains a previously unheard Doors performance at the venue dating from May 1966, also recorded by Nettie Peña*

Watch the actual fog roll in at . . .
Jesse James'
London Fog
8919 Sunset Blvd. 652-9480
"The most unique club on The Strip"
Entertainment / Dancing Nitely
SHOWS — CELEBRITIES

post card

THE DOORS
(BAND from VENICE)
with
Rhonda Layne
go-go girl

RAY The Whisky was the hottest place in the city and we were playing at this pathetic little bar that sailors would come into, drunken businessmen would come into, it was just the worst possible crowd – when there was a crowd. Three quarters of the time there wasn't anybody in the place so it was The Doors, the bartender and the go-go girl in a cage. [Outside the club] a sign read, 'The Doors. Band from Venice with go-go girl Rhonda Layne'.

JIM I just enjoyed working. There's nothing more fun than to play music to an audience. You can improvise at rehearsals, but it's kind of a dead atmosphere. There's no audience feedback. There's no tension, really, because in a club with a small audience you're free to do anything. You still feel an obligation to be good, so you can't get completely loose; there are people watching. So there is this beautiful tension. There's freedom and at the same time an obligation to play well.

Below and opposite, bottom: The Doors at the London Fog, May 1966
Above: Reproduction postcard depicting the original sign outside the London Fog
Opposite, top: The exterior of the London Fog on Sunset Boulevard, Los Angeles, CA, 16 April 1966

London Fog

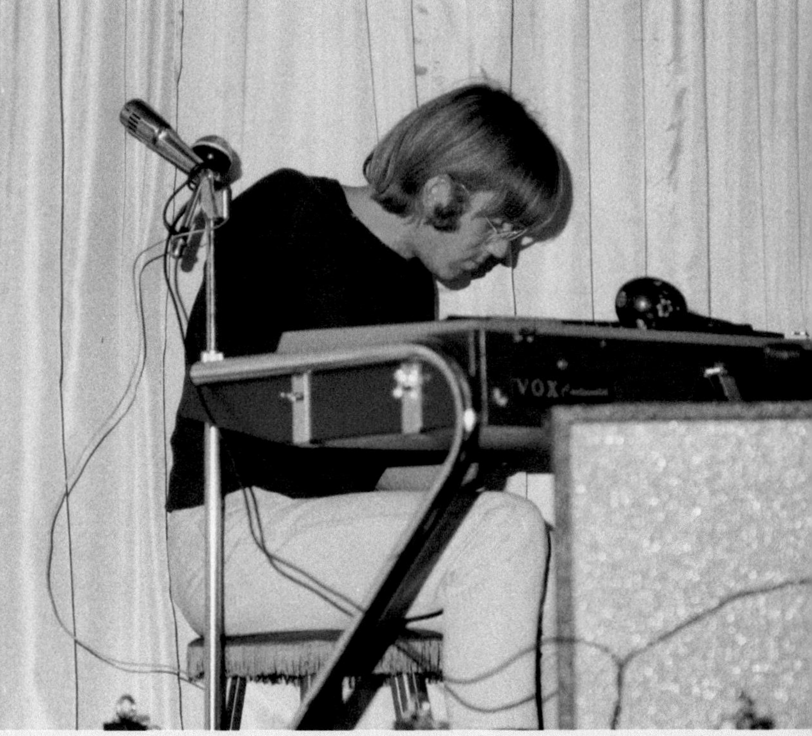
VOX

JOHN Since we had a kind of bizarre carte blanche to play what we wanted, we began experimenting. The long, jazzy instrumental solos in 'Light My Fire' and the stream-of-consciousness poetry of 'The End' were born at the Fog.

JIM There are songs I enjoy doing more in person than others. I like singing blues – these free, long blues trips where there's no specific beginning or end. It gets into a groove and I can just keep making up things. And everybody's soloing. I like that kind of thing rather than just a song. Just starting on a blues riff and seeing where it takes us.

ROBBY As much as our timing was lucky for getting the Fog gig, the timing of an offer from Ronnie Haran, the booker at the Whisky, was even more fortunate, considering that Jesse James, owner of the Fog, fired us that same night.

Night after night, performing in a near-empty club, Jim Morrison found his voice and The Doors crafted their sound. It was also here that Jim met Pamela Courson, who would be by his side for the rest of his life.

After a few months, the London Fog was on the verge of bankruptcy, and Jesse James told the band he was going to have to let them go. He said they could play through the weekend but they were out as the house band after that. It just so happened that at the same time, the Whisky a Go Go needed a new house band. Ronnie Haran arranged for The Doors to have an audition with the club's owner, Elmer Valentine. Although The Doors didn't impress Elmer, he gave them the job as a favour to Ronnie. The Doors were now officially the house band at the Whisky a Go Go.

ROBBY **IT WAS THE BEST CLUB IN TOWN WHERE EVERYBODY WANTED TO PLAY AND, ONCE YOU WERE THERE, YOU HAD PRETTY MUCH MADE IT.**

WHISKY A GO GO

Ronnie Haran

I came from New York to California to realise my ambition as an actress. I wanted to do Broadway plays and great movies but I got stuck doing television shows. It wasn't feeding me what I wanted so I quit. Because I was a starlet, we used to go to a place called P.J.'s on Santa Monica Boulevard. I would bring in people like Steve McQueen, Elizabeth Taylor, all my friends, so I was a magnet for the owners. One of the owners was Elmer Valentine. He was like a father to me, I adored him. I told him, 'Elmer, I need a job.' He said I could work at his new club called the Whisky a Go Go where I would assist the woman who did the publicity for the club and he'd pay me $50 a week. I said, 'Done. Love it.' The woman was a pillhead so three weeks later Elmer fired her and gave me her job.

The first thing I did was tell Elmer that we had to have a logo, so I created the original Whisky logo. Then I said that I wanted to start booking rock acts but we would have to get the age limit lowered to 18. The Whisky was always 21 and up because they served alcohol, but I found out that if we served food we could lower the age limit to 18. So, I created a menu. As soon as we lowered the age limit, Sid Bernstein, who represented The Young Rascals, got in touch, and so they were the first group I booked. From then on it was all rock and roll.

My phone would ring 20, 30 times a day with some man telling me that he had a group that was going to be bigger and better than The Beatles, wanting to get them into the Whisky. I never paid attention but if a musician that I respected told me about a band and they weren't too far away, then I would consider going to see them. Somebody told me about this band at the London Fog. I went down with Peter Asher and his manager – I didn't want to go alone to this shithole dive. I didn't even want to sit down for fear of catching crabs. We walked to the back and heard four or five songs. Peter wasn't impressed but I was mesmerised. With the combination of blues and jazz and what they did with 'Alabama Song' they were going to be the American Rolling Stones. Ray's countermelodies were brilliant, Robby's guitar playing was brilliant and Jim was hooked. It was about the combination of them all – if it was Jim by himself I would have felt nothing, the same with the rest of them. They had the formula of great music and a good-looking lead singer. As we were leaving I handed a business card to Ray, and said, 'I would like to make you the house band at the Whisky. Call me.'

It must have been a week or two later and I couldn't believe they didn't call me. I thought they had lost my card when finally I got a call on the night they were fired from the London Fog.

They were the first house band at the Whisky, playing every night. One of the things that kept getting them fired was that their sets would go on for an hour and a half and they would do 'The End' and Jim would do his, 'Fuck you Elmer, fuck your mother', and so on. I had a network of groupies that were my team. So, when Jim got the band fired (which happened on more than one occasion), I would go to the girls and ask them to make 50 calls a day to Elmer. They would call and say, 'When are The Doors going to be there? When are The Doors going to play?' And so he would rehire them.

I was also the manager of Love, who were signed to Elektra, so I knew label boss Jac Holzman. I picked him up from the airport one day to drop him at his hotel and I had to drop by at the Whisky on the way. We came in when The Doors were on stage. He told me, 'When I saw Love, I heard five bars of their music and I knew I wanted this band. But The Doors don't do it for me.' Yet he came back every night and he saw that the kids were mesmerised and everyone was worshipping them. And so he signed them to Elektra to do four albums. Robby later said to me, 'If not for you, maybe no Doors.'

Opposite: Whisky a Go Go, Los Angeles, CA, 1966

WHISKY A GO GO
8901 Sunset Blvd, LA

JOHN When people ask, 'What was your favourite gig?', I say Madison Square Garden. Mass adulation is excellent. But the most exciting point was early on in the clubs, or moving to a small concert hall when we were second on the bill. That's when it was like, 'Shit, we're going to make a living playing music. The train is going to leave the station.' That's the ultimate high.

RAY The Memorial Day weekend was probably when we started playing at the Whisky and we played there through the summer of '66. It was a magnificent summer because the freaks were coming from everywhere and the Whisky was freak central and they congregated on the Sunset Strip. It was really great, the feeling on the Strip was just amazing and had such an atmosphere. We were playing our asses off and getting better and better and stronger and stronger and all the girls were starting to fall in love with Morrison.

JIM I could put in a full day's work, go home and take a shower, change clothes, then play two or three sets at the Whisky. I loved it.

MARK VOLMAN *The Doors were an opening act for The Turtles many times at the Whisky a Go Go. We met them during the making of their first album, which they recorded in the small studio at Sunset Sound while we were recording our* Happy Together *album in the larger studio. Paul Rothchild, their producer, had lived a few houses away from me, so I was very aware of the process they were going through making the record. Lots of nights and many complaints about Jim Morrison not being at the studio or having trouble getting a song finished.*

They were a fun band to watch; I don't think I ever missed their show when they played with us. In those early shows they faced each other, the four of them. Apparently, they practised in the rehearsal hall facing each other and during their early shows they continued doing that so they wouldn't make any mistakes. Jim was a live wire. You never knew what was going to happen. He wasn't rude or obscene, just completely involved with his part of the image they portrayed off stage. He was one of those stars you just could not take your eyes off.

Promotional clippings for The Doors' Whisky a Go Go shows, with Them and Love
Opposite: The Whisky a Go Go on Sunset Boulevard, Los Angeles, CA, pictured here on 4 October 1966

ROBBY We played at the Whisky along with Them, Buffalo Springfield, B.B. King, Otis Redding.

When we started playing 'Light My Fire' every night it was always the song that got the best feedback from the audience so we knew it was going to be our big song.

I wish they had filmed those gigs because we had some renditions of 'The End' that were incredible. Stupidly, we never did get a good rendition of 'The End' on tape.

RAY The headliners of our initial engagement week? Them! Yes, my friends, Van Morrison and Them! Our favourite singer and perhaps our favourite band. 'Gloria' and 'Mystic Eyes' and John Lee Hooker's 'Boom Boom'. What great songs. What a great band. Jim was transfixed by Van, he studied his every move. He put the eye on him and he absorbed.

ROBBY It's funny, because we never knew Van Morrison or what he was like until he came to the Whisky, and there he was stomping around, throwing the mic just like Jim. Oh no, my God, another Morrison! In the early Whisky days he was a terror. You'd be afraid to come anywhere near that stage – he'd be drunk as hell, throwing the mic around, screaming and railing. He had some real devils inside.

GLORIA

Van Morrison

The Doors were pretty unique for the bands around at that time. They incorporated classical Indian raga, Chicago blues and, in some songs, psychodrama. Obviously, the Kurt Weill song was extraordinary.

On the last night the band and Jim joined me for 'Gloria' and 'Midnight Hour'. It was a lot of fun; we were in the zone. Jim had extraordinary energy. He had the ability to embody the song so absolutely that the audience had no choice but to go on that journey. He had spontaneity.

He was a great performer. We shared the same ethnicity and so were connected genetically like, as they say, a brother from another mother.

I don't know if I was aware of my influence in their music generally, although it was obvious in 'Gloria'.

They were fortunate in that they were able to recreate the energy and spontaneity of their live performances in a studio environment. 'Break On Through', 'End of the Night' and 'When the Music's Over' are the tracks that stand out for me.

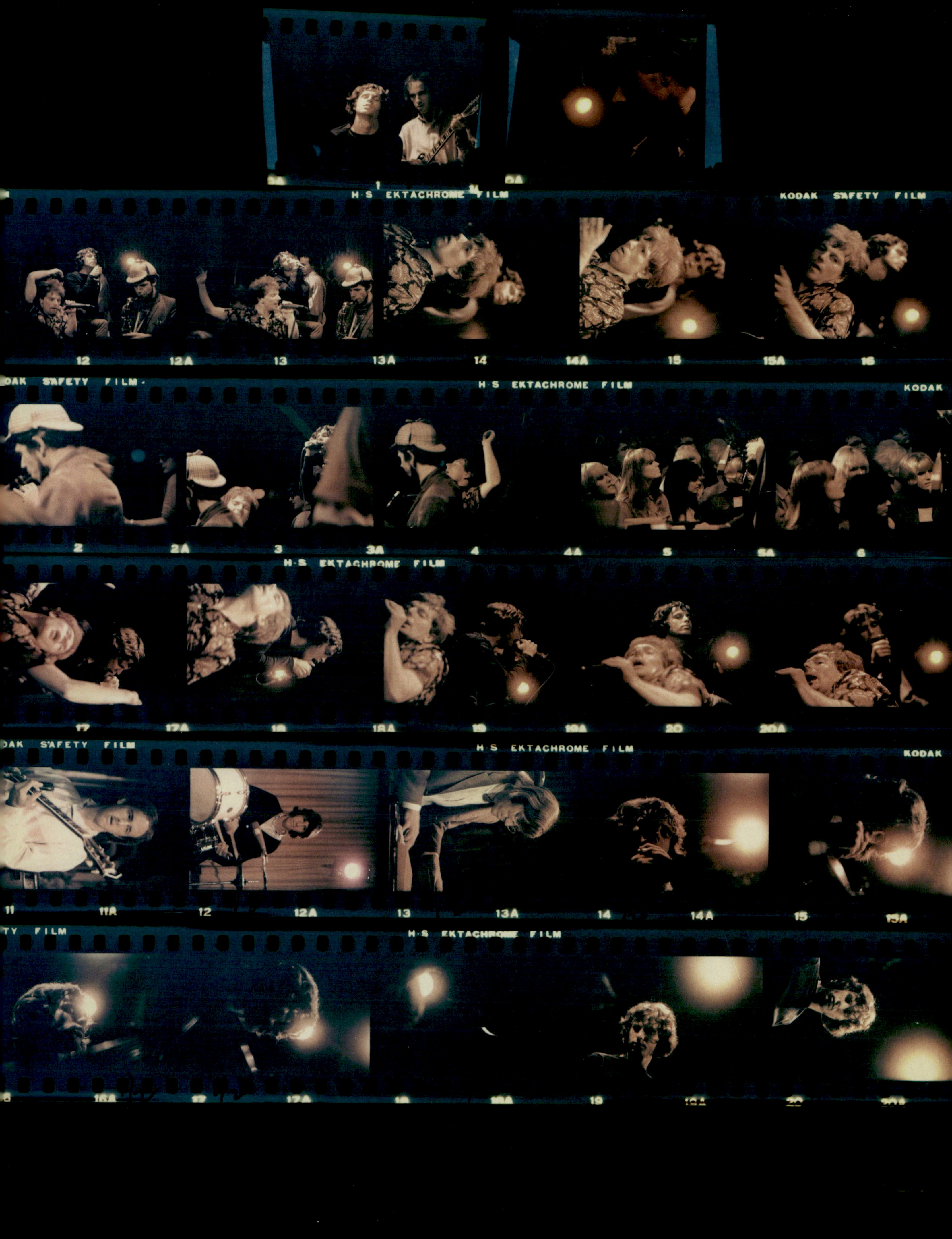

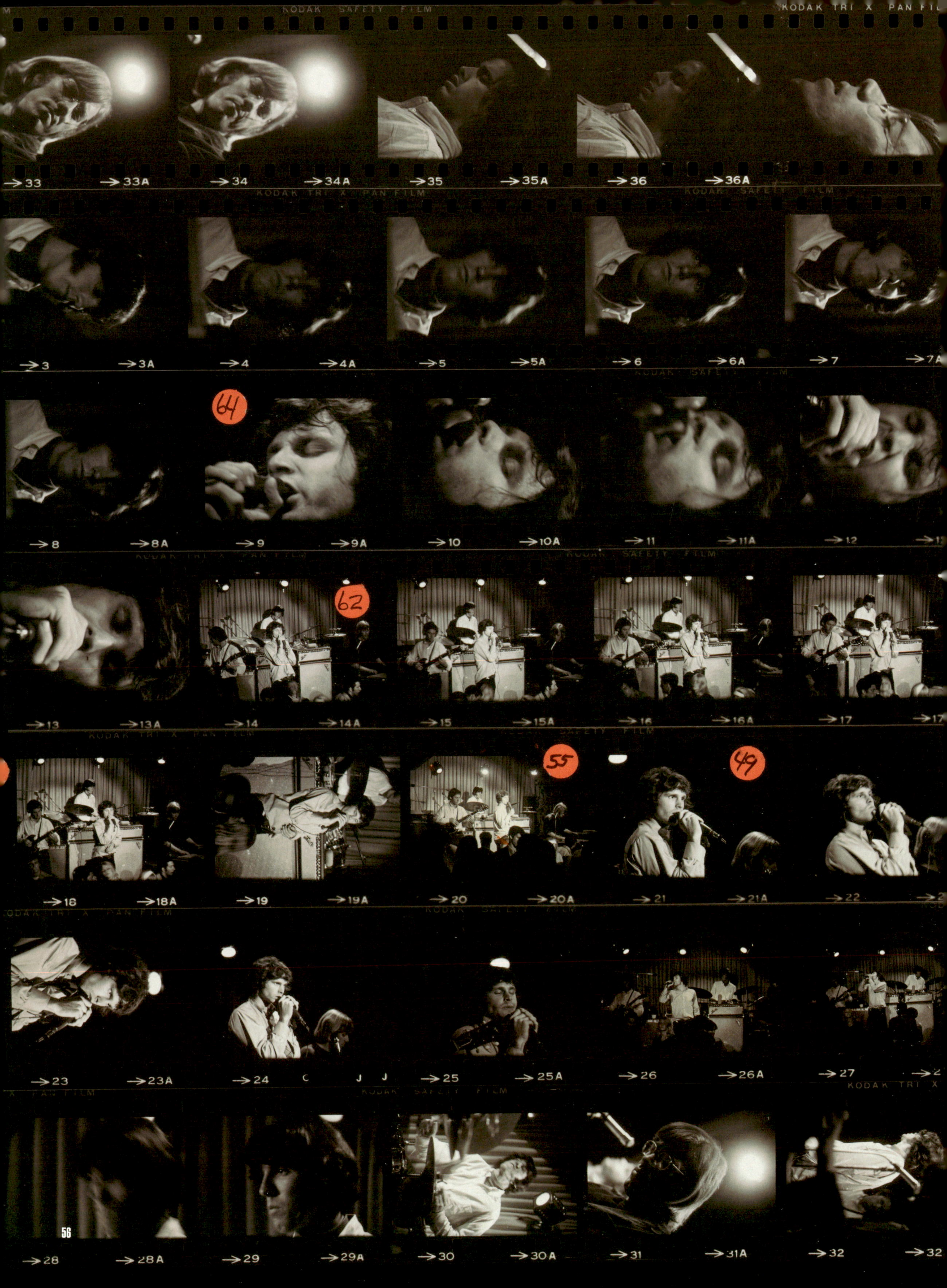
KODAK SAFETY FILM
KODAK TRI X PAN FILM
→33 →33A →34 →34A →35 →35A →36 →36A
→3 →3A →4 →4A →5 →5A →6 →6A →7 →7A
64
→8 →8A →9 →9A →10 →10A →11 →11A →12
62
→13 →13A →14 →14A →15 →15A →16 →16A →17
55
49
→18 →18A →19 →19A →20 →20A →21 →21A →22
→23 →23A →24 →25 →25A →26 →26A →27
→28 →28A →29 →29A →30 →30A →31 →31A →32

RAY Finally, some record people started coming by. Ronnie Haran brought Jac Holzman from Elektra and he fell in love with the band.

ROBBY Elektra Records found us at the Whisky a Go Go. Although we were signed to Columbia Records long before that, we had trouble with them so we got out of the contract. The president of Elektra heard us one night at the Whisky and wanted to sign us.

JOHN Columbia dropped us. Billy James was the West Coast PR guy and I looked on his desk and saw the Columbia pick up and drop lists and we were on the drop list. That night at the club, I told everybody and they were like, 'Oh fuck!' I thought it was a good thing, trying to be optimistic. Elektra were the only ones that stepped up. We were excited to be on a little boutique label with Paul Butterfield and Judy Collins and Love. It was pretty hip.

JIM Elektra at that time was very new to the rock field. Love was their first rock group and represented their first singles potential. They had been mainly an album label. After they signed Love, the president of the company heard us play at the Whisky. He told me he didn't like us [at first]. [But] he kept coming back and finally everyone was convinced we'd be very successful. So he signed us up.

JAC HOLZMAN *In May of 1966 I had flown to LA and was picked up at the airport by Ronnie Haran in her white convertible. Arthur Lee was playing the Whisky and expected me to drop by. It was 11 p.m. LA time, 2 a.m. New York time. I was beat, but I went. Arthur urged me to stick around for the next band. Whoever they were, Arthur had a high opinion of them, and I had a very high opinion of Arthur's opinion, so I stayed. It was The Doors and they did nothing for me. Jim was lovely to look at, but there was no command. Perhaps I was thinking too conventionally, but their music had none of the rococo ornamentation with which a lot of rock and roll was being embellished – remember, this was still the era of The Beatles and* Revolver. *Yet, some inner voice whispered that there was more to them than I was seeing or hearing, so I kept returning to the club. The fourth evening, I finally heard it. Jim generated an enormous tension with his performance, like a black hole, sucking energy out of the room into himself. The bass was Ray Manzarek playing a second keyboard, piano bass, an unusual sound, very cadenced and clean. On top of Ray, Robby Krieger laid shimmering guitar. And John Densmore was the best drummer imaginable for Jim – whatever Morrison did Densmore could follow, with his jazz drummer's improvisational skill and sensitivity. They weren't consistent and they needed some fine tuning before they would be ready to record, but this was no ordinary rock and roll band.*

RAY Elektra was a very intellectual label. They had folk music and poetry, but then they signed Love from Los Angeles and they signed the Paul Butterfield Blues Band so they were moving into rock and roll and Jac was looking for another band to sign. When we did 'Alabama Song (Whisky Bar)', the 1927 Kurt Weill/Bertolt Brecht song, I think that's what sold it to him. He thought, not only do they look good and are cute and rock and roll, but these guys are actually smart.

JAC HOLZMAN *I toyed with the idea of taking them into the studio myself, but I wasn't the ideal producer for them. Paul Rothchild was.*

Pages 52–3 and 55: The Doors and Them performing together, Whisky a Go Go, Los Angeles, CA, June 1966
Opposite: The Doors, Whisky a Go Go, Los Angeles, CA, 1966

The Elektra Corporation · 51 West 51st Street, New York, New York 10019 · JU 2-7711

TO: All ELEKTRA Ditributors and Promotion men
FROM: John Densmore of The Doors

I've been playing for six years. I don't really have too much to say about all this. I took piano lessons when I was ten. They tried to get me to play Bach. They tried for two years. When I was in junior high I got my first set of drums. I played symphonic music in high school (tympani snare), then I played jazz for three years. I used to play sessions in Compton and Topanga Canyon. Since last year it's been rock 'n roll and these creeps.

FULL REAL NAME: John Paul Densmore
BIRTH DATE & PLACE: December 1, 1944, in Santa Monica, California
PERSONAL DATA (Height, weight, and coloring): 5'9.5", 135 lbs., white-light?
FAMILY INFO (Names of parents, brothers, and sisters): Ray Densmore, Margaret Densmore, Ann Densmore, Jim Densmore
HOME INFO (Where located and description): 10610 Wilkins Avenue, Los Angeles, California-baroque
SCHOOLS ATTENDED: University High, Santa Monica City College, Los Angeles City College, San Fernando Valley State
MARRIAGE INFO: not married
INSTRUMENTS PLAYED/PART SUNG: drums, piano, tympani, vibes
FAVORITE SINGING GROUPS: none in particular-Beatles are the best
INDIVIDUAL SINGERS: Van Morrison, Jimmy Reed
ACTOR/ACTRESS: Charles Bronson, Peter Sellers, & Claudia Cardinale
TV SHOWS: old movies, rock 'n' roll shows
COLORS: blue
FOODS: vegetables, Chinese food, Zen macrobiotics, meat, fish
HOBBIES: listening to all kinds of music
SPORTS: tennis, basketball
WHAT LOOKED FOR IN A GIRL: sensitive
WHAT DO YOU LIKE TO DO ON A DATE?: communicate in one way or another
PLANS/AMBITIONS: musical production or engineering (musical)

elektra

RAY The first time I spoke to Jim about his parents, back in Venice on the beach, he said, 'My parents are dead.' I was shocked. 'You mean, you're an orphan? How long have they been dead? Since you were a kid, or what? I mean, who raised you?' 'Oh, my parents raised me.' I breathed a sigh of relief. He looked away. Kind of turned his back to me. 'It hurts, doesn't it?' He didn't respond. He just looked out at the water, then he spoke softly, to the ocean. 'They're not really dead.' I couldn't hear him over the roar of the waves. He turned to me. 'They're not dead. I just made that up.' I couldn't believe it. What a thing to say about your family. 'Why?' was all I could muster. He hemmed and hawed. 'I just … I don't want to see them.' And then the real shocker. 'Ever again.' 'What does your father do?' 'He's in the Navy. They just made him an admiral. He's in Vietnam.' And there it was. Death. Vietnam. Military. Professional killers. Admiral! No wonder Jim was conflicted.

The Elektra Corporation · 51 West 51st Street, New York, New York 10019 · JU 2-7711

TO: All ELEKTRA Ditributors and Promotion men
FROM: Robby Krieger of The Doors

The first music I heard that I liked was Peter and the Wolf. I accidentally sat and broke the record (I was about seven). Then I listened to rock'n'roll -- I listened to the radio a lot -- Fats Domino, Elvis, The Platters...
I started surfing at fourteen. There was lots of classical music in my house. My father liked march music. There was a piano at home. I studied trumpet at ten, but nothing came of it. Then I started playing blues on the piano -- no lessons though. When I was seventeen, I started playing guitar. I used my friend's guitar. I didn't get my own until I was eighteen. It was a Mexican flamenco guitar. I took flamenco lessons for a few months. I switched around from folk to flamenco to blues to rock'n'roll.
Records got me into the blues. Some of the newer rock'n'roll, such as the Paul Butterfield Blues Band. If it hadn't been for Butterfield going electric, I probably wouldn't have gone rock'n'roll.
I didn't plan on rock'n'roll. I wanted to learn jazz; I got to know some people doing rock'n'roll with jazz, and I thought I could make money playing music.
In rock'n'roll you can realize anything that you can in jazz or anything. There's no limitation other than the beat. You have more freedom than you do in anything except jazz -- which is dying -- as far as making any money is concerned.
In The Doors we have both musicians and poets, and both know of each other's art, so we can effect a synthesis. In the case of Tim Buckley or Dylan you have one man's ideas. Most groups today aren't groups. In a true group all the members create the arrangements among themselves.

FULL REAL NAME: Robert Alan Krieger
BIRTH DATE & PLACE: January 8, 1946, in Los Angeles
PERSONAL DATA (Height, weight, and coloring): 5'9", 135 lbs., brown hair, green eyes
FAMILY INFO (Names of parents, brothers, and sisters): Stu, Marilyn, Ron
HOME INFO (Where located and description): Laurel Canyon-Groovy
SCHOOLS ATTENDED: Uni High, Menla UCLA, Cal at Santa Barbara
MARRIAGE INFO: no
INSTRUMENTS PLAYED/PART SUNG: guitar
FAVORITE SINGING GROUPS:
INDIVIDUAL SINGERS: Van Morrison, Jimmy Reed, James Brown
ACTOR/ACTRESS: Brando, W.C. Fields
TV SHOWS:
COLORS: all
FOODS: peanuts
HOBBIES: music
SPORTS: surfing
WHAT LOOKED FOR IN A GIRL: soul
WHAT DO YOU LIKE TO DO ON A DATE?: do as much as possible
PLANS/AMBITIONS: produce

The Elektra Corporation · 51 West 51st Street, New York, New York 10019 · JU 2-7711

TO: All ELEKTRA Ditributors and Promotion men
FROM: Jim Morrison of The Doors

You could say it's an accident that I was ideally suited for the work I am doing. It's the feeling of a bowstring being pulled back for 22 years and suddenly being let go. I am primarily an American, second, a Californian, third, a Los Angeles resident. I've always been attracted to ideas that were about revolt against authority. I like ideas about the breaking away or overthrowing of established order. I am interested in anything about revolt, disorder, chaos--especially activity that seems to have no meaning. It seems to me to be the road toward freedom--external revolt is a way to bring about internal freedom. Rather than starting inside, I start outside--reach the mental through the physical. I am a Sagittarian--if astrology has anything to do with it--the Centaur--the Archer--the Hunt--But the main thing is that we are The Doors. We are from the West. The whole thing is like an invitation to the West. The sunset - This is the end The night The sea The world we suggest is of a new wild west. A sensuous evil world. Strange and haunting, the path of the sun, you know? Toward the end. At least for our first album. We're all centered around the end of the zodiac. The Pacific - violence and peace - the way between young and the old.

FULL REAL NAME James Douglas Morrison
BIRTH DATE & PLACE December 8, 1943, Melbourne, Florida, USA
PERSONAL DATA (Height, weight, and coloring): 5'11", 145lbs., brown hair, blue-gray eyes
FAMILY INFO (Names of parents, brothers, and sisters): Dead
HOME INFO (Where located and description): Laurel Canyon, L.A. - nice at night
SCHOOLS ATTENDED St. Petersburg Junior College, Florida State Univ., UCLA
MARRIAGE INFO Single
INSTRUMENTS PLAYED/PART SUNG Lead voice
FAVORITE SINGING GROUPS Beach Boys, Kinks, Love
INDIVIDUAL SINGERS Sinatra, Presley
ACTOR/ACTRESS Jack Palance, Sarah Miles
TV SHOWS News
COLORS Turquoise
FOODS Meat
HOBBIES Horse races
SPORTS Swimming
WHAT LOOKED FOR IN A GIRL Hair, eyes, voice, walk
WHAT DO YOU LIKE TO DO ON A DATE? Talk
PLANS/AMBITIONS Make films

JIM **I just didn't want to involve them. It's easy enough to find out personal details if you really want them. When we're born we're all footprinted and so on. I guess I said my parents were dead as some kind of joke. I have a brother, too, but I haven't seen him in a [while]. I don't see any of them.**

My desire for Family
The meeting
Rid of managers & agents
The horros of business

The Elektra Corporation · 51 West 51st Street, New York, New York 10019 · JU 2-7711

TO: All ELEKTRA Ditributors and Promotion men
FROM: Ray Manzarek of The Doors

I grew up in Chicago and left when I was 21 for Los Angeles. My parents gave me piano lessons when I was around nine or ten. I hated it for the first four years -- until I learned how to do it -- then it became fun, which is about the same time I first heard Negro music. I was about 12 or 13, playing baseball in a playground; someone had a radio tuned into a Negro station. From then on I was hooked. I used to listen to Al Benson and Big Bill Hill -- they were disk jockeys in Chicago. From then on all the music I listened to was on the radio. My piano playing changed; I became influenced by jazz. I learned how to play that stride piano with my left hand, and knew that was it: stuff with a beat -- jazz, blues, rock.
At school I was primarily interested in film. It seemed to combine my interests in drama, visual art, music, and the profit motive. Before I left Chicago I was in theater. These days, I think we want our theater, our entertainment to be larger than life. I think the total environmental thing will come in.
I think The Doors is a representative American group. America is a melting pot and so are we. Our influences spring from a myriad of sources which we have amalgamated, blending divergent styles into our own thing. We're like the country itself. America must seem to be a ridiculous hodgepodge to an outsider. It's like The Doors. We come from different areas, different musical areas. We're put together with a lot of sweat, a lot of fighting. All of the things people say about America can be said about The Doors.
All of us have the freedom to explore and improvise within a framework. Jim is an improviser with words.

FULL REAL NAME: Raymond Daniel Manzarek
BIRTH DATE & PLACE: February 12, 1939, in Chicago
PERSONAL DATA (Height, weight, and coloring): 6', 160 lbs., blond, blue eyes
FAMILY INFO (Names of parents, brothers, and sisters): Raymond, Helen, Rick, Jim
HOME INFO (Where located and description): Hollywood
SCHOOLS ATTENDED: UCLA
MARRIAGE INFO: Married
INSTRUMENTS PLAYED/PART SUNG: organ, piano, bass
FAVORITE SINGING GROUPS: no good new groups at this date
INDIVIDUAL SINGERS: Muddy Waters, Jacques Brel
ACTOR/ACTRESS: Marlene Dietrich, Orson Welles
TV SHOWS: documentaries, news, sports
COLORS: blue
FOODS: oysters, snails, prime ribs
HOBBIES: projecting the feel of the future
SPORTS: tennis, swimming
WHAT LOOKED FOR IN A GIRL: compatibility, reality
WHAT DO YOU LIKE TO DO ON A DATE?: dinner, movies, ice cream, drive to beach
PLANS/AMBITIONS: films

Bios written as part of an Elektra press release

Whisky

ROBBY Paul Rothchild worked for Elektra for years before we got there and it seemed like everything I listened to was produced by him. So, when they said that he was going to be our producer I thought, 'Wow, this is meant to be.'

RAY We just worked and worked at perfecting the songs and expanding the songs. 'The End', for example, was a short song with an Indian motif, a song of goodbyes, as Jim would describe it. So we played the body of the song and it was over in two minutes and there we were in the club and we just kept playing. Just kept the beat going. I would play the bass with my left hand and I had a little Indian flute that I would play into the microphone. We started fooling around with it and Jim started adding poetry to it. He would just drop things in and some things never got used, some things did, some things evolved, and it expanded until it became the 11-and-a-half-minute epic that it finally did become.

JOHN Musically, Ray and I were one. His left hand was the bass and bassists and drummers are pals. We were the sonic bed for Robby to float on and Jim to put words to. Together we were the rhythm section. When we did audition for a bass player we realised we sounded like a white blues band. We thought a keyboard bass would make us different. One night we were doing a gig at the Fillmore and Owsley Stanley, the chemist who invented LSD, came and saw us backstage and said, 'You guys have a hole in your sound. You need a bass player.' When he left, I turned to Ray and said, 'Hey, we're making the acid king nervous. I think we're on to something here!'

RAY There was one night at the Whisky where Jim had taken way too much acid but he wanted to [start our set with] 'The End'. John and I told him [we couldn't do it straight away]. The club was jumping and 'The End' was too slow. But Jim really wanted to do it. So we started to play it and it was so hypnotic that night that the entire club little by little came to a stop. First the dancers stopped dancing and just looked at Jim. Then the waitresses even stopped serving drinks and we were just about at the point where we were waiting for Jim to come in with some poetry, not knowing exactly what he was going to do. And that was the first time he said the forbidden 'F word'. 'Mother I want to ...' As he screamed out the forbidden word, John, Robby and I smashed on everything we had and just blasted the place with power. It shook everyone out of their trance and they all started dancing and freaking and going crazy. We played for another five, ten minutes, ended the song, and left the stage.

This is the end, beautiful friend
This is the end, my only friend
The end of our elaborate plans
The end of everything that stands
The end

No safety or surprise
The end
I'll never look into your eyes again

Can you picture what will be
So limitless and free
Desperately in need of some stranger's hand
In a desperate land

Jim Morrison on stage at the Whisky a Go Go, 1966

JOHN **WE WERE EXPERIMENTING WITH LSD AND ACROSS THE POND THE BEATLES WERE DOING THE SAME THING. IT'S THE MYCELIUM NETWORK – UNIVERSAL UNDERCURRENTS ACROSS THE GLOBE.**

RAY That night the owner came running backstage and said, 'Morrison, you are the filthiest, foulest person. You can't be saying that stuff about your mother on stage and in public! You can't kill your father and say those things about your mother. You guys are fired. Don't you come back here ever again. You want to come to the Whisky? You pay to get in.'

NILE RODGERS *'The End' was where it was at for me. I had a whole new language, an entirely new vocabulary. It was a massive musical influence on me because I went from playing classical music, loving modern jazz, playing soul music, because that's what all my friends listened to in South Central LA, and in one day I was into psychedelia. I remember taking acid with Dr. Timothy Leary, and this song was all I kept hearing. That stream-of-consciousness rambling sometimes is incredibly profound when you stand back and look at it.*

ROBBY When I took acid it was a brand-new thing and it was pretty amazing. It really opened your eyes to the fact that there really is something out there happening but you don't know what it is. I think that was probably the most important thing that happened in the Sixties: LSD. Morrison ate acid like people smoked joints.

JIM I like people that shake other people up and make them feel uncomfortable.

Above and opposite: New York, NY, 1966

ONDINE
308 East 59th Street, NYC

the village VOICE, *March 23, 1967*

Opening night at Ondine, that Queensboro Bridge of the soul, vast enough to encompass local beasts of prey, an occasional Rolling Stone on holiday, and a generation of post-pubic passion flowers who come to be seen and—knock on Formica—felt.

There is a certain suavite about rubbing hips in a crowded East Side discotheque. Something sexy about all that free-floating after-shave. And on opening night, all that kicky glamour-amour makes it almost seem like more than hunting up fresh pussy. Almost.

First New York opening in a while. The Doors—fresh from Los Angeles with an underground album - of - the-hour—return. This time, they are worshipped, envied, bandied about like the Real Thing. Ultimate proof that rock is an artform is watching the pop aristocracy at play. The great danger is no longer blatant ignorance by the press—we've come too far for that—or corruption from The Men In Charge—everyone takes that for granted—but the carping, eroding adulation an emerging creator receives from the scene.

The word was out—or "in"—"The Doors will floor you." So not all the pretty people in New York were present at opening night, but enough to keep a few publicity agencies busy. Liquor flowed like motor oil. Hors d'oeuvres melted into one fishy aftertaste. Lights dimmed and flashed. Wide neckties, dampened at the knot, waved limply in all directions. Silver sequins rattled in the breeze of undulation.

The critics—who are a strange anachronism in this age of instant depth—stood quietly to one side while the "personalities" (whore at 17; celebrity at 25) kept the frenzy with metronome hips.

Pace is all on opening night. The "worms"—thin and stunted men whose bones begin and end in their fingers—burrowed through the dance floor picking up partners like humus. A creased girl in backless gold-lame inquired of her partner: "Are you gonna dance wid me or do I have t'pick someone up?"

A typical East Side opening—with this difference. The Doors are a vital new group, with a major album and a sound that gripe. Would they make it live?

The four musicians mounted their instruments. The organist lit a stick of incense. Vocalist and writer Jim Morrison closed his eyes to all that Arnel elegance, and the Doors opened up.

Morrison twitched and pouted and a cluster of girls gathered to watch every nuance in his lips. Humiliating your audience is an old game in rock 'n' roll, but Morrison pitches spastic love with a raging insolence you can't ignore. His material—almost all original—is literate, concise, and terrifying. The Doors have the habit of improvising, so a song about being strange which I heard for the first time at Ondine may be a completely different composition by now. Whatever the words, you will discern a deep streak of violent—sometimes Oedipal—sexuality. And since sex is what hard-rock is all about, the Doors are a stunning success.

You should brave all the go-go gymnastics, bring a select circle of friends for buffer, and make it up to Ondine to find out what the literature of pop is all about.

The Doors are mean; and their skin is green.

ROBBY WE WERE DOING FIVE SETS A NIGHT AND WE WERE HOT. I WISHED THEY WOULD HAVE RECORDED US LIVE.

JAC HOLZMAN *In October of 1966 we brought The Doors to New York and booked them into Ondine, a club cheek by jowl with the 59th Street Bridge made famous by Paul Simon. It was the first time they had been east.*

ROBBY New York was more glitz, showtime, with Andy Warhol and that whole scene. LA was like the Wild West compared to New York. New Yorkers were a lot more outgoing.

JOHN New York felt like a lonely town when you're the only surfer boy around (a Beach Boys line). And then I realised the intensity of it and it was like, 'Wow, this is the centre of everything.' Eventually, New York became one of our best audiences.

RAY We played a month there. Terrific place. Everything very mod, very slick, very neat, very clean, very tight. Very sophisticated crowd. All the Andy Warhols and Plastic Inevitable kinds of chicks and mod guys.

A review by Richard Goldstein in the Village Voice *for The Doors' opening show of their third residency at Ondine, published 23 March 1967*
Opposite: The Doors at Ondine during their second residency at the club in November 1966

Ludwig

FRANK LISCIANDRO *When I saw them at Ondine I thought they had improved so much since I had last seen them several months before on the Sunset Strip. They were really polished and professional. Jim was less shy, but also seemed more drunk.*

ROBBY We had amazing chemistry in the band. I've been in many bands since The Doors and not one of them had that spark. What was needed was four guys who were on the same cog of where they wanted to be in life. You can't have one guy who's a kid musician, another guy that's in it for the girls, for example. We were all in the same spot, psychically. The way we rehearsed was very automatic, no questions were asked. There was no leader either.

JOHN I found myself wanting to really comment on what was going on musically, especially with Jim, Ray and Robby on their solos. Just to push them or lay back or whatever was happening in the moment. My main thing is dynamics. I think this comes from the school orchestra, playing *fortissimo* and *pianissimo* and everything in between. That's music. You can drum that way. Like in 'The End', it'll be real soft, and then bam-bam! I drop these cannonballs on the tom-toms in a real quiet section! What the fuck am I doing? I didn't even know. But later I listened and thought, 'Oh, that heightened the tension, didn't it?' Bridges and verses, contrast them, loud and soft.

We really knew each other musically and we knew Jim too. The three of us used to talk about how we could make Jim move around. We didn't talk to him about this, but we knew how to rile him up and get him into a dance. Jim lived in the subconscious. He would jump off the stage and do anything, but there was a connection there and we could steer him sometimes. Then other times he would do whatever he wanted.

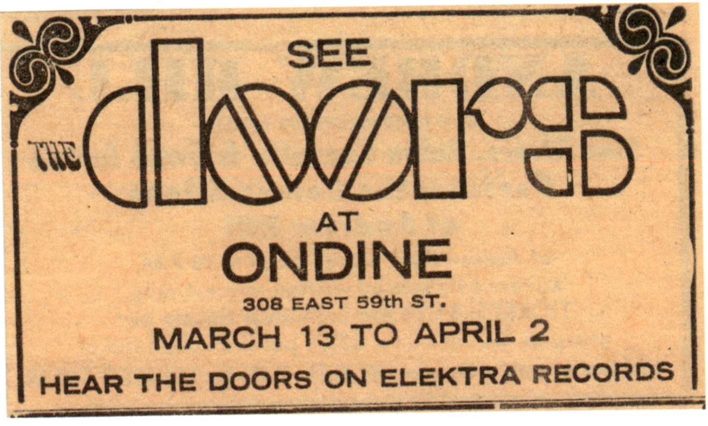
SEE THE doors AT ONDINE
308 EAST 59th ST.
MARCH 13 TO APRIL 2
HEAR THE DOORS ON ELEKTRA RECORDS

Cabaret Tonight

THE RIVERBOAT, Empire State Building, 34th Street and Fifth Avenue. Jimmy Dorsey orchestra, Bob Eberly and Helen Forres, singers.

THE LIVING ROOM, 915 Second Avenue. Susaye Green, singer. Held over: Bobby Short, singer.

ONDINE, 308 East 59th Street. The Doors, rock 'n' roll group.

Top: Ondine, New York, NY, November 1966
Above: Backstage at Ondine
Opposite, top: Andy Warhol at the Factory, 5 May 1968
Opposite, bottom: Exterior of the Ondine club, New York, NY

RAY Billie Winters, one of Jim's occasional amours, had booked us two weeks earlier into the most prestigious and hippest discotheque on the planet. She was friends with the owner, Brad Pierce, and he was buddies with Ondine's number one denizen ... Andy Warhol.

It was love at first sight on Andy's part. He knew the real goods when he saw it. And he saw it in Jim. To Jim, Andy was merely the entrée into decadence. The benign de Sade. The giggling Caligula of the Lower East Side. He held the keys to that gathering of quasi-artistic but beautiful young people known as the Factory – Andy's great loft of silver foil, silk screens, and anything goes. Jim was down there within the first week of our opening at Ondine. He loved it. He loved the games, the role playing, the attitude. The challenges to go further, to go beyond the self-imposed, societally sanctioned bounds of psychic control. To go beyond the pale.

SUNSET SOUND RECORDERS
6650 Sunset Blvd, LA

ROBBY We recorded the first two albums and part of the third at Sunset Sound. In those days studios had cottage cheese ceilings and shitty linoleum flooring, but this studio had a great echo chamber which we utilised quite a bit.

BRUCE BOTNICK *Recording The Doors was about the songs and performance. Paul Rothchild and I weren't supposed to 'create' The Doors in the studio, as they had already done that themselves. Our role was to be invisible, to document everything.*

PAUL ROTHCHILD *At the time, I think Sunset Sound Recorders was the best studio, mainly because of Bruce Botnick, one of the grooviest engineers I can conceive of, extraordinarily creative and very pleasant to work with. Bruce was completely sucked along into it and instead of sitting there at attention the way engineers tend to do, his head was on the console and he was just immersed. He'd done it all, made all the moves right.*

BRUCE BOTNICK *When Jim came into the studio, he had never officially recorded before and I didn't know what his microphone technique was like. My favourite vocal microphone is a long body Telefunken U47. I showed it to Jim and told him that would be his microphone, and he said 'Wow!' He told me that it was the same type of microphone he'd seen on a record cover of Frank Sinatra's album* Sinatra's Swingin' Session. *That's when I realised he was a big fan and could emulate Sinatra and Elvis when crooning.*

PERRY FARRELL *The closest persona or musician that I've heard to The Doors is Frank Sinatra because Jim Morrison sang in that kind of masculine, 'I've lived through it, here's what it's like' kind of way.*

JOHN Robby and I went to Ravi Shankar's Kinnara School of Music and were heavily influenced by that. Ravi didn't teach at the school, but he'd drop in and give a little lecture on 'Sublimating Your Sexual Drive into Your Instrument'.

ROBBY John was learning the tablas. Ravi showed up one time and told us, 'If you really want to be good at your instrument, you have to lay off sex.' Jim said something similar on the night before our first day in the studio. He called everybody to tell us that no one should have sex that night, to save it for tomorrow.

I first heard of Ravi Shankar when The Doors played in Berkeley for the first time at a theatre, around 1966. John and I met these Indian guys and we were kind of into Indian music so they suggested we check out this record by Ravi Shankar. I had never heard of him. It was a white album on the World Pacific label called *Ravi Shankar in London*. I just fell in love with it. I would go to sleep every night playing it and getting it into my brain. It really did affect my guitar playing quite a bit. There was an influence of Ravi on 'Light My Fire' and 'The End'.

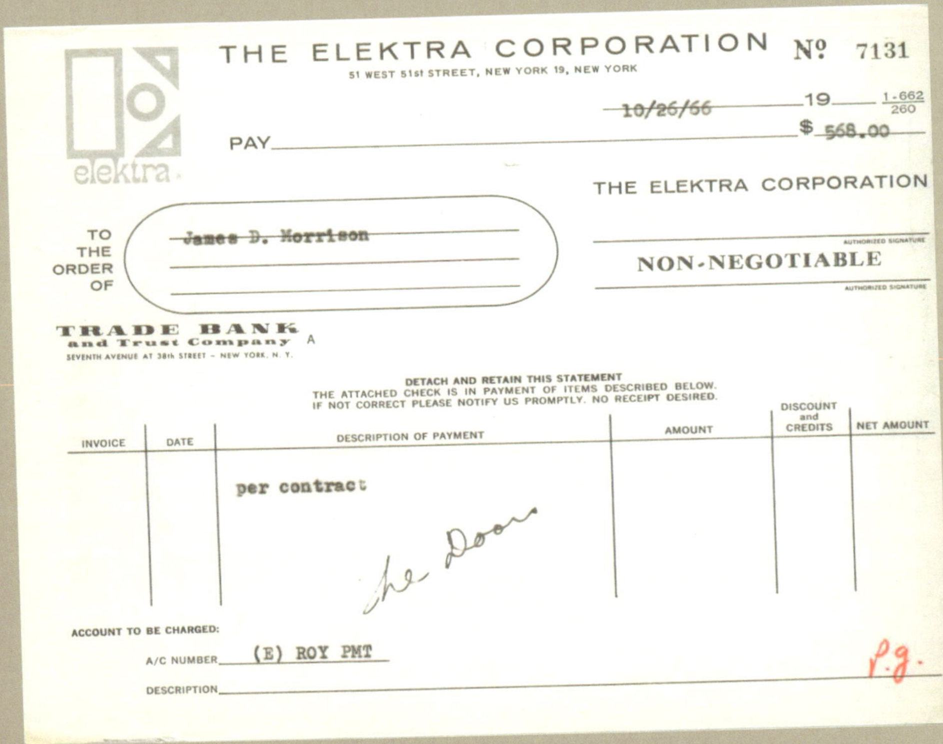

THE ELEKTRA CORPORATION № 7131
51 WEST 51st STREET, NEW YORK 19, NEW YORK

elektra

~~10/26/66~~ 19 1-662/260

PAY $ ~~568.00~~

THE ELEKTRA CORPORATION

TO THE ORDER OF ~~James D. Morrison~~

NON-NEGOTIABLE

TRADE BANK and Trust Company
SEVENTH AVENUE AT 38th STREET – NEW YORK, N. Y.

DETACH AND RETAIN THIS STATEMENT
THE ATTACHED CHECK IS IN PAYMENT OF ITEMS DESCRIBED BELOW.
IF NOT CORRECT PLEASE NOTIFY US PROMPTLY. NO RECEIPT DESIRED.

INVOICE	DATE	DESCRIPTION OF PAYMENT	AMOUNT	DISCOUNT and CREDITS	NET AMOUNT
		per contract The Doors			

ACCOUNT TO BE CHARGED:
A/C NUMBER (E) ROY PMT
DESCRIPTION

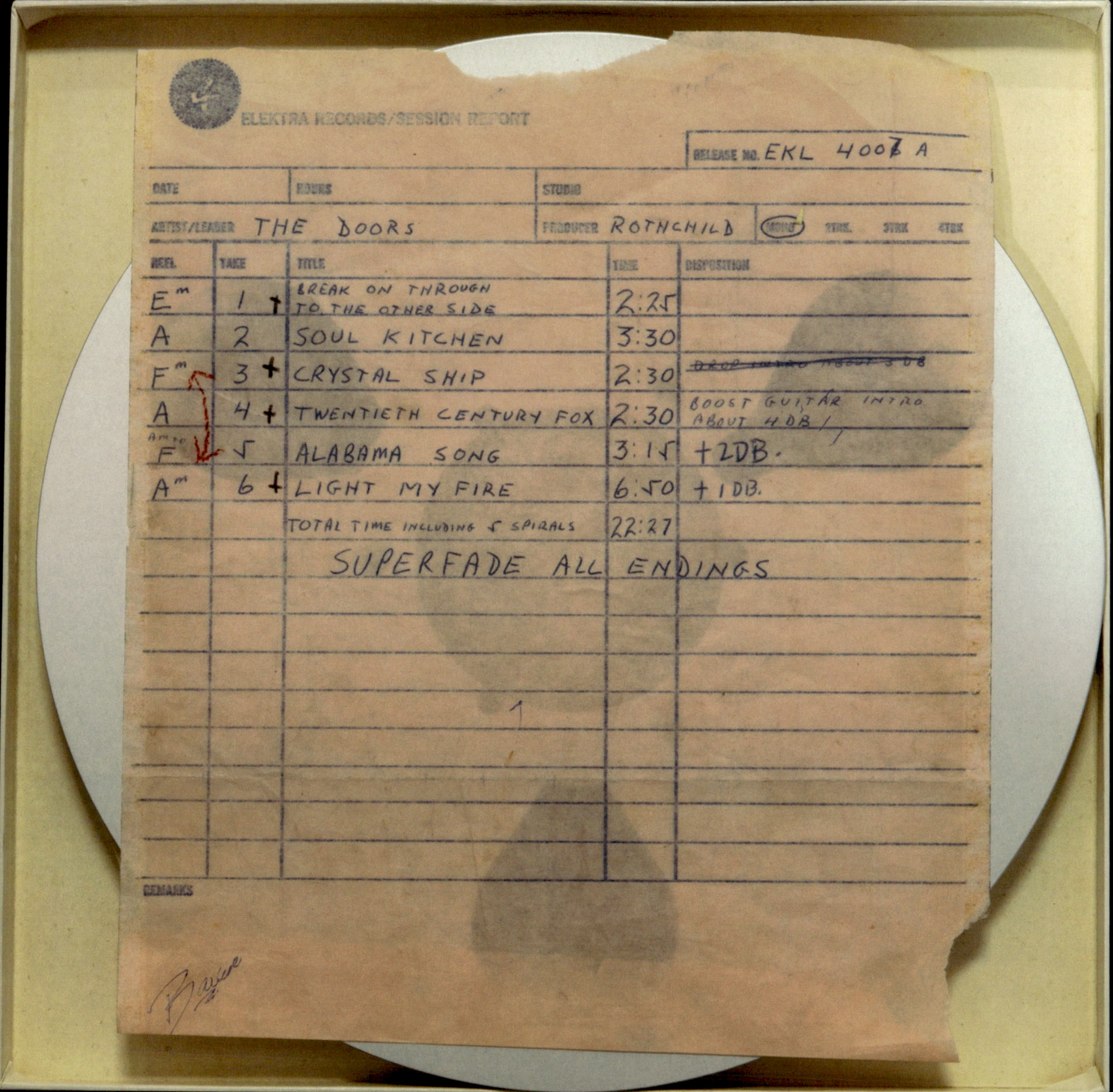

ELEKTRA RECORDS/SESSION REPORT

RELEASE NO. EKL 4007 A

DATE	HOURS	STUDIO
ARTIST/LEADER THE DOORS		PRODUCER ROTHCHILD — MONO 2TRK. 3TRK 4TRK

REEL	TAKE	TITLE	TIME	DISPOSITION
Em	1 +	BREAK ON THROUGH TO THE OTHER SIDE	2:25	
A	2	SOUL KITCHEN	3:30	
Fm	3 +	CRYSTAL SHIP	2:30	
A	4 +	TWENTIETH CENTURY FOX	2:30	BOOST GUITAR INTRO ABOUT 4DB
F	5	ALABAMA SONG	3:15	+2DB.
Am	6 +	LIGHT MY FIRE	6:50	+1DB.
		TOTAL TIME INCLUDING 5 SPIRALS	22:27	

SUPERFADE ALL ENDINGS

REMARKS

JIM The songs changed every time we did them. 'The End' was just a song that had more meaning, somehow, for all of us. It was a concept that we could bring more ideas into. Over the months, playing it every night, it changed gradually from a very simple melody idea to a kind of epic.

PAUL ROTHCHILD *It was one of the most beautiful moments I've ever had in a recording studio, that half hour when 'The End' was recorded. I was emotionally wrung. Usually as a producer you sit there listening for all the things that are right and all the things that are about to go wrong. You're following every instrument simultaneously, you're following the feeling, the mood, all the way through. In this take I was absolutely audience. I had done my job, there was nothing for me to do once the machines were rolling. I was no longer producer; I was just completely sucked up into it. The studio was totally darkened, the only light visible was a candle burning in the recording studio right next to Jim, whose back was to the control room, as he sang into his microphone.*

Original master tape and track listings for The Doors' first album

PAUL ROTHCHILD *I'd never been as moved in a recording studio as I was when that take went down. I was impressed by the fact that for one of the very first times in rock and roll history sheer drama had taken place on tape. This to me was very important, and it's also significant that Jim chose to use a purely classical image in modern dress to do this. The story he tells is basically the Oedipus legend.*

BRUCE BOTNICK *When recording* The Doors *and* Strange Days *at Sunset Sound, Jim was in the vocal booth and the guys were in the main studio with headphones looking at one another through glass windows. They recorded live to tape in the studio to capture the feel. The guys would come in for a 1 p.m. start and record, and then go to the Whisky and do a couple of shows. Recording at night was unusual in those early days, but on a rare occasion they'd come back in between shows and record some more. The whole album was recorded in five days.*

JOHN We were Jim's three musical sidekicks, and it took three of us to match the energy of this one person. We were lucky and talented enough to figure out the perfect sound bed for Jim to lie down in. When he first sang 'The End' *a cappella* it struck me as a goodbye love tune but over time as we played it in clubs the middle section stretched out into a king-sized bed for Jim to revel in. You could just feel the love and comfort that he got from surrendering to the drone-like guitar, the sustained organ, and the trance groove of this song. He unearthed the primal, sexual, edible underpinnings of all of our psyches.

RAY Jim's LSD intake did impinge upon the first recording sessions. Nothing disastrous other than when he went back to the studio after we had all left, because he 'knew' there was a fire. When he got to the studio the red work light was on. Hallucinating and seeing this red light, Morrison thinks, 'I knew it!' So he grabs the fire extinguisher and hoses down the entire studio.

ROBBY It wasn't on fire. It was the acid.

RAY Fortunately, it was just the instruments [that got wet]. The control room, where all the expensive shit was, he didn't go in. It was all our stuff that was all easily wiped off. I think at that point he realised what he had done so out the door he went, climbed over the fence and lost his shoe.

The next morning the owner of the studio, Tutti Camarata, called Jac Holzman to tell him that the studio had been hosed down. Jac said, 'Oh my God, is it a big loss?' And he said, 'No, it can be cleaned up, it's no big deal.' So Jac is like, 'Why are you calling me?' And Tutti said, 'Because we found Morrison's shoe.'

JAC HOLZMAN *After Tutti and I settled the Morrison misdemeanour, Tutti draped a fatherly arm over my shoulder and said, 'You're spending a lot of money on a band that can't behave itself. You've been a good customer and I'd hate to see Elektra hurt.' The $5,000 I had spent in studio time seemed like a lot to Tutti, who was used to bringing in a group of musicians who could knock out four tracks in three hours. I thanked Tutti for his concern and said I wasn't worried. Privately, I took a deep breath and hoped I was right.*

RAY [Another time,] Bruce Botnick had the LA Dodgers on and Sandy Koufax – one of the greatest pitchers of all time – was pitching. Bruce was recording with The Doors but he brought his portable television set, because he wanted to see the game. He couldn't put it in the control room, there was too much electrical equipment, too much static, so he found a place off to the side in the studio area, facing the control room window. Everything was fine.

We were in the middle of 'Light My Fire' and I was about to do my solo and Jim came out of the vocal booth and he started dancing around, having a great time. Then he came over to the TV set and noticed that it was on. He freaked out. This was our first recording session and a baseball game was on the TV set? Jim unplugged it, picked it up, and hurled it at the control room window which thankfully was double thick glass. It bounced off the window, fell on the floor, and shattered into 5,000 pieces.

PAUL ROTHCHILD *The lyric to 'Alabama Song' is strangely contemporary. There is one other verse in the song which The Doors didn't sing: the [one that goes] 'Show us the way to the next little dollar, oh, don't ask why.' It was out of context for them, not quite what they had in mind.*

RAY 'Alabama Song' – Dorothy's choice of Thirties Berlin cabaret for The Doors. Paul had brought in a strange device called a Marxophone. It was a turn-of-the-century autoharp with little hammers attached to a base that allowed you to lay it flat and play it somewhat like a keyboard. It gave off a ringing, jingle-jangle sound, all tinny and old-timey. It was a great choice for the song. We recorded the basic track, Jim put on a perfunctory guide vocal – he would get the master vocal later – and after a few passes and sound adjustments we had it. I put on the Marxophone overdub and we were done for the evening. 'Light My Fire' and 'Alabama Song', a good day's work.

ROBBY We used bass players on most of the records. On the first album, it was mostly the piano bass that Ray played with his left hand. I think the reason why some of The Doors' music is so hypnotic is that Ray sometimes had to play on autopilot. I overdubbed a couple of basslines too on the first album.

BRUCE BOTNICK *The Doors' first album was the only album that we recorded on four-track, half-inch tape. Eight-track, one-inch tape came into being in time for* Strange Days, *which is the format we used all the way through* L.A.Woman. *When we mixed we'd always make mono mixes for AM radio and stereo for the vinyl album. Mono never really left us. Both* The Doors *and* Strange Days *had mono vinyl releases and then Jac Holzman said, 'Let there be stereo.'*

JOHN We finished recording the album in days but the mixing down to the final two tracks for stereo took another couple of weeks. Mixing was tedious, but I liked the exactness that was necessary. The entire feel of a song could be changed by a slight drop or increase in volume on an obscure background instrument.

ROBBY We had no computers and only four tracks to work with. Organ and guitar on the first track, drums and piano bass on the second, vocal on the third, overdubs on the fourth. No click track, no autotune. Technology has opened up so many creative possibilities and streamlined the recording process in miraculous ways, but the ability to endlessly tweak and fine-tune everything to death has created way too many albums that sound perfect. I'm glad we recorded all The Doors albums when and how we did. The imperfections make them feel alive.

JOHN Technology is an aid but it's also dangerous, so you have to be careful how you use it. As they added more tracks – our first album was on four tracks – it was freeing to have more but I think some bands thought, well let's use them all! Let's put on a banjo, or an orchestra. But it's a trap. The song dictates the arrangement, not technology.

JAC HOLZMAN *Did I believe, when I signed The Doors, that their music would last, for 50 years now and counting? No. I believed they were musically distinctive, and worth the effort. It wasn't until we were mixing that I knew we had made an album that was historic.*

JIM THE FIRST ALBUM IS NOT REALLY SOCIALLY CONSCIOUS AT ALL. IT'S UNIVERSAL, PERSONAL STATEMENTS.

Advertisement in promotion of 'Light My Fire' in Cash Box, *27 May 1967*
Opposite: Outtake from the cover shoot for The Doors

ROBBY Jim didn't really like the cover of the first album even though it looked so good. He did complain about it but we all talked him into it. If you notice on the next album we were barely there at all, mostly on the back. He didn't want to be the star of the band.

JOHN At first I was like, 'Why is Jim's head so big?' and then I thought, 'Well he is kind of handsome.'

JIM Posing for a picture, can you imagine? You're only looking in the camera and posing. It's insane. I must have been out of my mind.

ROBBY Elektra had this silly idea that we should go down while they were putting up the billboard and have it look like we were helping to put it up. We wondered if it would be too commercial, but then we also thought no band had ever had a billboard like this.

JAC HOLZMAN *This was a new idea for the record business. No one in music had tried it before, but it was my way of saying to everyone in the music community of Los Angeles that Elektra had arrived, and we were big-time serious about a band that had a tenacious following. It was a message to radio and our distributors that we were willing to spend to make it happen.*

JOHN 'Break On Through' was chosen as the single, even though we were worried that the beat was too eccentric for the mass market. We had considered 'Twentieth Century Fox' as a single, but the chorus sounded too commercial, too cute, and we didn't want it to represent our sound, which we considered more hard edged.

JAC HOLZMAN *The short film Mark Abramson shot for 'Break On Through' helped us move The Doors around the country without transporting their bodies. It was one of the earliest pre-MTV clips aimed at the TV bandstand shows which were a staple of the late afternoon programming.*

It was Jac Holzman's idea to create a film to promote the The Doors' self-titled first album and their first single, 'Break On Through'. Seen by many as one of the first ever music videos, it was accompanied by a giant billboard on Sunset Boulevard to advertise the album, which was another of Jac's promotional innovations.

The film, directed by Mark Abramson, is shot on a dark soundstage with colourful stage lighting using Jac Holzman's 16mm camera. It features footage of the band playing live, which is then synced to the studio cut of 'Break On Through'.

Top: The Doors pose in front of their billboard, Sunset Boulevard, 1967
Above: Stills from the film promoting 'Break On Through'

CHATEAU
MARMONT

Break on Thru

ROBBY For 'Break On Through' I got the idea of the riff from the Paul Butterfield song 'Shake Your Money Maker', which is one of my favourites.

RAY 'Break On Through (To the Other Side)' is about opening the doors of perception, opening your mind up to break on through. Some people have said it's about death, but it's not about death, it's about expansion of consciousness. It's about breaking out of your chains, out of mundane existence, and breaking on through to the other side. The other side? That's freedom.

JIM More people should be involved, rather than designating all these powers to a few individuals. I think the average person, whatever that is, should be a part of it somehow and I think everyone feels that events are just going on without their knowledge or control. It's one of the tragedies of our time. I suppose it has always been that way but now it's just become so obvious. Decisions are made for you in which you have no part at all. I just lament the fact that so many people are content with living a very quiet, well-mannered, orderly life when so many obvious injustices are going on. They seem to ignore it somehow, or not care and just let it happen without ever becoming involved. I think that's sad.

ROBBY We'd put out 'Break On Through' as the first single but it didn't do very much. We wanted it to be number one but it didn't get there. But considering Elektra Records was a new company by most standards I don't think we were disappointed. We were pretty happy. They were a folk label originally, and flamenco. I listened to a lot of their stuff when I was in high school and I thought they were the best.

JOHN When the single of 'Break On Through' came out we convinced friends and relatives to start calling the stations to request it. Getting the band off the ground was a 24-hour obsession with each of us. If we weren't practising, we were sleeping. If we were eating, we were talking about the group.

One day I called the KRLA request line for what was probably the fortieth time. I said I was Fred Schwartz from West Covina and they said, 'We know who you are, and if you don't stop calling we'll pull the record!' I hoped I hadn't ruined our career before it began. 'Break On Through' slowly rose to number 11 in Los Angeles. It even made it to the bottom of the national charts, but just for a few weeks.

JIM MOST PEOPLE FEEL COMPLETELY VOID AND HELPLESS IN CONTROLLING THEIR OWN DESTINIES, IN CONTROLLING THE DESTINY OF HUMAN LIFE.

RESTRICTED
AREA
DO NOT
ENTER

ROBBY OUR FIRST FILLMORE SHOW WAS PROBABLY MY FAVOURITE CONCERT. WE KNEW WE HAD TO BE GOOD TO COMPETE WITH THE YOUNG RASCALS.

JAC HOLZMAN *Before the album was released I phoned Bill Graham in San Francisco and pleaded with him to book The Doors for the Fillmore before they broke wide. Though Bill and I trusted each other without question, selling him an unknown band was not going to be easy. After listening to my heavy pitch, Bill finally agreed but extracted one option for a repeat date within six months of the first booking – and both gigs for scale, hardly enough to cover the air fares. Bill Graham was doing a Jac Holzman on me! I gulped hard but agreed. San Francisco was the heart of spacy, rebellious rock and roll and The Doors had to be seen there.*

OVER AT THE FILLMORE this weekend, the Young Rascals, a tough, street-hip band from New York, headed a dance concert that included The Sopwith Camel and The Doors. It was a curious, if successful, show since the Camel is distinctly a low-pressure group in such a context and despite the popularity of their disc and their improvement on their tour, is not the kind of sound that grabs you.

The Doors are a weird group. They start off without much and gradually get into something which is not exactly the Frisco sound but some kind of Eastern-oriented improvisation that allows the drummer to build huge rhythmic climaxes. Both The Doors and the Young Rascals had excellent drummers, by the way, indicating, I think, a direction that will be taken by more rock groups in the future as the possibility of breaking through the straight jacket of strict time becomes a reality (as it has in jazz).

The light show on all walls was excellent but I was particularly struck by the projections from Head Lights (Jerry Abrams and Glenn McKay) which were really tuned in to the music.

JIM YOU HAVE TO BE IN A CONSTANT STATE OF REVOLUTION OR YOU'RE DEAD.

JOHN We went to the Bay Area and loved the whole scene. We felt like we were part of it. It felt kindred to be around other hippies. The middle of the country hadn't caught up yet. One time, Ray Manzarek, his girlfriend and I drove across the country because we were playing a club in New York and we got the car for free, as long as we paid for the gas, because it needed to be delivered to the West Coast. We stopped in a diner in Ohio and Ray and I had long hair and the guys there were asking the waitress for scissors so that they could cut our hair on the spot. So we felt a camaraderie with the guys in the Bay. Haight-Ashbury felt like the Sunset Strip or the Lower East Side in New York. There's always been a rivalry between the Bay Area and Southern California, just like the one between New York and LA. But it's healthy.

ROBBY We were never really protagonists of the flower movement. In fact, we were the complete opposite. What was happening with that trip is that the hippies were going all love and peace and everything is great, but really that was only one side of the coin and we were providing a glimpse of the other side as well. There always has to be a balance.

PAUL KANTNER *There was something that went on in San Francisco. It was the best rock and roll – in those days they called it 'tribal'. Jim was saying it was like a 'Dionysian experience'. It was like a religious experience. It's what religion should have been: total joy and exaltation. The Doors for me were one of the few Los Angeles bands that would excite that in their audience. They were one of the precursors to punk, new wave and heavy metal, I suppose.*

JIM There always has to be a revolution and that has to be a constant thing, not something that's changed things and that's it, the revolution has solved everything.

Above and opposite: Fisherman's Wharf, San Francisco, CA, 1967
Right: John Densmore in San Francisco
Opposite: Poster advertising The Doors' shows at The Matrix in San Francisco from 7 to 11 March 1967

RAY That evening was our first set at a San Francisco psychedelic ballroom. The Fillmore, Bill Graham's pleasure palace. We were the opening act behind Sopwith Camel and the headliners, The Young Rascals. We took the stage to a light smattering of applause and a few scattered boos after Bill Graham's announcement of 'Ladies and gentlemen, from Los Angeles, California … The Doors!' You see, San Francisco didn't like LA. Too plastic, not a real city. And here was a band being featured as coming from LA and calling themselves The Doors? Well, how pretentious and how very plasticine. 'Boo, hiss!'

BILL GRAHAM *Jim was very stubborn and very demanding. At the Fillmore in San Francisco he walked on stage one night and he was pretty loaded and he started waving the microphone over the audience. I got out there to try and stop him from dropping it, because it was quite a hard object. So I went on to the front of the stage and I tried to catch it and sure enough it landed right on my head and made a big lump. Of the 3,000 people, it had to hit me!*

BILL GRAHAM *After the show I told him that he had to be careful – he didn't want a lawsuit. And he said, 'It's part of my act. You're not going to tell me what to do.' So the next time he came back, he asked me to come up to the dressing room so that he could give me a gift. I opened the box and it was one of those jungle pith helmets, painted in psychedelic colours and it read, 'The Morrison Special'. He said, 'Now you're safe.'*

San Francisco, CA, spring 1967

ROBBY From playing to a small crowd at the London Fog to becoming famous didn't feel like a big deal to me. Jim got all the baggage that came with being the front man. I felt like I was in the background, along for the ride, which was fine with me.

JOHN *Shebang* was one of our first TV performances. We were clearly nervous. I mean, Jim won't even look at the camera or anything. I'm somehow positioned in the front. I'm the 'lead drummer'. Ridiculous!

RAY We really had no idea what we were doing. When the director started telling us what to do, we just looked at each other and said, 'I guess that's how it is.' We learned later that wasn't the case, but it was a great initial experience.

ROBBY We had no say whatsoever. There was a director telling us exactly what to do, and we did it. We just felt lucky to be there. *Shebang* was a local TV show, so it wasn't as big as *Dick Clark* – but it was great to be on there.

JIM I do think it's more difficult to manipulate TV and film than it is the press. The press has been easy for me in a way, because I am biased toward writing and I understand writing and the mind of writers; we are dealing with the same medium, the printed word. So that's been fairly easy. But television and films are much more difficult and I'm still learning. Each time I go on TV I get a little more relaxed and a little more able to communicate openly, and control it. It's an interesting process.

Appearance on KHJ's show Boss City, *Los Angeles, CA, late February 1967*
Opposite: Stills from The Doors' mimed performance of 'Break On Through' for the KTLA TV show Shebang, *Los Angeles, CA early March 1967*

VOX
AMP
SLO BLO
LINE
VOX Continental

RAY I played a Vox Continental, as played by all the English Mod bands. Anybody who played an organ had a Vox Continental. I was lucky enough to get one. On top of that I played the Fender Rhodes keyboard bass. It had 32 notes and it sat on the left-hand side on top of the organ. So I had the right hand for all the lead lines and on the left side I played the bass notes. It was like playing boogie woogie.

What was lovely about the little Vox Continental was that it was a portable suitcase-type instrument. You put it through a good amp, crank up the reverb, and you've got some real power. When we played at the Whisky, I could split eardrums with that California-style organ. I would squeeze down on the volume pedal until the sound became unearthly and people's heads would start turning. I could see their pain, and just at the point where I knew I was going over the edge, I would begin the lick and we would get into 'Summer's Almost Gone'.

ROBBY In March of '67 we played two packed weekend shows at the Avalon Ballroom with Country Joe and the Fish and then followed it up with several weeknight gigs at a much smaller club called The Matrix. They had a decent live recording set-up and they happened to roll tape while we were in town, so years later we were able to release a rare live album from the archives. Of course, we didn't draw much of an audience as an out-of-town band playing on a Tuesday, so it almost felt like we were back at the London Fog.

One time in Seattle, nobody came. There were like 20 people in this huge hockey rink. Jim was pissed and he wouldn't sing.

RAY We played a college town in Iowa. A beautiful old auditorium that held 1,500. There must have been 75 people in the whole damn place. But they loved it. They were a great little audience.

This page and opposite: Avalon Ballroom, San Francisco, CA, March 1967

COUNTRY JOE & THE FISH
THE SPARROW
THE DOORS

JOHN Dave Diamond, a local disc jockey who spun his records from the psychedelic depths of *The Diamond Mine* (the name of his radio show), invited Robby and me over to his house to show us piles of letters from listeners requesting 'Light My Fire' – the seven-minute version he was daring enough to play in an era of the strict three-minute format. He said we should consider cutting the song down to the standard three minutes and put it out as a single. We didn't like the idea of shortening our jazz solos, but Robby and I agreed with him that it could be a hit. Rothchild, however, was less than excited when we took the idea to him. Grudgingly he agreed to edit the song, saying he still didn't think the record had a chance.

RAY 'Light My Fire' is a seven-minute track and we had to do a version for the single so we had to cut it down to under three minutes. Paul Rothchild, a brilliant genius producer, and Bruce Botnick, our engineer, were Doors members five and six. I didn't know how Paul was going to cut it – you actually had to cut the tape in those days. Two days later he called us and told us he had it ready and wanted us to listen to it.

PAUL ROTHCHILD *Bruce and I had established a kind of rapport. He knew where I wanted things done and when, and when his work was done he did exactly the same thing, involuntarily, without volition.*

RAY We were all in the control room at Sunset Sound and the song started playing with the regular introduction, verse, chorus, and nothing seemed changed. But then he got to my solo and it cut to the end. There were no solos! Just straight back to the verses. I could have killed him! But he told us, 'Look, imagine you've never heard this song, you're 17 years old, you've never heard of The Doors. All you know is that a two minute and 45 second song is going to come on the radio called "Light My Fire". Does that work?' And you know what? It did.

JOHN In July 1967 'Light My Fire' hit number one on the charts and it stayed there for a month. It remained on the charts for an unheard of 26 weeks. A rumour spread like bushfire that the song was the anthem for race riots in Detroit that summer. That July we headed to New York for a club gig at the Scene and a series of interviews. It was all set up by the record company. When 'Light My Fire' started racing up the charts, we began crisscrossing the country on airplanes. This was to be our way of life for the next few years. Airports, baggage claim checks and limos became our steady environment. This time around in New York we were minor celebrities because *Newsweek*, *Vogue* and the *New York Times* all gave our album favourable reviews. It seemed as if they were trying to outdo each other with wild descriptions. *Time* magazine ran Jim's old quote from our Elektra biography: 'I'm interested in anything about revolt, disorder and chaos.' I'd hated the quote from the beginning. In spite of the attention it got, I had a feeling that it would lead to Jim's demise. Howard Smith gave us a terrific review in the *Village Voice*, calling Jim the first real male sex symbol since James Dean.

This page and opposite: New York, NY, September 1967

ROBBY **WHEN 'LIGHT MY FIRE' CAME OUT, THAT WAS REALLY A GAME-CHANGER.**

Try to excite
A cry in the night
Try to set the Night on Fire (S)

Interview

– What is the cloudburst sign?

–

– did you remember that you didn't remember?

–

JIM I like interviews because they're similar to answering questions on a witness stand. It's that strange area where you try and pin down something that happened in the past and try and honestly think about what you were thinking, what you were trying to do. It's a crucial mental exercise. An interview will often give you the chance to confront your mind with questions, which to me is what all art is about – a self-interview in which you pose yourself questions and try and come up with a reasonable answer. I like the interview form. I think it's going to become an increasingly important art form. I guess it has antecedence in the confession box, debating and cross-examination. Once you say something you can't retract it, it's too late. It's a very existential moment. I guess it's why talk shows are so popular, because it's right on the line, everyone is watching and you can't run back the tape and do it over, it's right there.

I'm the only one who can speak of such things that are relevant, & yet though I know I know I will remain silent & talk about peripheral matters. For instance –

ARE YOU READY FOR THE DOORS?

THEY ARE CREATING THE NEWEST AND THE WILDEST SOUND EVER —AND IT JUST MAY BLOW YOUR MIND!

JIM MORRISON

If you entered a room full of people and Jim Morrison was there, you wouldn't notice anyone else. That is the best way to describe the newest and most fabulous lead singer to hit what – for lack of a better expression — is called the pop scene.

Jim possesses a strange, captivating, somewhat suppressed sensuality combined with an almost childlike sensitivity and clarity which seem to imbue him with a special aura that glows about him wherever he goes. Jim moves through the ordinary world of people with the untamed grace and purpose of a strong, young, wild lion and, at the same time, he has qualities of innocence and ingenuousness which make him seem as lovable as a baby kitten.

Jim was born on December 8, 1943, in Melbourne, Fla. His full name is James Douglas Morrison, and he had the typical American allotment of one father, one mother and one younger brother. Restless and somewhat rebellious, he moved to California several years ago, where he began to endure the singular experience of "discovering himself". The search for the real Jim Morrison has not ended and perhaps it never will, but meanwhile he has crystallized from an everyday garden variety young college student into an incredibly fascinating and profoundly gifted performer and singer.

When Jim delivers all six feet of himself, moving sensuously under a flowing casque of light brown hair, into the spotlight and holds the microphone gently in his hands (almost as though it were a girl he is about to kiss) — he has already hypnotized his audience. What follows is even more spellbinding. The resonant, rhythmic style of singing oscillates between the earthiest of blues shouting to the tenderest of love ballads. It is a sound that is like an overwhelming shock-wave combined with an anguished plea from deep in the soul of a very lost and very lonely young man.

That is about as close as anyone will ever come to describing Jim Morrison, and what he *is* and what he *does*. But that is not all; there is the future. There will be more, for Jim Morrison moves faster than the speed of light and whatever surprises he has in store are right around the corner. Don't anticipate, just turn the corner — and follow him. He is waiting to take you into his unknown future.

•

RAY MANZAREK

Behind the vital, ever changing Jim Morrison there is a sound *other* than his voice. When the fingers of Ray Manzarek touch the keys of the electric organ you are suddenly a part of his music. It is as though the sonic vibrations enter you and literally lift you out of your chair. They take you somewhere — to a place you have never been — and while you are there, you don't ever want to come back to where you are now. Just as Jim gives himself totally to his song, Ray *blends* the sounds he is playing until they become one, blending and consuming every*thing* and every *person* within its wave-length.

Tall, thin, gentle Raymond Daniel Manzarek was born on February 12, 1942, in Chicago. His personal musical tastes run from Muddy Waters to Jacques Brel, illustrating that his range in his "private" life is as extraordinary as it is in his "music" life. Intelligent, quiet and stable, Ray is the backbone of the Doors.

•

JOHN DENSMORE

The heartbeat, then, is John Paul Densmore — Door drummer. Johnny plays the drums with a subdued kind of eloquence that is eye-catching but not distracting. He is kind and careful, and yet has a style all his own — qualities which show brilliantly when he is performing. He was born in Santa Monica, Calif., and has dark brown hair and blue eyes. When he removes himself from the pulsating climate of the Doors, John searches out old movies and good books — and if Jimmy Reed or Van Morrison are playing in town, you can count on finding John in the audience.

He is single (as are all the Doors) and doesn't "date," but instead searches for sensitive and spontaneous girls who would prefer to communicate on a personal level, rather than spend an evening partying or dancing.

•

ROBBY KRIEGER

The electric guitar as such has had many adventures, but none quite so different and expansive as those given to it by the skilled fingers of Robert Alan Krieger. A rock and roll and blues lover since his mid-teens, Robby evolved from trumpet to classical guitar, from blues to rock and roll, and to what now can only be called "the Doors' sound." When Ray and Robby start to *blend*, there is no end to the trip they can take you on. It is one of the higher experiences of popular music — as you probably know if you have ever listened to either of the Doors' fantastic Electra LP's, *The Doors* and/or *Strange Days*.

Sonically, Robby is only halfway up the Mt. Everest of the guitar. As he scales the higher, more dizzying peaks of the musical possibilities of the electric guitar, you may have to run fast to keep up. But it is worth it, for the Doors are the newest and the greatest — the end!

Be *ready* for them when they come your way!

18

Feature profiling The Doors, 16 magazine, December 1967
Opposite: Jim photographed by Gloria Stavers, 16 magazine's editor-in-chief, New York, NY, September 1967

NANCY SINATRA *'Light My Fire' is one of the most evocative songs ever written. I'm grateful to have run into it and recorded it.*

SLASH *When I first visited LA, 'Light My Fire' was on every car radio and on every stereo. You couldn't escape it. It was a living, breathing behemoth of a song and The Doors were the band everybody was talking about. It made quite an impression on two-year-old me. It was like Los Angeles was Doors town.*

BRUCE BOTNICK *Nobody is a good enough fortune teller to tell you the first time they hear something that it's going to be really important and stand the test of time. But I did relate to The Doors immediately; they were like nothing I'd ever heard before and somehow innately I knew what to do.*

JOHN We had no idea it was to become a classic and our biggest seller ever. Something in my bones did tell me that 'Light My Fire' was special. The transition from the verse into the chorus made something inside of me weep. On each song we had tried every possible arrangement, so we felt the whole album was tight. No excess. And Jim was happy with 'The End', his dark, poetic, stream-of-consciousness vision accompanied by Robby's sitar-like guitar. When the album was released, each of the band members got ten copies. I held off for a few days and then finally played the album for my parents. I was very proud of it but worried about their reaction to 'The End'.

ROBBY With the success of 'Light My Fire' a few songs from the first album were overlooked – 'Twentieth Century Fox', 'Alabama Song' and 'Back Door Man' didn't get the love they should have.

ROBBY We had a road manager, Bill Siddons, to take care of things on tour, but our attorney Max Fink recommended we hire two slick Hollywood characters as our career managers: Sal Bonafede and Asher Dann. Sal had previously managed Dion, and Asher was a real estate agent. Asher didn't have any experience managing bands, but he was a good drinker, which was an essential skill when dealing with Jim. Sal and Asher's theory was that if we got Jim really drunk the night before a show, he would wake up the next day all contrite and humble and therefore he wouldn't drink as much on the show night. This, of course, did not work. Asher took Jim out and got him hammered one night before we played the Scene in New York. The next night at the show, not only was Jim drunk, but when he started swinging the mic around like a lasso in the same fashion that had taken down Bill Graham, Asher jumped on the stage to try and stop him and our show suddenly turned into a wrestling match. We bought Sal and Asher out of their management contract early the next year.

JIM On a very basic level, I love drinking. But I can't see drinking just milk or water or Coca Cola. It just ruins it for me. You have to have wine or beer to complete a meal.

JOHN I wasn't at the Scene when Jim got on stage with Jimi Hendrix but I've heard the tapes. I hated it, Jim was so drunk.

Steve Paul's the Scene nightclub, New York, NY, 27 June 1967
Opposite: Lucky U Mexican restaurant, Venice Beach, CA, 1967

Gibson

Robby's lost Gibson (right) was a red '63 or '64 SG Special with the serial number 88779 and it had black P-90 pick-ups. He found a replacement – a red 1967 model (opposite and below) – soon after the original was stolen, but he began to think back to the magic of his first Gibson when writing his 2021 memoir Set the Night on Fire.

ROBBY I hope to find my first guitar. It's the one I wrote 'Light My Fire' with and played on the first two albums. I don't know what it is about the SG. It's just a psychedelic looking guitar and it sounds great too. It's got that double cutaway so it's easier to play up high. There's a lot of good things about it. I think the SG had a smoother sound compared to the Fender guitars of the day. The Fender stuff was twangier, and I never was a fan of that. I always have gone for smoother sounds, which I could get with the Gibson.

SUNSET SOUND
SUNSET
Sound Recorders

SUNSET SOUND RECORDERS

6650 Sunset Blvd, LA

ROBBY We had enough songs to do two albums and the minute the first one was doing well because of 'Light My Fire' they wanted us to keep going and do the next one.

BRUCE BOTNICK *It is the case with almost every artist that when they start to get recognised and they go on the road, they normally don't have much inspiration and spare time to write songs. The further down the road of success the artist got, the fewer and fewer new songs there were. When The Doors came into Sunset Sound Recorders Studio One, they already had 25 songs ready to go. That's why when we recorded* The Doors *through* Morrison Hotel, *we always had lots of songs to work with.*

Sunset Sound Recorders
6650 Sunset Boulevard Hollywood, California 90028 Phone HOllywood 9-1186 № 5631

To ELEKTRA CORP.
1855 Broadway
New York, N. Y. 10023

Date July 6, 1967
Customer's Order Number
Shipped Via To

OVERDUB: DOORS	
OVERDUBBING: 6 hours @ $35.00 per hour	210 00
4 hours @ $45.00 per hour	180 00
8-TRACK MACHINE: 10 hours @ $35.00 per hour	350 00
	740 00
Tax	29 60
	769 60

This invoice is your statement

JOHN We started our second album back at Sunset Sound that May. Elektra announced a record-breaking advance order of 500,000 copies, so we were excited about delivering the goods to a receptive audience. As we were feeling that Max Fink was an old-school lawyer, and we could use some new blood, my old girlfriend Donna Port urged us to see a friend of hers, Abe Somer.

The contract had options for two more albums, at the same royalty rates, but Abe felt with the huge success of 'Light My Fire' and the album having already sold a half million copies, he could vastly improve our deal. 'First of all, you should own your own songs. That's your gold, and it belongs to you. It's nothing to have your own publishing company. It costs $200 and we'll take care of the paperwork. Jac owning it is slightly immoral. Second, I think I can get a better overall deal. I'll call Jac in New York right now, and you'll see the guilt coming through the phone. Elektra may seem like a family, but wait until we audit them.'

ROBBY Abe made the case to Jac that he should give us 100 percent of our publishing. He didn't think Jac would actually go for it; he was using it as a negotiation tactic to make Jac compromise on other deal points. But Jac just said, 'OK' and handed it over, because he thought it sounded fair. It's almost impossible to imagine another record label being that way.

2 TRACK ☑ 4 TRACK ☐
TAPE SPEED 7½ ☐ 15 ☑
MASTER NO. 74014
DATE 9-20-67
MUNTZ STEREO-PAK INC.
16032 ARMINTA STREET VAN NUYS, CALIFORNIA — 787-2420
3183
ENGR. RECORDED ON # TONE AT HEAD ☐ TAIL ☐ NONE ☐ MASTER FROM Elektra

TITLE	TIME	REMARKS
SIDE ONE:		
STRANGE DAYS	3:05	
YOU'RE LOST LITTLE GIRL	2:57	
LOVE ME TWO TIMES	3:18	
~~UNHAPPY GIRL~~ I CAN'T SEE YOUR FACE	3:21	
HORSE LATITUDES	1:35	
MOONLIGHT DRIVE	3:00	
		17:38
SIDE TWO:		
PEOPLE ARE STRANGE	2:09	
MY EYES HAVE SEEN YOU	2:25	
~~I CAN'T SEE YOUR FACE IN MY MIND~~ UNHAPPY GIRL	1:55	
WHEN THE MUSIC'S OVER	10:59	
		17:38

Remake 9-27-67
2nd 4-TRACK
ALBUM TITLE STRANGE DAYS ARTIST The Doors
TIME SIDE A EDITED BY
TIME SIDE B APPROVED BY
CT
MUNTZ RELEASE NO. A-EKT-74014

Opposite: Ray and Robby with journalist Hank Zevallos during the recording of Strange Days*, Sunset Sound Recorders, Los Angeles, CA, May 1967*
Bottom right: Tape box from the Strange Days *sessions, September 1967*

This page and opposite: The recording of Strange Days, *Sunset Sound Recorders, Los Angeles, CA, May 1967*
Opposite, top right: Ray with producer Paul Rothchild (centre) and engineer Bruce Botnick (right)
Opposite, top and bottom right: Tape box from the Strange Days *sessions, September 1967*

RAY Recording is entirely different to playing in person. In the recording studio it's more like a laboratory. You can be much more selective about what you create, whereas in person there's a greater degree of spontaneity.

Strange Days is when we began to experiment with the studio itself, as an instrument to be played. It was now eight-track, and we thought, 'My goodness, how amazing! We can do all kinds of things – we can do overdubs, anything, we've got eight tracks to play with!' It seems like nothing today but those eight tracks to us were really liberating. It became a band of five: keyboard, guitar, drums, vocalist and the studio.

BRUCE BOTNICK *In any good relationship between artist, producer and engineer, there is a meeting of the minds, and a lot of it is unspoken. It's an understanding and there's a chemistry there. The six of us made those records together; it was a team effort.*

JOHN Paul Rothchild, our producer, was very open to listening to everyone's input in the recording studio. If he had been an old-time producer, we probably wouldn't have been invited to the mix, where the final sound is put together. But Paul was wise enough to know that the new groups were very concerned about every stage of recording.

The recording of the second album began very well. We polished up 'My Eyes Have Seen You', which was written in Ray's parents' garage before Robby even arrived, and rehearsed 'People Are Strange' for a couple of weeks. It turned into a catchy song with single potential.

Second Album By 'Doors' To Be Released

Susquehanna's Homecoming evening attraction, The Doors, has become the first group this year to receive a Gold Record for sales of its record, "The Doors," in excess of $1,000,000.

The group's second album, "Strange Days," will be released soon.

THE DOORS, in person, have become the best the West has to offer. In concert at the Village Theater several weeks ago, they were frightening and beautiful beyond my ability to describe. In the audience, young men with thoughtfully groomed beards contorted like Beatles fans in the days of Shea Stadium. Robbie, Ray and John excelled in musicianship, constantly adding to the perfection of their album (now number two in the country--!--and certainly indelible in the minds of the audience) and leaving no note unturned in their desire to communicate. And as it was meant to be, Jim stole the show. "I tell you, I tell you, I tell you we must die!" "Hope not," he added. Our hearts stopped. "The men don't know, but the little girls, they understand... Don't 'cha?" The audience gasped. The first show was the unexpected by way of the familiar, anti-climaxing nicely with "Light My Fire." The difference between "records" and "live," the subtleties of "new" and "old-as-new" were illustrated with utter clarity. Jim brilliantly carried the audience from anticipation to excitement to over-the-edge fright and joy. And the second show, opening with "When the Music's Over," made the first an introduction. If "Horse Latitudes" had shaken us stem to stern, still we didn't know how lost we were till Jim spoke, without accompaniment, the Sophocles section of "The End." And then fell, worshipping some young lady knelt before the stage. And suddenly flew into the air, a leap to make Nureyev proud. And finally swung his microphone on its cord, around his head, towards the audience, more and more violent, prepared to release--everything; and we knew he'd do it. One of us would die. "This is the end," he sang into the now-frustrated, un-violent microphone, "my only friend," and Jim was wonderful shrugging his shoulders and letting the boys carry on in "Light My Fire." The Doors are now the best performers in the country, and if the albums are poetry as well as music, then the stage show is most of all drama, brilliant theater in any sense of the word. Artistic expression transcending all form, because you knew as Jim died there for you on stage that that wasn't mere acting--but it was all for art. Christ, they say, became the perfect criminal, negating all crimes in his own most heinous one. Absolving the world by absorbing all sins. And Jim dies a little more each day, pulling towards him all the violence around him, frightening and beautiful as he strains to perfect his art. And every day more of a pop star, pied piper of mice and the flower kids, and when the music's over.... When I first heard a dub of Strange Days, I thought of Rap Brown's troubles and suggested that in six months everyone connected with this album might be in jail. But I wasn't kidding. Cancel my subscription... ::: WABC in New York will not play records over 3½ minutes long until they're in the top 20 nationwide. WMCA is trying to follow a similar policy (records affected include "All We Need Is Love," "Ode to Billie Joe," "Pooneil," "Whiter Shade of Pale," "We Love You" and "Dandelion"). And WOR-FM doesn't really play better music, only more. And they still publish a weekly "best-selling" chart. Who's in charge here? ::: The MONKEES had to cancel a concert in Detroit because of the riots. ::: Rays of hope: APOSTOLIC, the first twelve-track recording studio in the country, is now open at 53 East 10th Street in New York. This may be a real boon to the development of local rock groups; it's certainly friendlier and more aware than the average studio.

Crawdaddy

ROBBY John and I were staying in Laurel Canyon at our Lookout Mountain house when Jim dropped by. I had seen Jim in every type of mood, but I had never seen him so depressed. He kept saying things like, 'What's the point, man?' At first, I thought it might be a pity play to get the girls to feel sorry for him, but it soon became clear that this was genuine despair. I don't know what was weighing on him. He wasn't drunk, as far as I could tell. He didn't specifically say he wanted to end it all but his attitude was heavy enough that it seemed like it might be on the table. We all tried to cheer him up, but nothing was working. As the predawn light filtered through the windows, I suggested we all take a walk up to Appian Way to watch the sunrise.

It worked. The sun brightened both the sky and Jim's mood. When we got back to the house he explained the revelation he'd had: 'When you're strange ... people are strange. It's your own mind that makes everything seem fucked up even when it isn't. It doesn't come from the outside. It comes from within.'

Jim immediately scribbled down some rough lyrics, I added a guitar part, and within a week we recorded 'People Are Strange' for the *Strange Days* album. I thought it was a nice, quirky little song, but I had no clue at the time that the Laurel Canyon sunrise had just inspired one of The Doors' biggest hits.

JOHN During the recording of the *Strange Days* album, Morrison's attitude was more confident. For all of us the studio was becoming a familiar place, we were more relaxed there. It was almost like a second home. Botnick was using more and more microphones on my drums, which my ego liked. Getting the sound on the drums took forever; I had to play each drum and cymbal over and over individually in simple, monotonous patterns until Rothchild was satisfied with what he heard.

JIM I think the music got progressively better – tighter and more professional and more interesting. [In 1967] there was a great renaissance of spirit and emotion and revolution sentiment, but when things didn't change overnight people resented the fact that we were still around doing good music.

The Doors with engineer Bruce Botnick and producer Paul Rothchild during the recording of Strange Days*, Sunset Sound Recorders, Los Angeles, CA, 1967*
Right: 'People Are Strange' ad, 1967
Overleaf: Crawdaddy *piece on The Doors, Issue 11, September/October 1967*

Making Records

The World consists of rival gangs incessantly warring, roaming the earth, raping & pillaging the planet

ROBBY After we did 'Light My Fire' and 'The End', which were both long songs, we thought we better do another long one. Ray was listening to Herbie Hancock's 'Watermelon Man' one day, which inspired the bassline for 'When the Music's Over'.

RAY I knew Jim was a great poet. There's no doubt about that. That's why we put the band together in the first place. I loved his poetry. He was doing ecological poetry: 'What have they done to the earth?' The words were well edited. Jim was good that way when it came to songs. He put his words into an entirely different context, a musical context, a hit single in a three-minute context.

NILE RODGERS *I think about the lyric, 'What have they done to the earth, what have they done to our fair sister?' I never thought about ecological things when I was younger because people really didn't talk about the environment that much. I'm not certain if that's what Jim was talking about but if he were, that was way ahead of its time. When The Doors go into that instrumental section and they just take off, it feels like they're free-form improvising. It's amazing, it's just like bebop. It felt to me like the super-hip jazz players that were all around my house and the music that I listened to with my mom.*

Strange days have found us
Strange days have tracked us down
They're going to destroy
our casual joys
We shall go on playing or find a new town

Strange eyes fill strange rooms
Voices will signal their tired end
The hostess is grinning
Her guests sleep from sinning
Hear me talk of sin you know this is it

Strange days have found us
and thru their strange hours we linger alone
Our bodies confused
memories misused
we run from the day
to a strange night of stone

JOHN We certainly made Jim's voice sound strange on the title cut. For 'Unhappy Girl' Rothchild actually had Ray overdub the chord changes backwards on the piano while listening to the song backwards, and then played it back forwards. The backwards piano track sounded like some melodic percussion instrument – a rattle or shaker – playing the correct chords.

BRUCE BOTNICK *A special place during the sessions for* The Doors *and* Strange Days *was the famous Sunset Sound Recorders Studio One echo chamber. The chamber was made of six layers of glued and screwed plaster dry wall and had 40 coats of resin, which made it sound and feel like you were in a huge wooden room. Because most of us were meditating with the Maharishi and also consuming copious quantities of cannabis, we'd go into the echo chamber, shut the door, and in the dark reach out psychically and feel the space, one of the many fond memories of the Summer of Love.*

Although it has been said that if you can remember the Sixties you weren't there, I know we were there – in the echo chamber.

Years later, going back to the eight-track tapes for the band's 40th anniversary and later Atmos rereleases, I found that for a majority of the songs we didn't record more than a couple of takes. The feel and spontaneity of the performance was everything.

Above right: Advertisement for Strange Days *featured in* Cash Box*, 28 October 1967*
Above left: Jim's handwritten notes for 'Strange Days'
Opposite: A page taken from Jim's notebook

JOHN We all loved the photograph on the album cover, with the posters of the first album in the background all ripped and torn.

ROBBY The cover for *Strange Days* was Jim's idea. The first album had this big image of him with these three little guys in the back and he was embarrassed by that, so he overdid it on the next one and didn't want any of us on the front. There is a little poster on the street which does have us on, though. The alleyway where they took the picture was right where Ravi Shankar lived.

JIM I hated that cover on the first album. So I said, 'I don't want to be on this cover. Put a chick on it or something. Let's have a dandelion or a design.'

Originally, I wanted us in a room surrounded by about 30 dogs, but that was impossible because we couldn't get the dogs and everybody was saying, 'What do you want dogs for?' I said that it was symbolic that it spelled God backwards. Finally we ended up leaving it up to the art director and the photographer. We wanted some real freaks, though, and he came out with a typical sideshow thing. It looked European. It was better than having our fucking faces on it, though.

Strange Days

Gatefold for Strange Days
Opposite: Bronson Caves, Los Angeles, CA, 1967

JIM I LIKE TRAVELLING AROUND, THAT'S THE BEST PART OF THE BUSINESS.

RAY We moved all around the country, playing and promoting the new album for the people in Iowa, Colorado, New York, Oklahoma, Massachusetts, Maryland, Pennsylvania, California. The University of Michigan homecoming dance – what a disaster! Jim got drunk, John and Robby stormed off the stage in a fit of pique, I played guitar until the football players – men of great bulk in black broadcloth – and their diminutive dates in pink taffeta started booing and throwing paper cups of punch at the two stoners on the stage playing John Lee Hooker Chicago blues. It was a total fiasco but Jim Osterberg, a.k.a. Iggy Pop, was there and it changed his life. The sheer outrageousness and audacity of Jim Morrison convinced Iggy that a life of anarchic rebellion was the only way to fly.

JOHN Our stage presence, especially Jim's, evolved to meet the size of the growing audience. First we played the clubs, then second bill at small 2,000-seat auditoriums like the Cheetah. I couldn't believe my eyes. Someone had turned Lawrence Welk's Aragon Ballroom on the Santa Monica Pier into a mock spaceship called the Cheetah. Across the gleaming hardwood floor Jim ambled slowly onto the ten-foot-high island-like stage. A cocky smile flashed across his face. He knew he belonged there.

The Doors return to the Whisky a Go Go for the first time since their dismissal in August 1966, 16-21 May 1967
Opposite: The audience at the Town Hall, Philadelphia, PA, 18 June 1967

JIM The bigger the audience the better. I like playing any place where there's a large crowd of enthusiastic people to watch us. In an intimate club atmosphere you can be more subtle. In a large arena you have to be more theatrical but they're both interesting. You're not aware of individuals like you are in a smaller place. In a smaller place you can see individuals. In a large place all you see is a mass.

JOHN The managers ran us ragged. They booked us anywhere and everywhere. We played the Earl Warren Showground once, which is for horses, not music. We were on the same bill as the Grateful Dead. When we were doing the soundcheck, I went to the centre of the circular room, clapped my hands and there was so much reverberation. It was more than I had ever heard. It was frustrating.

The Mountain Will Really 'Rock' Next Weekend

RAY They came for the show and not the music. They came to watch Jim become the 'wild man'. They didn't want intense psychic acts in the ether by the black-leathered lead singer. They wanted a freak show, a geek show, as the band played its most famous songs. Jim's reputation for outrageousness had set up an expectation in the minds of the cud types in the audience.

JIM KERR *There were two Jim Morrisons. There was the wild man, almost pagan Morrison, the boorish, the abusive; and then at the same time, his father said, 'Let it be known that Jim was quite a polite, quiet young man.'*

KFRC Fantasy Fair — Magic Mountain Music Festival

. . . A gathering of beautiful things, created and collected by the artisans and craftsmen of Northern California, and represented by the exhibitors listed on the Fantasy Fair Map.

. . . A variety of "happenings." When you arrive at the Fantasy Fair, you will be immediately surrounded by color and motion, the good vibrations of thousands of people flowing with the natural beauty of Mt. Tamalpais. The major happening is you, your feeling of good will, and your knowledge that the Fair and the Mountain are a part of you, therefore yours to enjoy. The woods and meadows are an open invitation to wander and enjoy yourself to the limits of your imagination. And because they are yours to enjoy, we hope that you will groove with the surroundings, doing everything you can to keep them in their natural state.

. . . For your enjoyment, The Fantasy Fair staff has prepared the Geodesic Dome Light Chamber. The Dome can accommodate 150 people per 8 minute show. We invite your participation in the wonders of the Dome, and ask that at the end of each show, you move out to make room for others waiting on line. You are also invited to enjoy out the giant slide, the tree swings (on the way to the valley of dancing), the vast assortment of strolling or sitting musicians (find many of them under trees or behind rocks,) and dozens of other surprises prepared by Fantasy Fair volunteers for your pleasure and participation.

Music will be performed hourly in the Amphitheater from 8 A. M. until 6 P. M. We ask that after each performance the seats be cleared to make way for people who may be waiting for the next performance.

The Fantasy Fair wishes to express extreme gratitude to the artists in the performing groups, who have graciously donated their valuable time and exceptional talents, and all the bands performing in the Valley of Dancing.

This page and opposite: KFRC Fantasy Fair and Magic Mountain Music Festival, Sidney B. Cushing Amphitheatre, Mill Valley, CA, 10 June 1967

THE DO
5 B 2
BALCONY
JUNE
18
1967
SUN. EVE., at
Est. Price $2.39
City Tax .12
TOWN
Broad & Race
Phila., Pa.

JIM Sex is just one part of my act. There are a lot of other factors. It is important I guess, but I don't think it is the main thing, although all music is a very nature-based thing. So they can't be separated. But the sex thing has been picked out because it sells papers.

RAY 1967 WAS THE SUMMER OF LOVE.

JOHN The summer of 1967 was one of travelling the country from coast to coast, from gig to gig, studio session to studio session. We were trying to crack New York again, appearing at the Scene in June while the Monterey Pop Festival, the first of its kind, was going on in California. I was depressed that we were in this dumpy club across the country while all of the important groups of the Sixties were in Monterey. Of course, we weren't even invited! Later, Derek Taylor, one of the organisers, was to say that we'd been overlooked. Bullshit. They knew about us. They were afraid of us. We didn't represent the attitude of the festival: peace and love and flower power. We represented the shadow side. My flower child half strongly wanted to be tripping and dancing at the festival, but I was in the demon Doors.

Previous pages: Town Hall, Philadelphia, PA, 18 June 1967
Left and opposite, top: Fantasy Faire and Magic Music Festival, Northridge, CA, 15 July 1967

Fantasy Faire, Music Show Headlined By Top Groups

RAY Getting high, taking the psychedelic substances, feeling part of the Earth, feeling a part of the planet and feeling your brothers and sisters – white, black, brown, purple and green, we were all brothers and sisters made of the same flesh. Made of the same energy, that's what The Doors were all about. That's what the Sixties were all about.

JOHN The days and weeks blurred as we performed continually. I began dreading the drive down to the airport to get on another flight. Especially with Jim. Sometimes it felt like I was trapped on an airplane with a lunatic. I thought that if these other passengers knew what was going on in Jim's mind they would head for the exit, find a parachute, and jump out, 'cause he's gonna open the exit door anyway. He'll wait till we're good and up in the air. On one flight during this tour, Jim got so loud and drunk that the stewardess summoned the captain. Jim snapped to attention, said 'Yes, sir', and quickly sat down at the captain's mere presence. Interesting.

JIM I think the major influence in the next decade or so will be the people, connectors you could call them, who are able to assemble huge masses of people under one spot as we've witnessed at pop festivals. The rock music enthusiasts have created some of the most exciting music and theatrical events on the planet. I think they're fantastic.

ROBBY The Fantasy Faire Festival wasn't as well documented as the Monterey Pop Festival or Woodstock, but it was actually the first major outdoor music event of its kind. Tens of thousands of people, 30 bands, multiple stages, art installations, vendors, food, drugs, and a big inflatable Buddha. It's largely forgotten about now but we had never seen anything like it. And, of course, I forgot to bring my guitar. I left it at the motel, which was 30 miles away, so I had to borrow one – possibly from one of the guys from Jefferson Airplane. We used to borrow stuff from them quite a bit.

ROBBY *The Ed Sullivan Show* was the biggest show you could play on at that time. If there was a show of that calibre today I would definitely play on it, but only if we had total control over the lyrics. The producers told us we couldn't use the word 'higher' on national television. I'm glad they didn't do the same thing for radio too.

JOHN At one point during rehearsal, Ed says to us, 'You know, you boys are too serious. You should smile. You look good when you're smiling and laughing.' Thanks for that stage direction, Mr. Sullivan.

RAY So Jim sings the word 'higher' after we promised he wouldn't. After the show the producer rushes into the dressing room and screams, 'We were going to book you for six more shows, but now you'll never play *The Ed Sullivan Show* again!' So Jim says, 'That's fine, because we just *did* play *The Ed Sullivan Show.*'

JIM I THINK OF MYSELF AS AN INTELLIGENT, SENSITIVE HUMAN BEING WITH THE SOUL OF A CLOWN. IT ALWAYS FORCES ME TO BLOW IT AT THE MOST IMPORTANT MOMENTS.

Bronson Caves, Los Angeles, CA, 1967
Opposite: The Ed Sullivan Show, *New York, NY, 17 September 1967*

JOHN MY FEELINGS ABOUT LIVE PERFORMANCES WERE BITTERSWEET.

JOHN Was the magical hour on stage worth all the craziness and rootless feeling of the road? Jac Holzman, who was, after all, president of a folk label, had Paul Simon over for dinner and played him some of our demos for our second album. He told Paul The Doors were going to be the biggest group in America, and Simon agreed. Simon also agreed to have us play second bill with Simon and Garfunkel at Forest Hills. Ten thousand people!

We went out on stage and Jim didn't give an inch. He didn't try to connect to the audience in any way. At the end of our set, during the 'Father, I want to kill you' section, Jim put all the bottled-up hatred and rage and whatever was bothering him into slamming the mic down and screaming. It lasted about one minute. The audience woke up a bit and started thinking about what they were seeing.

RAY They were the kings of New York and we were the opening act. And it was terrible. In that very prestigious tennis centre of the US Open we had the worst reception of our entire career. The audience had come to see smarm and were instead getting rock abyss from the opening act. And they hated it! Boos, catcalls, heckling, jeers and whistles assaulted us as we tried to weave a little night music around their empty heads. But they didn't want electric, they didn't want Jung, they didn't want The Doors. They wanted their soft boys. They wanted to be coated with honey-tongued harmonies. They did not want intensity. It was ultimately a battle between soft folk-rock (very nice, very inoffensive) and West Coast psychedelic jazz-rock. We lost. Badly. Jim said it was the worst gig he had ever played and the worst audience he had ever experienced.

JIM I don't think our particular style of music holds up very well in a huge outdoor event.

Rock leader says mystic religion popular

The Shaman

medieval shamanism

JIM I must have been about four when my mother, father and I were driving to the desert at dawn and a truckload of Indian workers had hit another car or something. But they were scattered all over the highway, bleeding to death, so the car pulls up and stops. That was the first time I tasted fear. A child is just like a flower that's floating in the breeze. The reaction I get now, looking back, is that the souls of those dead Indians, maybe one or two of them were running around, freaking out, and leaped into my soul. And they're still in there.

Indians scattered on dawn's
Hiway bleeding. / Ghosts
crowd the young child's
~~Fragile~~ egg-shell mind

RAY He saw this accident and he says the souls of one or two of those dead Indians jumped into his body and are still in there. He's the only guy I ever knew who was really interested in that sort of thing and could sort of become it on stage. It wasn't part of his background at all – he came from a military background and a very standard American upbringing. Yet there was this other side of him too and I always wondered where it came from and he told me that story and I thought, 'That's it, man, that explains it.'

The shaman was the medicine man. He wasn't necessarily in charge of healing but he was the visionary, the seer of the tribe. The people would have special feast days and ceremonies where everyone would sit around and play on drums and rattles and the shaman would stand in the middle of this circle of people and go into a trance. His spirit would leave his body and he would go on these psychedelic voyages in which he would see what might be wrong with somebody in the tribe, what the weather was going to be like next year, what the harvest would be like, what kind of psychic crisis this tribe might be going through. He was a spiritual guide and Jim Morrison was that same kind of guide on stage.

Top: New York, NY, September 1967
Above: Jim on the cover of Crawdaddy, *1967*

RAY THE CONCERTS BECAME A SHAMANISTIC RITE.

ROBBY It wasn't easy with Jim. That's why we had meditation. I think that really helped and after all, it's where we all met. Even though Ray didn't keep it up, he was still a meditator at heart and we needed that to balance Jim's craziness.

ALICE COOPER *He would fall out of windows drunk and never go to the doctor with broken limbs and perform that day. I saw him jump out of an MG one night going along Topanga Canyon.*

JAC HOLZMAN *My moments with Jim were generally peaceful. In my experience, Jim was a person who would break out in a rash occasionally, and he would do something like chop up a typewriter in the office, so we would just deduct the cost of the typewriter from the next royalty cheque. That wasn't a big deal. I found him to be extremely soft and willing to talk. He would try to get me to go drinking with him, which I wouldn't do because I knew I was out-classed. Once when I declined he said, 'Jac, you've got to get more out there on the edge.' And I said, 'Jim, I agree with you, being out there on the edge is important; the trick is not to bleed.'*

NEW HAVEN ARENA

26 Grove Street

On 9 December 1967, Jim Morrison did something that no musician had done before, and that was to get arrested on stage during a live performance. The Doors had just released their second album, Strange Days*, to critical acclaim and were nearing the end of a gruelling, months-long tour. On 8 December, their gig at the Rensselaer Polytechnic Institute in Troy, NY was, by all accounts, a disaster, with the crowd not responding to the music or Jim Morrison. Jim left the gig dejected and depressed. The next day the band was off to a gig in New Haven, CT. The New Haven Arena was an old ice hockey facility built in 1927. By the time The Doors performed there in 1967, the building had seen better days. It had old wooden doors and windows that were easy to pry open, and fans would routinely take advantage of that to sneak into concerts. To address this, the arena management would hire New Haven police officers to come along a few hours before showtime to check every nook and cranny to ensure no freeloaders were hiding out. On the night of The Doors' concert, 35 of New Haven's police showed up at around 7 p.m. to search the building for any stowaways.*

VINCE TREANOR *I had met Bill Siddons, who was soon to become the band's manager, at several other concerts and I would help him after the shows to pack up the equipment. I had taken to sort of following them around. New Haven started out to be just another show.*

Police Shut Up 'Door' After Alleged Obscenities

'Doors' Arrested...

'Doors' Chief, 3 Others Booked

RAY New Haven was a tough little town. We got to the concert and Jim got there a little early and went backstage by himself into the dressing room and a girl came in and they made out. A cop walked in and Jim explained that he was in the band, but [the cop] tried to clear them out. They started fighting and the cop pulled out his mace and shot Jim in the face with it. Finally, our manager showed up and said, 'This is the lead singer of the band!' He showed him the official pass that Jim didn't have. So the cop split and we took Jim into the dressing room. Jim was really wrecked from it, his face was all red.

VINCE TREANOR *Jim's face, of course, was still somewhat red and his eyes were still a little bit bloodshot, tearing a little bit. In his plight, he sort of gave me a nod and went on stage, because at that point his mind was obviously preoccupied with other things. I had met John and Robby beforehand, behind the steps. But, as always, Jim was that quiet, reserved type, so this was the first real up-close look that I had, and unfortunately he was not at his best at that point. He had been maced, and then he'd been washed and bathed and anointed and was coming up onto the stage when I saw him. He was a little tiddly and thoroughly outraged at what had happened, although I would say he was mollified a little bit by the apologies and backslapping and all that had gone on with the police.*

RAY We got on stage and halfway through the set Jim decided to tell the story of what happened and put the cops down and then he started working the audience up, screaming about the cops, so they ran on stage and took him away. He was making them look bad but he was telling the story the way it happened. The cops looked like fools.

New Haven Police Close 'The Doors'

Professor Claims Police Started Concert Scuffle

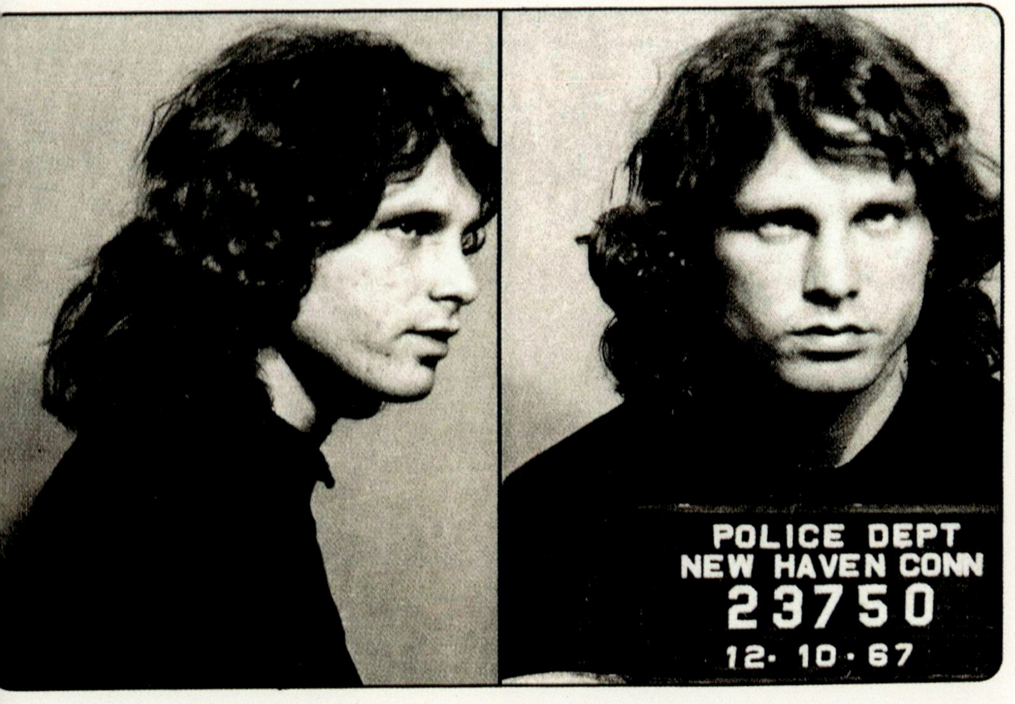

Ruckus Raising Rock 'n Roller Released on Bond

New Haven College
Interfraternity Scholarship Fund

Presents in Concert

the "Doors"

at New Haven Arena
Saturday, Dec. 9, 8:30 PM

Tickets at Yale Co-op, Cutler's Music Store

'The Doors' Arrested in New Haven

JIM If I had known beforehand that New Haven had a history of things like that I would have been more skilful in coping with it. But to me it was just another town. I'd heard the name but I didn't know anything about it. They had a history of that sort of incident. The charges were dropped, so obviously it was a mistake. I think it was the fact that I was pointing out the police's existence, talking about them in a performance and I guess they thought it was trespassing the bounds of art and reality.

RAY When the heat was on, when the narcs were backstage looking for dope, and when the vice squad were backstage with photographers and tape recorders, waiting for obscenities, it was hairy.

JIM I wouldn't have done it that night except that I was a little indignant about the way I was treated. I thought it was unjustified.

RAY If you've got any brains at all, you have to realise that the lead singer gets all the attention, both good and bad. He gets all the attention, but he also gets busted. He gets all the shit, he gets all the crazies who come around, people with the drugs and the booze.

JIM I WAS JUST LETTING OUT SOME VERY PERSONAL FEELINGS THAT I HAD.

Jim's mugshot after his arrest during the show, 10 December 1967

FIRE
ESCAPE

WAITING FOR MORRISON

Joan Didion

IT WAS SIX, seven o'clock of an early spring evening in 1968 and I was sitting on the cold vinyl floor of a sound studio on Sunset Boulevard, watching a band called The Doors record a rhythm track. On the whole my attention was only minimally engaged by the preoccupations of rock and roll bands (I had already heard about acid as a transitional stage and also about the Maharishi and even about Universal Love, and after a while it all sounded like marmalade skies to me), but The Doors were different, The Doors interested me. The Doors seemed unconvinced that love was brotherhood and the Kama Sutra. The Doors' music insisted that love was sex and sex was death and therein lay salvation. The Doors were the Norman Mailers of the Top 40, missionaries of apocalyptic sex. Break on through, their lyrics urged, and light my fire, and:

Come on baby, gonna take a little ride
Goin' down by the ocean side
Gonna get real close
Get real tight
Baby gonna drown tonight
Goin' down, down, down.

On this evening in 1968 they were gathered together in uneasy symbiosis to make their third album, and the studio was too cold and the lights were too bright and there were masses of wires and banks of the ominous blinking electronic circuitry with which musicians live so easily.

There were three of the four Doors. There was a bass player borrowed from a band called Clear Light. There were the producer and the engineer and the road manager and a couple of girls and a Siberian husky named Nikki with one grey eye and one gold. There were paper bags half filled with hard-boiled eggs and chicken livers and cheeseburgers and empty bottles of apple juice and California rosé. There was everything and everybody The Doors needed to cut the rest of this third album except one thing, the fourth Door, the lead singer, Jim Morrison, a 24-year-old graduate of UCLA who wore black vinyl pants and no underwear and tended to suggest some range of the possible just beyond a suicide pact.

It was Morrison who had described The Doors as 'erotic politicians'. It was Morrison who had defined the group's interests as 'anything about revolt, disorder, chaos, about activity that appears to have no meaning'. It was Morrison who got arrested in Miami for giving an 'indecent' performance. It was Morrison who wrote most of The Doors' lyrics, the peculiar character of which was to reflect either an ambiguous paranoia or a quite unambiguous insistence upon the love-death as the ultimate high. And it was Morrison who was missing.

It was Ray Manzarek and Robby Krieger and John Densmore who made The Doors sound the way they sounded, and maybe it was Manzarek and Krieger and Densmore who made seventeen out of twenty interviewees on American Bandstand prefer The Doors over all other bands, but it was Morrison who got up there in his black vinyl pants with no underwear and projected the idea, and it was Morrison they were waiting for now.

'Hey listen,' the engineer said. 'I was listening to an FM station on the way over here, they played three Doors songs, first they played "Back Door Man" and then "Love Me Two Times" and "Light My Fire."'

'I heard it,' Densmore muttered. 'I heard it. So what's wrong with somebody playing three of your songs?'

'This cat dedicates it to his family.'

'Yeah? To his family?'

'To his family. Really crass.'

Ray Manzarek was hunched over a Gibson keyboard. 'You think Morrison's going to come back?' he asked to no one in particular.

No one answered.

'So we can do some vocals?' Manzarek said. The producer was working with the tape of the rhythm track they had just recorded. 'I hope so,' he said without looking up,

'Yeah,' Manzarek said. 'So do I.'

My leg had gone to sleep, but I did not stand up; unspecific tensions seemed to be rendering everyone in the room catatonic. The producer played back the rhythm track. The engineer said that he wanted to do his deep-breathing exercises. Manzarek ate a hard-boiled egg. 'Tennyson made a mantra out of his own name,' he said to the engineer. 'I don't know if he said "Tennyson Tennyson Tennyson" or "Alfred Alfred Alfred" or "Alfred Lord Tennyson," but anyway, he did it. Maybe he just said "Lord Lord Lord"'

'Groovy,' the Clear Light bass player said. He was an amiable enthusiast, not at all a Door in spirit. 'I wonder what Blake said,' Manzarek mused. 'Too bad Morrison's not here. Morrison would know.'

It was a long while later. Morrison arrived. He had on his black vinyl pants and he sat down on a leather couch in front of the four big blank speakers and he closed his eyes. The curious aspect of Morrison's arrival was this: no one acknowledged it. Robby Krieger continued working out a guitar passage. John Densmore tuned his drums. Manzarek sat at the control console and twirled a corkscrew and let a girl rub his shoulders. The girl did not look at Morrison, although he was in her direct line of sight. An hour or so passed, and still no one had spoken to Morrison. Then Morrison spoke to Manzarek. He spoke almost in a whisper, as if he were wresting the words from behind some disabling aphasia.

'It's an hour to West Covina,' he said. 'I was thinking maybe we should spend the night out there after we play.'

Manzarek put down the corkscrew. 'Why?' he said.

'Instead of coming back.'

Manzarek shrugged. 'We were planning to come back.'

'Well, I was thinking, we could rehearse out there.'

Manzarek said nothing.

'We could get in a rehearsal, there's a Holiday Inn next door.'

'We could do that,' Manzarek said. 'Or we could rehearse Sunday, in town.'

'I guess so.' Morrison paused. 'Will the place be ready to rehearse Sunday?'

Manzarek looked at him for a while. 'No,' he said then.

I counted the control knobs on the electronic console. There were seventy-six. I was unsure in whose favor the dialogue had been resolved, or if it had been resolved at all. Robby Krieger picked at his guitar, and said that he needed a fuzzbox. The producer suggested that he borrow one from the Buffalo Springfield, who were recording in the next studio. Krieger shrugged. Morrison sat down again on the leather couch and leaned back. He lit a match. He studied the flame awhile and then very slowly, very deliberately, lowered it to the fly of his black vinyl pants. Manzarek watched him. The girl who was rubbing Manzarek's shoulders did not look at anyone.

There was a sense that no one was going to leave the room, ever. It would be some weeks before The Doors finished recording this album.

I did not see it through.

Previous pages, above and opposite: **Waiting for the Sun** ***album cover shoot, Malibu, CA, 1968***

PAUL FERRARA *I was given the job of photographing the* Waiting for the Sun *album cover. I wanted to do something that showed them in a glamour type portrait for their third cover. They had one album with four heads and the second with a juggler. I wanted the sunrise behind them, which was kind of hard on the West Coast. The easiest thing to accomplish was a sunset that doubled for a sunrise. Late one afternoon I rounded up the four suspects and loaded them into the Rambler station wagon.*

We arrived in Malibu just before sunset and drove to the top of the canyon. I placed a couple of shiny boards in front of them that reflected the setting sun behind them back onto their faces. I needed some height to see the pink of the sunset, so I climbed on top of my car and shot from there with a Hasselblad camera I had rented. Of all the album covers they did, I still think it is the most flattering. I was very pleased with and proud of the result.

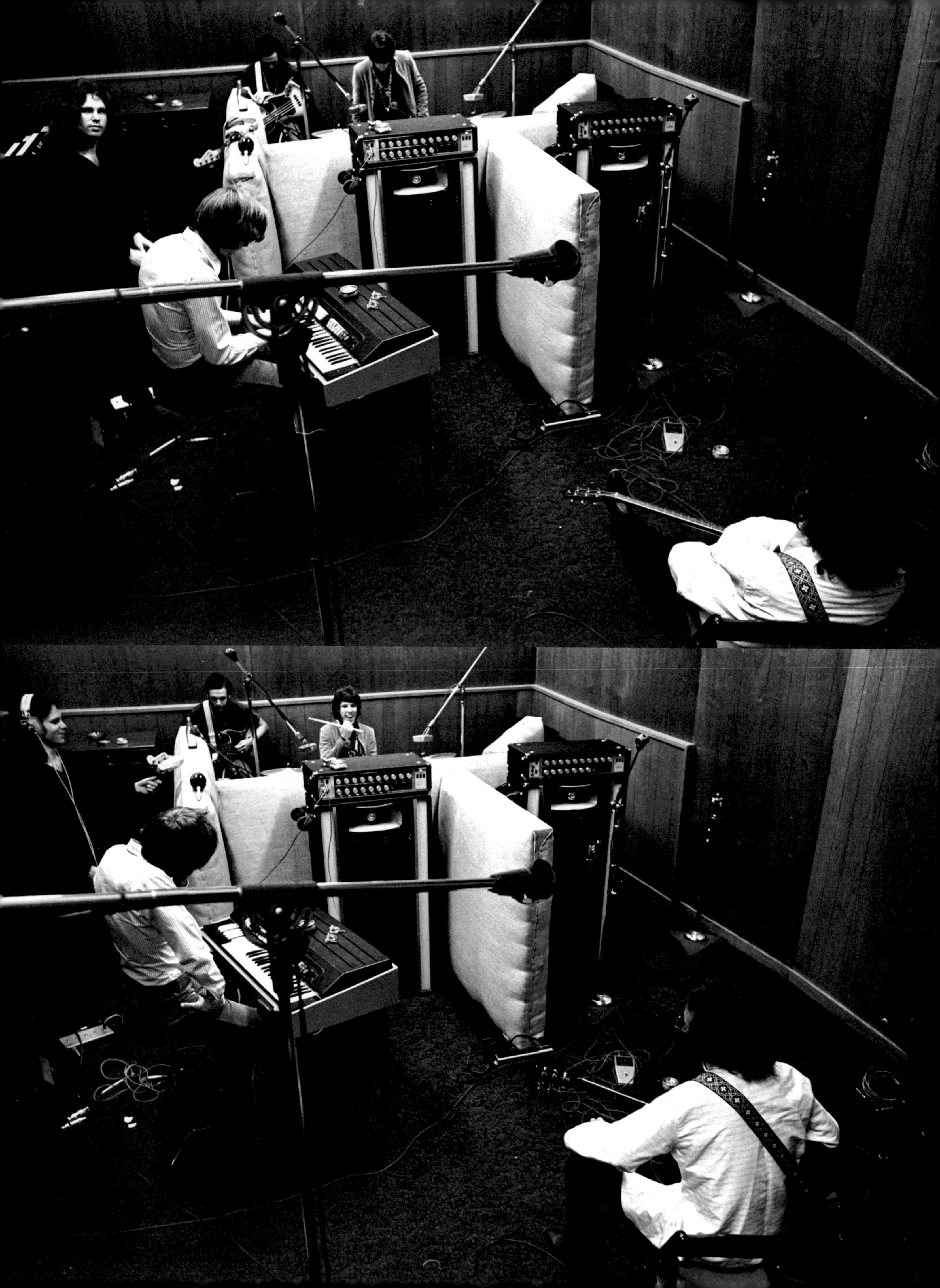

TTG RECORDING STUDIOS
1441 North McCadden Place, LA

PAUL ROTHCHILD *Things were wonderful in the Sixties, because it was an era of intense experimentation. Everyone was trying to out-hip each other. With The Doors, we tried to strike a very fine line between being very fresh and original and being documentary – making the record sound like it really happened live, which it did for the most part. At the same time we wanted it to sound new. I didn't want it to sound gimmicky by using things that sounded really trendy. For instance, everybody was using wah-wah pedals because Hendrix had just hit and guitar players were blown away by what he did with wah-wah. I prohibited Robby Krieger from using wah-wah because I wanted people to still be listening to Doors records in 20 years. If you sound like everyone else, nobody's going to notice you, now or in the future. If, on the other hand, we stayed true to the original musical concept, this music would survive.*

RAY We recorded *Waiting for the Sun* at TTG in Hollywood. It was located next to Stan's Drive-in, a car-hop Fifties anachronism of Suzie Q fries and patty melts and cherry lime rickeys. Hot-rod eating, California style. Good stuff. I filled up on plenty of those corkscrew Suzie Qs during the making of *Waiting for the Sun*.

ROBBY The biggest problem with the album was the production process. We were no longer bound by time or budget constraints, so Paul indulged by spending hours and hours dialling in drum sounds and tweaking everything obsessively in pursuit of a perfection that only he could hear. Our first record was fun and fast. Our second record was experimental and exciting. *Waiting for the Sun* was when recording turned into a chore. Paul's approach was to have us do endless takes, hacking and slashing at a song all night until we beat the life out of it, and then have us come in fresh the next day and nail it. Sometimes it worked, sometimes it didn't, but there was no talking him out of his methods.
I can't argue with how great the album sounds and I'm glad Paul cared enough to put in so much effort, but I don't know if it was worth the loss of morale and spontaneity.

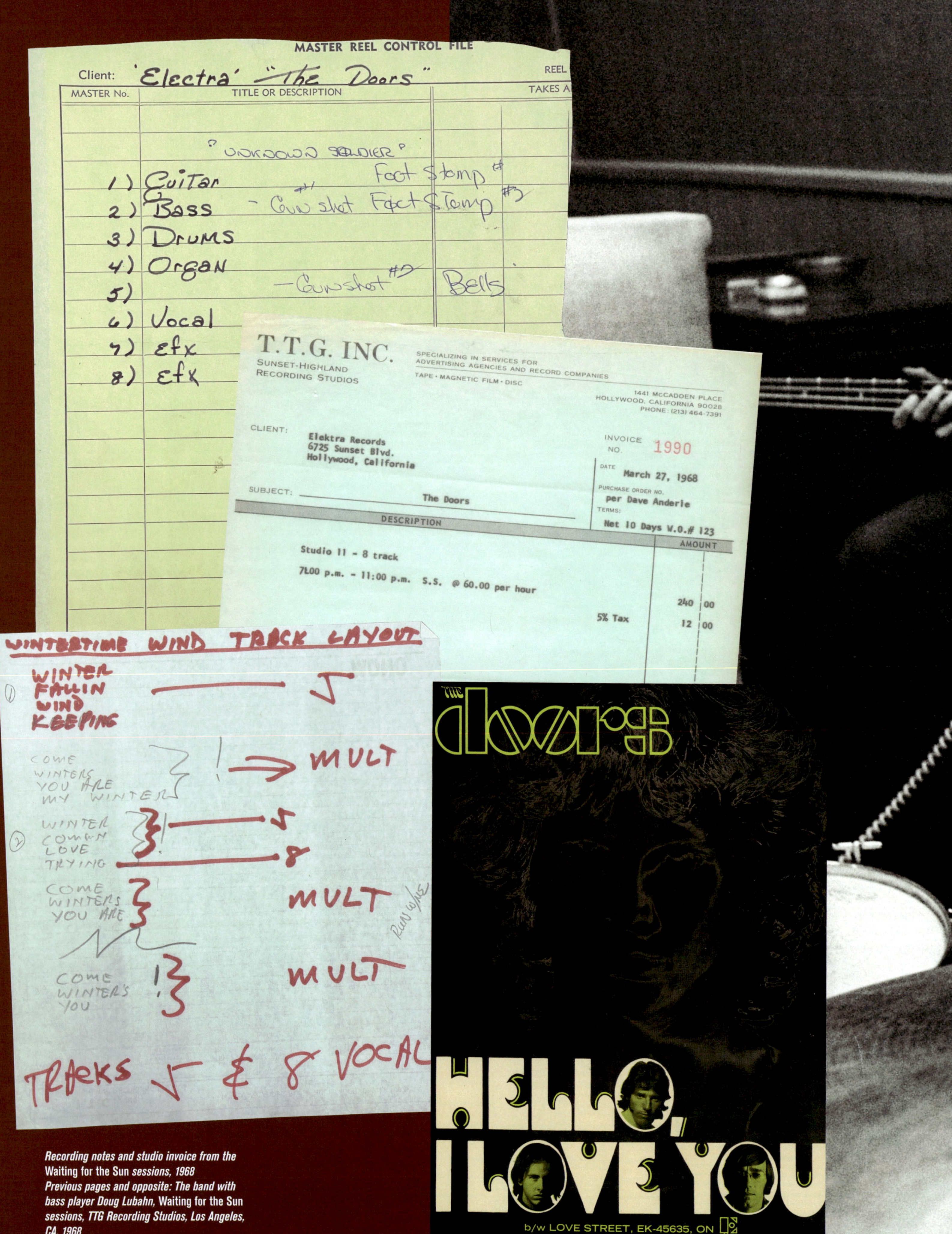

MASTER REEL CONTROL FILE

Client: 'Electra' "The Doors"

REEL

MASTER No.	TITLE OR DESCRIPTION		TAKES
	"UNKNOWN SOLDIER"		
	1) Guitar	Foot Stomp #1	
	2) Bass	- Gun shot #1 Foot Stomp #3	
	3) Drums		
	4) Organ		
	5)	- Gunshot #2	Bells
	6) Vocal		
	7) efx		
	8) efx		

T.T.G. INC.
SUNSET-HIGHLAND RECORDING STUDIOS

SPECIALIZING IN SERVICES FOR ADVERTISING AGENCIES AND RECORD COMPANIES
TAPE • MAGNETIC FILM • DISC

1441 McCADDEN PLACE
HOLLYWOOD, CALIFORNIA 90028
PHONE: (213) 464-7391

CLIENT: Elektra Records
6725 Sunset Blvd.
Hollywood, California

INVOICE NO. 1990

DATE March 27, 1968

PURCHASE ORDER NO. per Dave Anderle

TERMS: Net 10 Days W.O.# 123

SUBJECT: The Doors

DESCRIPTION	AMOUNT
Studio 11 - 8 track	
7:00 p.m. - 11:00 p.m. S.S. @ 60.00 per hour	
	240 00
5% Tax	12 00

WINTERTIME WIND TRACK LAYOUT

① WINTER FALLIN WIND KEEPING —— 5

COME WINTERS YOU ARE MY WINTER → MULT

② WINTER COMIN LOVE TRYING —— 5 —— 8

COME WINTERS YOU ARE MULT

RUN W/WE

COME WINTER'S YOU MULT

TRACKS 5 & 8 VOCAL

Recording notes and studio invoice from the Waiting for the Sun *sessions, 1968*
Previous pages and opposite: The band with bass player Doug Lubahn, Waiting for the Sun *sessions, TTG Recording Studios, Los Angeles, CA, 1968*

ROBBY AFTER A CERTAIN POINT JIM WOULD RELAPSE INTO THIS OTHER PERSON WHO RAY CALLED 'JIMBO'. YOU NEVER KNEW WHAT WOULD HAPPEN, ALL YOU KNEW WAS THAT IT WOULDN'T BE GOOD.

Waiting for the Sun *sessions, TTG Recording Studios, Los Angeles, CA, 1968*

RAY The album was fun to record. The ballads were sensitive and beautiful. The rockers like 'Five to One' were insane hard-on over-the-top crunchers and all was well with the creative process ... except for Jim's drinking. It was starting to become excessive. He would say, 'I'm depressed, let's go get a drink,' or 'I feel great, why don't we get a drink.' Too much booze and too much 'Jimbo'.

Jimbo was another personality altogether – a mean and desperate man. A man of roughness and crudeness. A man on a hell-bent-for-leather quest for domination, power and kicks. And he was Jim's doppelgänger.

ROBBY Some of my favourite Doors songs are the less commercially appealing tunes on *Waiting for the Sun*. When I wrote 'Yes, the River Knows' I tried to pull at the same inspirational thread that had brought 'Light My Fire': the four elements. This time it was water instead of fire, balanced out with a lyric comparing a break-up to a drowning death to once again keep up with Jim's darkness (he loved the line about 'mystic heated wine' even though I only squeezed it in there for rhyming purposes). Ray gave the song life by playing a grand piano instead of his Vox Continental. It's my favourite thing Ray ever played.

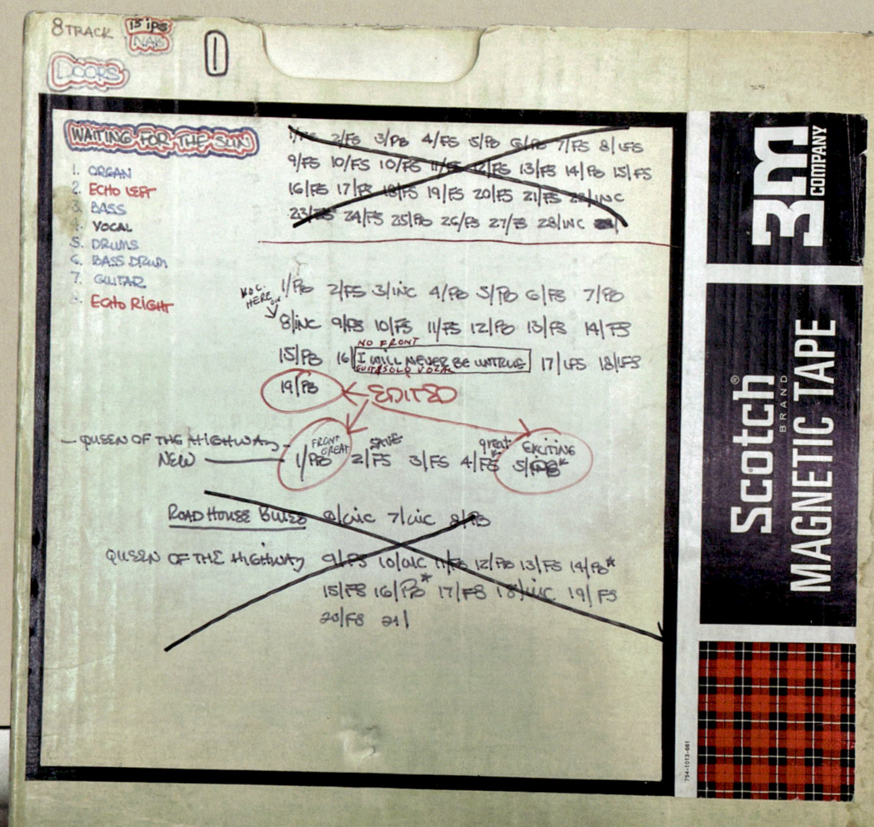

JIM RECORDING STUDIOS TEND TO GET A LITTLE DRY AND MONOTONOUS. I GUESS THE REAL FUN IS IN PERFORMING.

Waiting for the Sun sessions, TTG Recording Studios, Los Angeles, CA, 1968
Opposite, bottom right: Touch, Elektra's monthly newsletter, May 1968

JIM Each album got a bit more socially aware of the whole landscape, perhaps to the detriment of the music. Our later recordings get back to the blues, which is what we do best.

TOUCH

A Monthly Newsletter From The ELEKTRA RECORDS Publicity Department

DOORS - "NOW YOU ARE THE SUPERGROUP"

Item: They sold out the Fillmore East in New York for four shows--the only attraction thus far to do so--concluding with a 2½ hour set (!) which was called by everyone who heard it, an historic event in pop music chronicles.

Item: Eight pages in Life Magazine--an extraordinary story with even more extraordinary photographs--were devoted to them, which is another historic event for an American group.

Item: Albert Goldman abandoned the book he was reviewing (something about contemporary sexuality) in New York Magazine, went on to write--in the book review column--a powerful essay on Jim Morrison, claiming that Morrison was what the book should have been about anyhow. Commented one PR expert (Steve Paul, if you must know who), "Now that's the kind of break that means you're very, very big."

Item: Goldman again, this time in New American Review, a rather highbrow collection of fiction, essays, and poetry, concluded an essay entitled "The Emergence of Rock" with a long passage on The Doors, ending thus: "Ultimately, what is most impressive about The Doors is the completeness of their commitment. Whether it be acid, sex, ritual, or rock, they are further into it than any other group. Perhaps this explains the air of dignity that accompanies all their actions. No matter how wild or strange this group behaves, one feels they are in the American grain--indigenous artists like Walt Whitman or Charlie Parker."

Item: Jim Morrison was photographed for Vogue by Richard Avedon.

Conclusion: As an old friend of The Doors and a close observer of their origins and ascent said to them backstage at the Fillmore East after their legendary gig, "Now you are the Supergroup."

EARTH OPERA EXCEPTED AS PRESS REACTS AGAINST "BOSTON HYPE"

As we suspected way back, no one with two ears and a brain was ever going to believe that there was such a thing as a "Boston Sound," so whenever we were asked about the geographical origin of our brilliant Earth Opera, we responded by saying that they were from Cambridge, Massachusetts, and that their sound was their sound, and that it was a coincidence that other labels were picking up on groups from the Boston area. And when we heard they were calling it "The Bosstown Sound" (why not "Plymouth Rock"?), we figured Earth Opera was definitely better off disassociated from the whole make-believe thing, which looked about to backfire anyhow, for the

ROBBY I used a Gibson Maestro fuzztone on 'Hello, I Love You', which I wasn't crazy about, but it was all that we had. To tell you the truth I think they overdid it with the fuzz on that song. I would have toned it down a little bit but that was a mix thing.

I think sometimes effects are an easy way to cover up mistakes and not hear what you're really playing. I try to keep it down to just what's necessary. The box that I use now is from the Nineties – it's an analogue Boss pedal called an ME-10 and even that has too much stuff on it.

JOHN I thought the words to 'Hello, I Love You' were brilliant and they were around forever but we could not get the arrangement right. Then Robby added the fuzztone and it was like, 'Woah'. Rothchild kept saying that it was going to be a hit. He was terrific, he taught us how to make records, but eventually he got too dictatorial, having us do take after take.

Opposite and overleaf: TTG Recording Studios, Los Angeles, CA, 1968

ROBBY I thought the video for 'The Unknown Soldier' was pretty cool, pretty weird. We brought our Indian instruments: I brought a sitar and John had his tabla drums and Ray had his tanpura, which is like a bass for Indian music. In the video Jim was getting shot as the 'unknown soldier'. It was a bit of a weird idea but I think it worked. It was pretty avant-garde, especially with the Vietnam War going on.

JOHN It's really fulfilling that we became the soundtrack for some of those struggling through Vietnam, people making love, smoking a joint for the first time. That's something to feel good about.

THE UNKNOWN SOLDIER

b/w WE COULD BE SO GOOD TOGETHER EK-45628

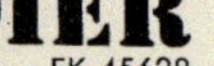

Theories of War:

Destruction derby
The funnelling of young seed

To break the peace
The slow insidious growth
of pain & culture

Like earthquakes, to unite

Keeping the boys in line
Physical Education
Sent from the exercise line
back to the bus

The Laotians 80% out of money
economy, Think world is flat
& all Laotians

A promotional film of The Doors current single, "The Unknown Soldier," has been unveiled by filmmakers Mark Abramson and Edward Dephoure. Mot a filmed performance, the movie uses the single as its soundtrack, while footage shows Doors in various staged activities (including the execution of Jim Morrison), intercut with documentary film showing various aspects of war... and peace.

A bit outré for national TV, alas, the film will be shown at concerts, in clubs, and in underground and college theatre outlets. If you are interested in showcasing the flick, please contact us about obtaining a print. "The Unknown Soldier" must be seen as well as heard.

JIM Young people are probably opposed to wars because they're the ones who always fight the wars. They're the human fodder, war machine. There just seems to be no way around it. There's just no cause.

I think young people got tired of being grist for the mill. It's a funny thing. From the comfortable position of your TV set in your living room, the horror of it makes it glamorous. It's the drama of life and death right there, the struggle. And we're all infected in youth, from little kids running around playing war and cowboys and Indians. Somehow, it's just ingrained in you from the beginning. That it's somehow heroic, proving yourself in battle.

Previous pages: Robby Krieger, 1968
Top left: Stills from 'The Unknown Soldier'
Top right: Excerpt of Jim's handwritten 'Theories of War'
Above: Portion of Elektra's monthly newsletter Touch *reprinted in* Broadside *magazine, 1968*

ROBBY 'Not to Touch the Earth' became most notable for its last line: 'I am the Lizard King. I can do anything.' Jim wasn't speaking about himself; it was a proclamation from one of the characters he had created in the poem, but it became Jim's eternal nickname. I chuckle inside a little every time I hear it. It always makes me think back to the green welder's jacket with the sewn-on lizard skin that he was wearing when I first met him. I wish Jim could witness the unintentional cultural impact of that single whispered lyric. It has been referenced in everything from *The Office* to *SpongeBob SquarePants*.

RAY The press loved it. It was their new hook for him. Jim would now be known as 'the Lizard King'. Hell, the people loved it too.

Waiting for the Sun *sessions, TTG Recording Studios, Los Angeles, CA, 1968*
Right and opposite bottom: Notes from the Waiting for the Sun *sessions*

PAGE (2)

2- GET TOGETHER O M T
2- " " O M T
3- GET TOGET
2- GET
1- GET

2 uhh

3-4 COME ON HONEY
GO ALONG HOME AND WAIT FOR ME BABY
~~GONNA~~ I'LL BE THERE IN A LITTLE WHILE
YOU SEE I GOTTA GO OUT IN THIS
CAR WITH THESE PEOPLE
AND UHH

1 GET TOGETHER O M T
GET TOGETHER O M T
GETT GOTTA GET GOTTA 2-4 TH BAR

1. WINTERTIME LOVE
2. SUMMERS ALMOST GONE
3. YES THE RIVER KNOWS
4. NOT TO TOUCH THE EARTH
5. FIVE TO ONE
6. HELLO I LOVE YOU
7. SPANISH CARAVAN
8. LOVE STREET
9. WE COULD BE SO GOOD TOGETHER
10. MY WILD LOVE GOES RIDING
11. UNKNOWN SOLDIER

JIM I find the music gives me a kind of security and it makes it a lot easier to express myself.

"WINTER TIME LOVE"
LEFT | LC | MID | RC | RIGHT
DRUMS | ORGAN VOCAL | HORNS | BASS DBL VOCAL | GUITAR

"LOVE STREET"
GUITAR | DRUMS | VOCAL PIANO | ORGAN | BASS

"SUMMERS ALMOST GONE"
ORGAN | BASS PIANO 1 | VOCAL | DRUMS PIANO 2 | GUITAR

"YES THE RIVER KNOWS"
BASS | L-PIANO | VOCAL SKINS | R-PIANO CYMBALS | GUITAR

"HELLO I LOVE YOU"
GUITAR W/ FUNKY ORGAN | LEAD #1 DRUMS | HARMONY VOCAL | LEAD #2 BASS | GUITAR

"FIVE TWO ONE"
BASS GROUP | ORGAN CLAPS & GROUP | LEAD VOCAL LEAD INTRO & FADE | GUITAR | DRUMS

"NOT TO TOUCH THE EARTH"
DRUMS GUITAR | BASS ORGAN | VOCAL (VOCAL INTRO, ORGAN FILL, DRUM FILLS) | GUITAR | ORGAN

"SPANISH CARAVAN"
GUITAR ORGAN | BASS DRUMS | VOCAL | HORNS BASS | GUITAR PERCUSSION

"WE COULD BE SO GOOD TOGETHER"

T.T.G. INC.
SUNSET-HIGHLAND RECORDING STUDIOS
SPECIALIZING IN SERVICES FOR ADVERTISING AGENCIES AND RECORD COMPANIES
TAPE · MAGNETIC FILM · DISC
1441 MCCADDEN PLACE
HOLLYWOOD, CALIFORNIA 90028
PHONE: (213) 464-7391

INVOICE NO. 1933

CLIENT: Elektra Records
6725 Sunset Blvd.
Los Angeles, California

DATE March 13, 1968
PURCHASE ORDER NO. per Jack Holzman
TERMS: net 10 days W.O.# 63

SUBJECT: Doors

DESCRIPTION	AMOUNT
Studio 11 - 8 track	
6:00 p.m. - 12:00 midnight O.D. @ 60.00 per hour	360 00
5% Tax	18 00

JIM I had a book on snakes and reptiles and the first sentence of it struck me very acutely: 'Reptiles are the interesting descendants of magnificent ancestors.' Another thing about them is that they are a complete anachronism. If every reptile in the world were to disappear tomorrow, it wouldn't really change the balance of nature one bit. They're a completely arbitrary species. If any creature could survive another world war, or some kind of total poisoning of the planet, I think somehow reptiles would find a way to make it. Also, we must not forget that the lizard and the snake are identified with the unconscious and the forces of evil. They're the devil's gang.

VINCE TREANOR *During 1967, Jim had developed a fantasy legend:* Celebration of the Lizard. *Jim described it as a series of events or thoughts told by a group of boys who had camped in the desert. As they sat around a campfire at night, each told a different story. Each story was to blend in with the one before and lead into the story following. It was almost like an opera with the boys providing the musical setting for the stories.*

JIM The lizard and the snake are identified with the unconscious and the forces of evil. *Celebration of the Lizard* was kind of an invitation to the dark forces. It's all done tongue-in-cheek. I don't think people realise that. It's not to be taken seriously. It's like if you play the villain in a Western it doesn't mean that that's you. It just an aspect that you keep for show. I don't really take that seriously. That's supposed to be ironic.

FRANK LISCIANDRO Waiting for the Sun, *released in July 1968, contained, on the inside of the gatefold cover, the complete text of* The Celebration of the Lizard, *a Jim Morrison rock theatre work mixing poems, songs, music and sound effects. Jim had hoped the band would record and release the piece as one side of* Waiting for the Sun. *In the event, only one excerpt of* Celebration, *'Not to Touch the Earth', was included on the album. In July 1969, The Doors recorded a performance of the whole piece at the Aquarius Theatre in Hollywood, California, incorporating some additional lines from Jim. The recording was later released on the band's 1970 album* Absolutely Live.

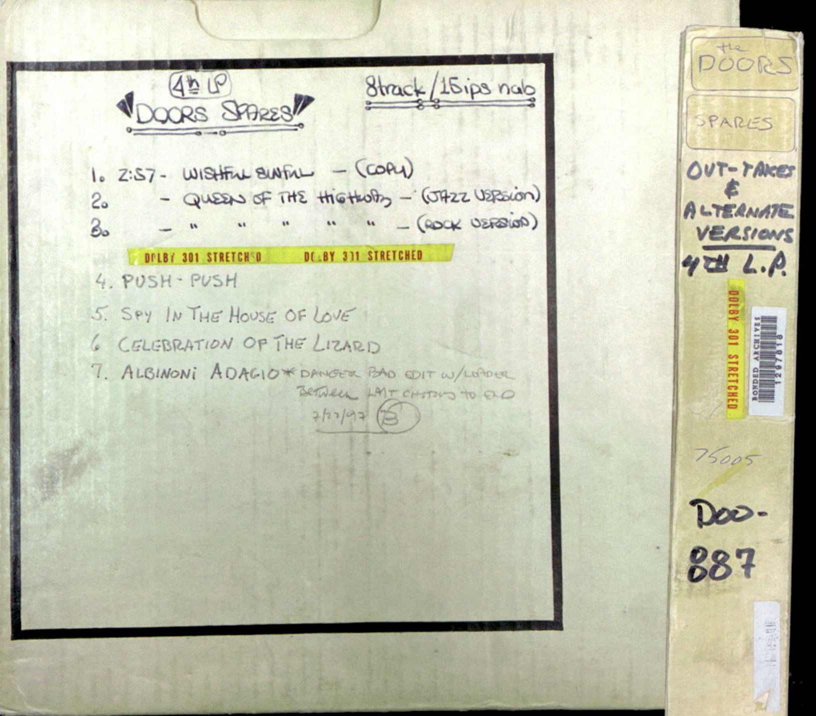

Don't stop to speak
or look around.
Your gloves & fan
are on the ground.
We're getting out of town
We're going on the run
& you're the one
I want to come.

Not to touch the earth
Not to see the sun
Nothing left to do
But run run run

RAY ***Celebration of the Lizard*** **was tongue in cheek but it also made me a little nervous. 'I am the Lizard King, I can do anything.' Jim got himself a snakeskin suit. Was he building his own myth here or was he kidding? It was a combination of the two. If he was kidding, well, he had to be careful with the notoriety. You have to remember, the muse comes through, we get blessed, we don't own it. With writing, sometimes it flows, sometimes it doesn't. So, don't get too caught up in how great you are.**

We wanted the world to be aware that Jim Morrison was a brilliant poet. He was a great rock and roll man who would get on stage and go crazy in front of your very eyes. All the things that people said about him, that they loved and hated him, I understand, because I loved and hated him too. He said some really great things that had nothing to do with the Sixties or the Seventies or the Eighties. It was about being alive on this planet right now.

JIM I really admire poets that can get up, with or without a microphone, in front of a group of people and just start reciting their poetry.

Jim Morrison, photographed in New York by Yale Joel for an April 1968 **LIFE** *feature by Fred Powledge titled 'Wicked Go the Doors: An Adult's Education by the Kings of Acid Rock'. In the article, Powledge wrote about Jim: 'Once you see him perform, you realise that he also seems dangerous, which, for a poet, may be a contradiction in terms.'*

DOORS WORKSHOP
8512 Santa Monica Blvd

RAY We needed a place to rehearse. We no longer had the beach house in Venice, and Robby's parents had moved to an ersatz Frank Lloyd Wright house that was not hospitable to kick-ass rock and roll. We needed something professional. A piece of commercial property that would allow us to have creative space and an office. I scoured West Hollywood, an area that was central to everybody, and then I found it, on the corner of La Cienega and Santa Monica. It was a little two-storey building with a large room downstairs, two rooms upstairs. Perfect. Music on the first floor, business on the second. Elektra was half a block away on La Cienega, Duke's – the great health-food-style coffee shop/restaurant – was a block west on Santa Monica, the legendary Barney's Beanery was a block east on Santa Monica. Right across the street was the Alta Cienega Motel, where Jim spent many a night after fights with Pam, and the Phone Booth – a topless bar where Jim also spent many a night … resulting in many arguments with Pam that resulted in his spending many a night across the street at the Alta Cienega Motel.

From 1967 to 1971, The Doors' world was centred around their Workshop on Santa Monica Blvd. Across the street was the Phone Booth, a strip club where Jim liked to relax after a long day of recording, and next door to that was the Alta Cienega Motel, where Jim would sleep off the effects of his night at the Phone Booth. Also next door to the Workshop was the Extension, the sister club of the Phone Booth, where Jim loved to take friends and interviewers.

RAY We immediately moved into The Doors' 'workshop'. We bought a couple of desks, a file cabinet, lounge chairs, a small refrigerator, and a couch for the upstairs office. A pinball machine and another couch for the rehearsal room downstairs. Siddons moved the equipment in, set it up, and we were a go. We fired Bill Siddons and hired Vince Treanor – a Boston pipe organ fanatic and electronics genius – as our equipment manager and immediately rehired Siddons as The Doors' official manager. Bill would now be responsible for all the phone calls coming in. He would deal with Elektra in terms of publicity, promotion and distribution. And he would book our gigs. He would tell us what requests and gig offers came in during the week at our Friday band meeting. It was a big job for a 22-year-old surfer, but he was up to the task. And Vince was a godsend.

Jim (opposite, top) and the full band (top right) outside the Doors Workshop, Los Angeles, CA

Tropicana – naked
Acid. Christ, its
you, a femal human.

JIM I STARTED THAT WHOLE SCENE AT THE TROPICANA. PUT IT ON THE MAP.

ROBBY Jim didn't have a house. He would live in a motel or wherever he happened to be that night. He would end up sleeping there. He was always thinking about songs. When he was alone, he would have a notebook and that's what he would do. I guess he considered himself to be more into the whole trip than the three of us were.

JIM We used to have lots of fun there. It's boisterous. Them were there, nice guys.

Tropicana Motor Hotel
8585 Santa Monica Blvd.
(U. S. 66) HOLLYWOOD. Calif.
Phone: OLympia 2-5720

74 luxurious air-conditioned rooms in Hollywood near Beverly Hills. Close to movie and TV studios. 10 minutes to beaches. 24 hour switchboard service. Coffee shop. TV in rooms. Lovely year around heated swimming pool. Popular prices. Family kitchenette suites and apartments.

TROPICANA
MOTOR HOTEL
& APARTMENTS
8585 SANTA MONICA BL.
LOS ANGELES, CA. 90069
110

Although Jim preferred staying at the Alta Cienega, he also spent a lot of time at the famous Tropicana (and Duke's coffee shop), which was right across the street
Opposite: John Densmore in Los Angeles, CA, 1968

VETERANS COLISEUM
1826 W McDowell Rd, Phoenix

ROBBY The whole point of the band was to make records, get them out there, let people hear it and then go on the road and play the music for the people. Throughout the entire career of The Doors you could describe our performances as erratic, spontaneous, mesmerising and chaotic.

JIM Who isn't fascinated with chaos? More than that, though. I am interested in activity that has no meaning, and all I mean by that is free activity. Play. Activity that has nothing in it except just what it is. No repercussions. No motivation. Free ... activity.

Arizona Veterans Memorial Coliseum, Phoenix, AZ, 17 February 1968
Opposite, bottom right: Promotional poster using imagery from the Phoenix show, 1968

VINCE TREANOR *Everything went well in Phoenix and though Jim had been drinking it was not excessive. They played 'Light My Fire' and finished the set with 'The End'. Jim did a good job of entertaining the crowd. They played their hearts out. The audience loved the show, everything went smoothly and everyone was satisfied. That is what counts. Jim was entirely unpredictable so one could never know whether the show was going to be perfect or miserable.*

JIM I like any kind of reaction I can get, I enjoy it. Anything just to get people to think. If you can get a whole room of drunk, stoned people to wake up and think, then you're really doing something because that's not what they come for. They come just to lose themselves.

JOHN During the performances I could feel this exchange of power. They were rituals, not concerts. It was like some kind of seance. I couldn't get enough.

FILLMORE EAST
105 2nd Avenue, NYC

JOHN In the early days, it was scary at times. Like at the Fillmore in New York. Jim would get hurt, not from the audience attacking us or anything, but because it got so heavy. You wondered if something weird was going to happen because Jim was so intense. We were all together: us and the audience. It was incredible, it was like a community.

Jim would stick the microphone down into people's mouths and it would get rowdy. He would wait, and there would be long silences where we'd be riffing forever until I'd run out of fills. And he'd wait longer but he'd do it just to get the audience to squirm a little and then he would scream.

Doors Opening

The Doors, rock combo, will appear at the Fillmore East on Friday and Saturday evenings of next week.

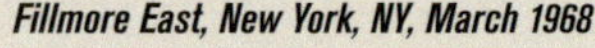
Fillmore East, New York, NY, March 1968

JOHN **IT WAS A RELIGIOUS EXPERIENCE BETWEEN US AND THE AUDIENCE.**

JIM It was less theatrical, less artificial, when I began. But later the audiences we played for were much larger and the rooms wider. When you're a small dot at the end of a large arena, you have to make up for that lack of intimacy with expanded movements.

I think people enjoy being in crowds. It gives them a feeling of power and security to rub up against hundreds of other people that are like them, it reinforces their trip. It has something to do with swarming theory. The idea of when the population starts stripping out the food supply, the animals or insects swarm together. It's a way of communicating and working out a solution, signalling that there is a danger. In nature a balance is worked out. For example, in LA, New York and many big cities you feel crowded. You feel psychologically crowded and physically crowded. People get very neurotic and paranoid and things like rock concerts are a form of human swarming to communicate this unease of overpopulation.

Fillmore East, New York, NY,
22 March 1968
Opposite: Northern California Folk-Rock Festival, San Jose, CA, 19 May 1968

Hip God of Rock

JOHN The Northern California Folk-Rock Festival was a good gig although if anyone offered security a six pack of beer they would let them on stage so the security wasn't too good. We were just getting our stage presence together for larger arenas.

ROBBY I didn't mind fans crowding the stage, it happened all the time. But the Hells Angels were there, which I didn't really like.

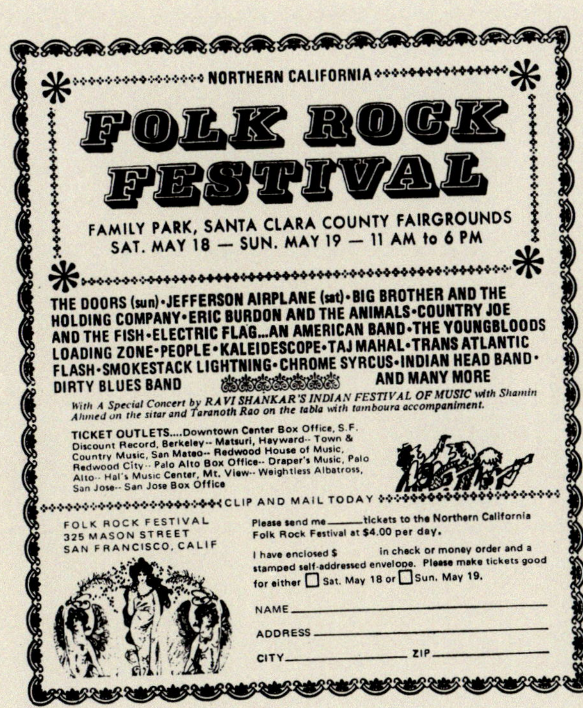

JIM IT WAS NECESSARY TO PROJECT MORE, TO EXAGGERATE – ALMOST TO THE POINT OF GROTESQUENESS.

RAY I'd say as far as the groups are concerned there seems to be a lot more action on the West Coast than in New York. I hadn't heard too many groups from New York that were exciting. I liked The Blues Project but that was about it. San Francisco and LA were really filled with a lot of good groups. Everything was going on out there. It's hard to put a label on it, you can't really call it flower music or psychedelic music, it was a whole new thing that was starting. It was an American thing.

New York, NY, 1968

This page: John in silhouette, 1968
Opposite and overleaf: Hollywood Bowl, Los Angeles, CA, 5 July 1968

ROBBY WE WERE ONE OF THE FIRST GROUPS TO PLAY THE HOLLYWOOD BOWL. WE HAD BROUGHT CAMERAS TO FILM THE SHOW, SO IT LOOKED GREAT. BUT IT WASN'T A GREAT GIG.

JOHN We got a call from Jimmy Miller, The Stones' producer, and he said that he and Mick would like to come to the Bowl. Mick Jagger! They drove up to our office to go to dinner with us. We went to Mu Ling's Chinese restaurant on Sunset Boulevard, but unfortunately, since there were too many people in our entourage, we had to sit at two separate tables.

Mick sat at the other table. Jimmy Miller talked up a storm, but I wanted to hear the interaction between the two lead singers, and maybe put my two cents in. As we drove to the back of the Bowl, it felt like attending a huge baseball game. I felt a twinge of nervousness looking at the crowd as we walked into the dressing room. I got a piece of paper and we agreed to the first three or four songs. Out of the corner of my eye, I could see Mick watching very attentively.

DOORS BIG DRAW

ROBBY Mick got on really well with Pam. I don't think that bothered Jim but for some reason he took a massive dose of acid before the show at the Hollywood Bowl, which wasn't that unusual except that this was our first show to be recorded and televised. The acid actually made him self-conscious in a way but it was still kind of cool.

Acid popular, taken at least once or twice
by most everyone I knew
'grinding your wheels'
I can attest to its power. Saw many
astonishing things

HOLLYWOOD BOWL

2301 Highland Avenue, LA

JOHN The Hollywood Bowl didn't look as impressive in the daylight as it did at night, but unfortunately the night light didn't save our performance. We were worried about the acoustics at the outdoor amphitheatre, where there were no walls to bounce the sound off.

We had played outdoor concerts successfully before, but you couldn't hear the sound coming back to you and it could be difficult to judge how loudly to play. We didn't want to take any chances, so Vince Treanor, our dedicated and obsessed road manager, built additional amplifiers, 52 speakers in all, with 7,000 watts of power. For a four-piece band!

ROBBY The amps were spread all the way across the Hollywood Bowl stage. At soundcheck it sounded really good, really loud, and then this guy walked over and said that we weren't allowed to play at over 100 decibels at the Hollywood Bowl. We were probably at 150 and getting louder, so in the end we had to turn them all off, apart from our one amp each. My guitar sounded horrible. It didn't have the sound that I wanted.

JOHN Robby was very unhappy. I was actually pleased, because as a drummer I always fought to be heard. Whenever Ray and Robby turned up a knob, I had to use more muscle. Unfortunately, 80 decibels was not enough to fill 18,000 seats with the punch we relied on.

JOHN I wanted to show The Stones' lead singer how good we could be. Not that night. I wished we were better. Several close friends were right in the front seats and I couldn't even look at them. Jim wore a cross and smoked a lot of cigarettes, which seemed out of character for him. He wasn't born again and it was the first time I ever saw him smoke. I detected some self-conscious image-building.
The audience lit matches when we played 'Light My Fire', a trend that continues at rock concerts today, but as beautiful as it looked from the Bowl stage, there was little spark coming from the music. It wasn't a bad show; it was just off. I couldn't put my finger on what went wrong. The mood of the show wasn't there. We didn't have enough power and Jim's crucifix didn't help. I had noticed Roger Daltrey of The Who sporting a cross on TV, so I asked Jim why he had followed suit. 'I like the symbol visually, plus it will confuse people.' 'What went wrong?' I asked Robby, walking back under the shell to the dressing rooms. He replied, 'Jim took acid right before going on.' 'GOD DAMN IT!' I hurled my drumsticks to the floor. It's one thing to take it on your own time, but the Hollywood Bowl?

Later, Jagger was very kind when *Melody Maker*, the English music magazine, asked him how he liked The Doors. He said, 'They were nice chaps, but they played a bit too long.'

HOLLYWOOD BOWL ASSOCIATION
LEASE

THIS AGREEMENT entered into this 11th day of June, 19 68, between the SOUTHERN CALIFORNIA SYMPHONY-HOLLYWOOD BOWL ASSOCIATION, a California corporation, with its principal office at 2301 North Highland Avenue, Hollywood, California, (hereinafter called ASSOCIATION) and SIGHT AND SOUND PRODUCTIONS

with its principal office at 9301 Wilshire Boulevard, Beverly Hills, California 90210 (hereinafter called LESSEE).

WITNESSETH:

1. ASSOCIATION hereby leases to LESSEE the amphitheatre commonly known as the Hollywood Bowl, including the use of the appurtenances and equipment hereinafter specified, for the purpose of presenting the program entitled "THE DOORS" and for NO OTHER PURPOSES WHATSOEVER on condition that the said program be promoted, advertised, and presented so as not to reflect unfavorably upon the acknowledged long standing cultural and civic reputation of ASSOCIATION, the said Hollywood Bowl or the "Symphonies Under The Stars" season of ASSOCIATION.

2. The term of this Lease shall be the period from 1:00 P.M. on Friday, July 5, 19 68, until 11:30 P.M. on Friday, July 5, 19 68.

3. In consideration of the foregoing Lease, LESSEE agrees to pay ASSOCIATION the following amounts:

a. The sum of $ 500.00 (Five Hundred Dollars)
This sum is payable upon execution of this Lease.

(1) The ONLY artists, performers and/or speakers who are to appear in connection with the program are the following:

The Doors

(2) The following are:

(a) The purposes for which the leased premises are to be used:

Concert

(c) The schedule of actual program hours:

8:30 P.M. to 11:00 P.M. (Set-up and rehearsal to begin at 1:00 P.M.; rehearsal to conclude by 5:00 P.M.)
In the event the program is not condluded by 11:30 P.M., Lessee agrees to pay Association, in addition to the amounts set forth in Paragraph 3 and 4 above, an amount equal to 2 1/2% (two and one-half percent) of the gross receipts, exclusive of Federal and/or local admission taxes, for each additional 15 (fifteen) minutes or portion thereof.

(d) The scale of admission prices to be charged:

$6.50, $5.50, $4.50, $3.50, $2.50.

This page: Contracts for the Hollywood Bowl performance
Opposite and page 177, top: Hollywood Bowl, Los Angeles, CA, 5 July 1968

Drugs are a bet w/ your mind

Introduced in 1966 as the Kalamazoo K101, Gibson's portable organ was renamed the G101 the following year. This is the one used by Ray Manzarek, with his Rhodes Piano Bass sitting on top. He initially used a Vox Continental, but eventually had to replace it.

RAY The Vox Continental fell apart and it was no longer made in England. I'd go out on a gig and in half a set I'd break about six or seven keys. So at that point I switched over to the Gibson Kalamazoo. It had a little more versatility than the Vox; it could make the sort of piano-ish sound I used on 'Back Door Man', plus it had a little knob sticking up on the volume pedal which could bend the note a half-step down. We used it on 'Not to Touch the Earth'.

VINCE TREANOR *The Kalamazoo had a greater variety of tone and Ray liked the sound of it. More importantly, Ray liked the feel of the keyboard. It was rugged and had a flat top that Ray could use to perch the piano bass on.*

By the standards of synthesisers that were to come, it was fairly simple. But it was polyphonic, reliable and could survive all the rigours of road trips.

In the late Sixties, Harrison Ford was yet to become a household name – except to those in the Hollywood Hills and Laurel Canyon who hired him for his carpentry and house remodelling skills. Although he was striving towards becoming an actor, getting a few bit-parts here and there, he paid the bills working with his bare hands and, by all accounts, he was an expert at his craft. During this period, it also came about that he was hired to work for The Doors. Ford had become friends with the band's photographer, Paul Ferrara. In early 1968, Paul had the idea of filming The Doors in concert and creating a documentary (later to become Feast of Friends*).*

The band gave Paul the approval to proceed and in April of 1968 he began recording Doors concerts and behind-the-scenes footage with his friend Babe Hill, who recorded audio for the project. Paul realised he needed a bit more help, so he asked another friend, Harrison Ford, if he could be a grip and assist with the filming. Ford joined the Feast of Friends *crew and worked with them for a little over a month. The first shoot was at the Sixth Annual Renaissance Pleasure Faire in Calabasas, where Ford learned how to use all the filming equipment. He was now ready to go on the road with The Doors. He assisted in filming three concerts: the Northern California Folk-Rock Festival in San Jose, Bakersfield Civic Center, and the famous Hollywood Bowl show.*

After filming was complete, Ford went back to focusing on his carpentry work, having picked up a couple of new clients from his time with The Doors. First, he installed custom cabinets in Paul Rothchild's house. Then, when Jim Morrison's girlfriend Pamela Courson opened up her boutique, Themis, in 1969, Ford did all of the interior carpentry work. He would later say that he knew he could never be a rock star after experiencing life on the road with The Doors. He just couldn't keep up with them.

FEAST OF FRIENDS

ROBBY Around the time we opened the office, Jim had built up an entourage: Frank Lisciandro, Paul Ferrara and Babe Hill. Frank and Paul were his classmates at UCLA film school, so we hired them to tag along with us on the road and shoot what would become our *Feast of Friends* documentary. We weren't thrilled about spending band money to employ Jim's drinking buddies, but they were a major improvement over some of the other characters he sometimes hung around with. And today their footage survives as some of the most crucial visual evidence of The Doors' existence.

JIM It was a little 40-minute documentary on a rock and roll band travelling around the States.

FRANK LISCIANDRO *I shot some of* Feast of Friends *with Paul Ferrara. I did some of the scenes at the Hollywood Bowl. There was so much footage and the band would ask me to take a look at it. There wasn't any structure to it, which is what it needed, so they hired me to work on it. I already had a good job working with an educational film company but I made up my mind by thinking, 'This is my one chance to work with The Doors,' so I took it.*

Opposite: Stills from Feast of Friends, *1968, including one (top right) in which Harrison Ford can be seen behind Jim*
Above: Feast of Friends *original master reel*

PAUL FERRARA *We were proud of what it was; it fully captured the experience of The Doors in concert and at play. The reviews were good for the most part. Jim became the spokesman for the film, which established him as a rock star who was also interested in cinema.*

JIM I was at this film festival in San Francisco for *Feast of Friends* and the audience consisted of young people, well under 30, hip young people and they booed the film. We're on a monstrous ego trip and people resent it. They hate us because we're so good. Maybe it will change, it's a question of longevity. It's that old thing of on a first novel they usually give the kid a break and they pat him on the back, and on the second they really chop him up. Then if he does a few more and shows he has staying power they say, 'Well, welcome back to the fold. The human family embraces you.' I think it will be the same with us, we just have to hold out for a while and everyone one day will realise, 'Wow, they're just like old friends, they've been around for years. They're part of our national psyche. I guess we'll accept them.' But now we're kind of in an in-between.

SINGER BOWL
Flushing Meadows, NYC

VINCE TREANOR *We drove to the Singer Bowl and arrived late afternoon. We set up on stage. This was my rule. We set up first and when we were done the other bands could do what they wanted, but they could not move or use our equipment. They would set up in front.*

The Who arrived and they began to demand that we move off stage. They even agreed to help with the exchange – all working together to get the job done. They agreed to help us set up and I conceded the stage to them.

The Who were nearly half an hour late. The crowd were half an hour angry. Things did quiet down when they came on and the performance was good if you liked their style of music.

As soon as The Doors appeared, they were greeted with a thunderous assault of screaming fans and segments of the crowd began moving from the ground level seating towards the wooden bars around the stage. A cordon of policemen was stationed around the front and sides of the platform to hold back this onrush of people. Morrison fiercely jostled his way through these guardians to face the crowd.

JIM It's a real drama: you get a triangle situation with the audience, the police and the stage. When you don't have that, when you have a dialogue, it's just a conversation between two people. A bunch of uniformed officers lining up in front of the audience does turn it into something that it's not intended to be. It's an incitement. If you find yourself in that situation you just have to go with it.

VINCE TREANOR *Morrison vainly attempted to shush the audience. This had no effect. Following the opening stanzas of the song, he drifted into an expansive passage of poetry. With decidedly steady pacing, he advanced through a series of poems until he unexpectedly burst into a blood-curdling scream, which was followed by Krieger's guitar set on some wildly unrestrained echo. Proceeding from this flare-up into 'The End' Morrison was continually assailed with clamorous screams of 'Morrison is King!' from the crowd.*

By now, no one remained seated and the police were forming a barricade in front of the stage.

The music was over and they turned out the lights. The Doors left the stage in great haste as the crowd was beginning to get out of hand. The police formed a flying wedge to get the band through the crowd and left us alone in the middle of this now churning mass of humanity.

The riot was not caused by Jim, the music or anything like it. The riot was the result of several factors: a very hot and humid night, the breakdown of the stage, a long delay between the end of The Who's performance and the time The Doors came on stage, and a large number of people, located on the ground behind the stage, who were very angry over paying a lot of money for seats and then watching the back of some amplifiers.

Right: Stills from Feast of Friends, *taken from the Singer Bowl show*
Opposite: Singer Bowl, New York, NY, 2 August 1968

New York Show Is a Riot

JIM If there were no cops there, would anybody try to get on stage? Because what are they going to do when they get there? When they get on stage, they're just very peaceful. They're not going to do anything. The only incentive to charge the stage is because there's a barrier. If there was no barrier, there'd be no incentive. That's the whole thing. I firmly believe that. No incentive, no charge. Action–reaction. Think of the free concerts in the parks. No action, no reaction. No stimulus, no response. It's interesting, though, because the kids get a chance to test the cops. You see cops today walking around with their guns and uniforms and the cop is setting himself up like the toughest man on the block, and everyone's curious about exactly what would happen if you challenged him. What's he going to do? I think it's a good thing because it gives the kids a chance to test authority.

JOHN **THERE WAS ONE NIGHT WHERE WE WERE INTRODUCED AS 'JIM MORRISON AND THE DOORS'. JIM DRAGGED THE ANNOUNCER OUT AND SAID, 'EXCUSE ME, REINTRODUCE THIS BAND. IT'S THE DOORS.'**

Washington, DC, August 1968

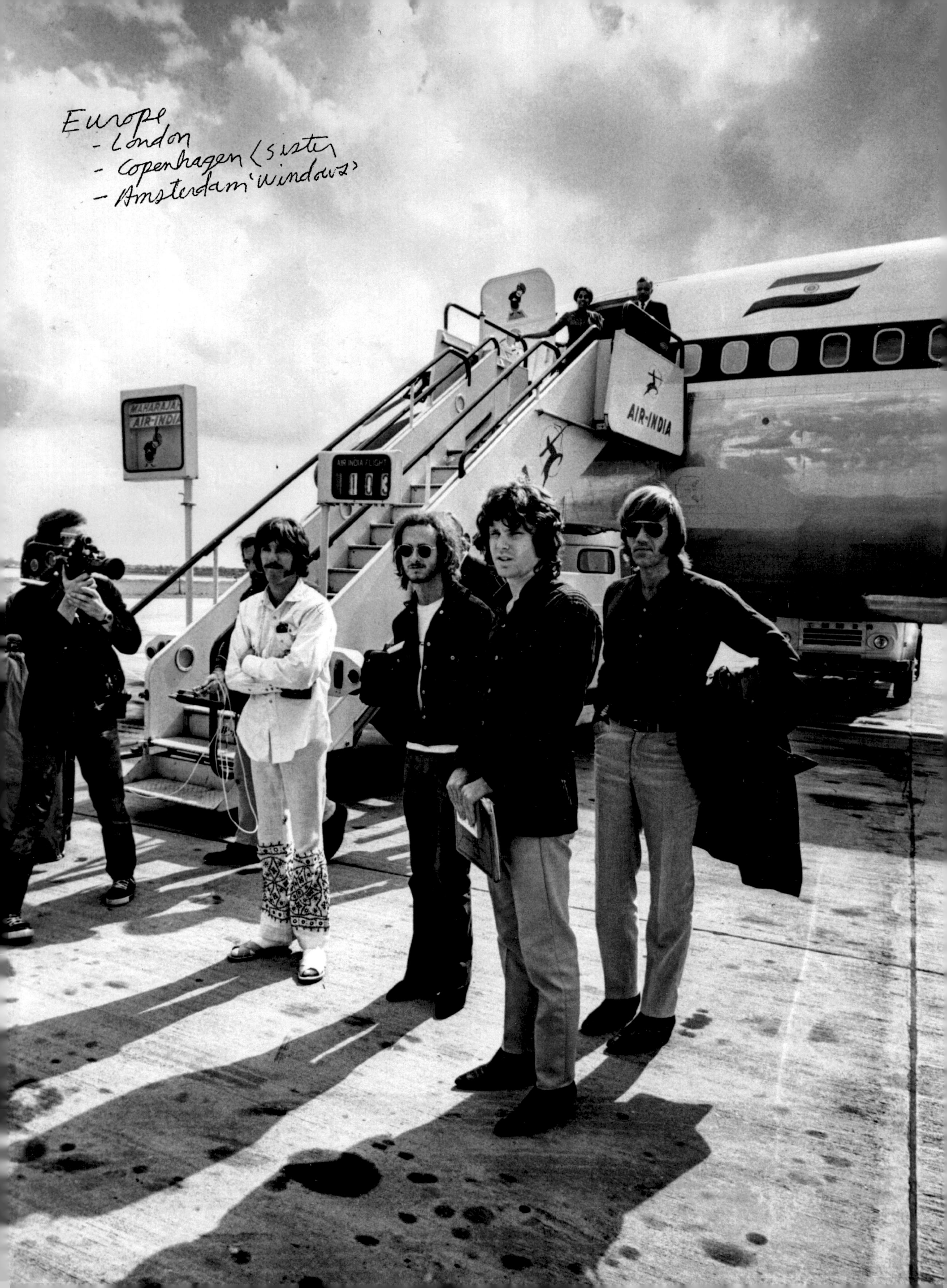

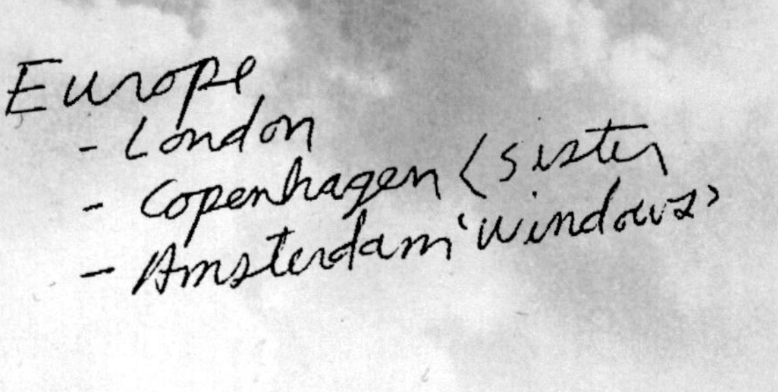
Europe
- London
- Copenhagen <sister
- Amsterdam 'windows>

JOHN At first our records were underground favourites, but by the third album, 'Hello, I Love You' was a hit across the Atlantic. So in September of '68, we went for two weeks to conquer Europe.

JIM Just living in one country all your life you don't realise there's the rest of the world. I expected London to be black and white, like you see in photographs or movies. Most English movies are really grey and kind of foggy, even the ones in colour.

ROBBY A lot of people make it real big by developing most of their potential in a foreign country. Like Jimi Hendrix: he was nothing here but when he went to England he got very big and then he made it big in the US.

JIM I didn't realise they turned out everyone like sausages on [*Top of the Pops*]. I doubt if we'll do it again.

JOHN **RUMOUR HAD IT THAT WE WERE GETTING A REPUTATION IN ENGLAND AS A SERIOUS GROUP WITH POLITICAL OVERTONES.**

EUROPEAN TOUR

The Doors Are Open *TV documentary, London (3–7 September)*
Top of the Pops *TV performance, London (5 September)*
Roundhouse, London (6–7 September)
4-3-2-1 Hot and Sweet *TV performance, Frankfurt, Germany (13 September)*
Kongresshalle, Frankfurt, Germany (14 September)
Concertgebouw, Amsterdam, Netherlands (15 September)
Falkoner Centret, Copenhagen, Denmark (17 September)
Danish TV performance, Copenhagen (18 September)
Konserthuset, Stockholm, Sweden (20 September)

Right: Backstage at Top of the Pops, *Lime Grove Studios, London, UK, 5 September 1968*
Opposite: The Doors landing in London, 2 September 1968

JIM KERR *In 1968, The Doors were probably at their commercial peak in the US and therefore there was great anticipation surrounding their debut in the UK. Part of that anticipation was to do with Morrison's stage antics, which had got him into a lot of trouble in the States. Some establishment figures were hostile – in particular campaigner Mary Whitehouse, the most conservative of them all, who wrote to whoever was in charge to say that we shouldn't be encouraging these 'degenerates', as she described the band.*

JOHN The BBC put together a documentary of our time in London, filled with political footage. They made us out to be the quintessential revolutionary American band. It was a little heavy handed. I don't think that much of our image was consciously built.

Above and opposite, right: Press conference, ICA Gallery, London, UK, 4 September 1968
Opposite, left: Promotional materials for The Doors and Jefferson Airplane's concerts at the Roundhouse, London, UK, 6–7 September 1968

The doors
MIDDLE EARTH
NEW ROUNDHOUSE, CHALK FARM, 636-6311
September 6th and September 7th, 7.30-Dawn
Members 25/- in advance, 30/- at the door
Guests 35/- in advance, 40/- at the door
Tickets available from MIDDLE EARTH
94 Great Portland Street, London, W.1
Cheques and P.O.s to be made payable to
MIDDLE EARTH LTD.
Please send s.a.e. with your application

JEFFERSON
AIRPLANE
MIDDLE EARTH
NEW ROUNDHOUSE, CHALK FARM, 636-6311
September 6th and September 7th, 7.30-Dawn
Members 25/- in advance, 30/- at the door
Guests 35/- in advance, 40/- at the door
Tickets available from MIDDLE EARTH
94 Great Portland Street, London, W.1
Cheques and P.O.s to be made payable to
MIDDLE EARTH LTD.
Please send s.a.e. with your application

RAY The Roundhouse was the hippest venue in London. It was positively psychedelic. Liquid light projections, swirling colours and amoeba shapes of psychedelic intoxication. And 100-year-old dust everywhere!

Roundhouse, London, UK, 6 September 1968

ROUNDHOUSE
Chalk Farm Road, London

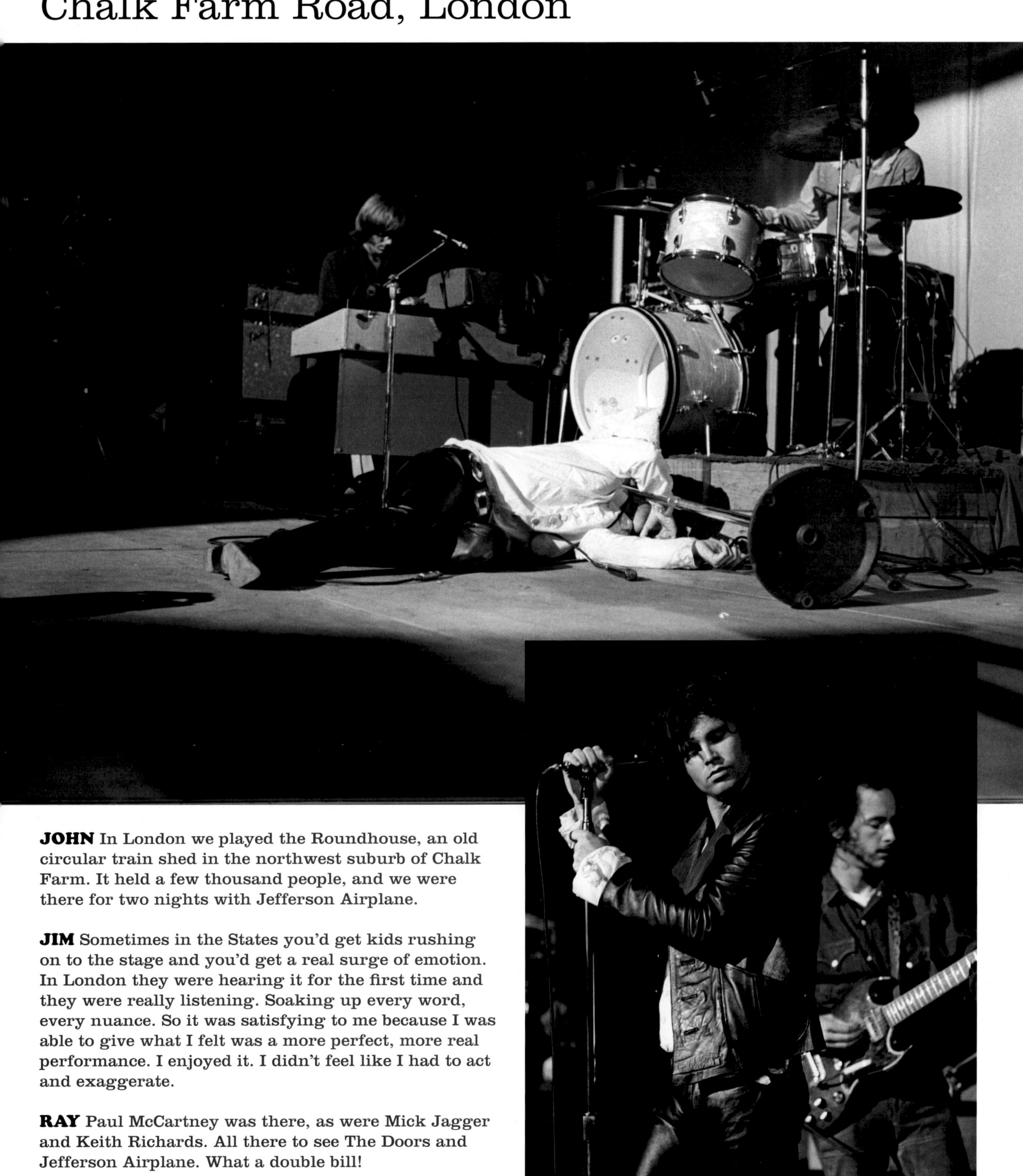

JOHN In London we played the Roundhouse, an old circular train shed in the northwest suburb of Chalk Farm. It held a few thousand people, and we were there for two nights with Jefferson Airplane.

JIM Sometimes in the States you'd get kids rushing on to the stage and you'd get a real surge of emotion. In London they were hearing it for the first time and they were really listening. Soaking up every word, every nuance. So it was satisfying to me because I was able to give what I felt was a more perfect, more real performance. I enjoyed it. I didn't feel like I had to act and exaggerate.

RAY Paul McCartney was there, as were Mick Jagger and Keith Richards. All there to see The Doors and Jefferson Airplane. What a double bill!

MIDDLE EARTH PRESENTS

THE DOORS JEFFERSON AIRPLANE

AT THE NEW ROUNDHOUSE, CHALK FARM

SEPTEMBER 7 7-30 - DAWN

25/- NO 115.....

ROBBY THEY LOVED IT! IF WE HAD JUST PLAYED, THEY DUG THAT TOO, BUT THEY REALLY DUG THE POLITICAL SIDE.

acoustic
acoustic

THE DOORS at the Roundhouse
by Robin Denselow

THE DOORS, the most important American group of the moment, were unleashed on London this weekend, with two concerts at the Roundhouse, in the early hours of Saturday and Sunday morning. Back home they are hailed as the sociological phenomena of the age, the ultimate expression of McLuhanism in practice, the tribal voice of the global village, and so forth. Maybe—they're certainly impressive (and the lead singer, Jim Morrison, is the most outstanding pop personality that America has produced since Elvis Presley)—but their experiments are based on some well-established traditions.

ROBBY In Europe the kids were very politically oriented. If we said anything related to politics, they'd go into a furore.

PAUL KANTNER *They were ready for us in England by 1968. I think it was at an underground level but a very big underground level so it was large. The Roundhouse in London was an old train turning shed and it was just like San Francisco – people were maniacal to be different and the whole psychedelic thing had swept across the Atlantic.*

JIM It was beautiful. That was one of the best concerts we've ever done. I thought the film was very exciting and to be on television was incredible. The guys that made the film had a thesis of what their film was going to be before we even came over. We were going to be the political rock group and it gave them a chance to whip out some of their anti-American sentiments, which they thought we represented. I still think they made a very exciting film.

This page, opposite and overleaf: Roundhouse, London, UK, 6 September 1968

JIM AS WE TRAVELLED AROUND AND PLAYED TO LARGE GROUPS OF PEOPLE, THE WORDS COULDN'T HELP BUT REFLECT WHAT I WAS RUNNING INTO.

Falkoner Centret, Copenhagen, Denmark, 17 September 1968

KONGRESSHALLE

Theodor-Heuss-Allee, Frankfurt

RAY In Germany they really had no idea what The Doors were doing, and it all went completely over their heads. But we were a bit naive as well. At one concert we thought, 'Hey, let's play "Alabama Song". That's German, so they'll like that one.' That was the worst possible thing we could have done because Brecht and Weill were Communists and we were playing in West Germany. A total disaster.

Above: Kongresshalle, Frankfurt, Germany, 14 September 1968
Opposite: An outdoor TV appearance in Frankfurt's historic Römerberg, 14 September 1968

JOHN The people behind us [opposite] are completely bored to death. It's an example of me playing so lightly that the sound you're hearing could never be what I was playing live. But we were trying to get a foothold in Europe.

ROBBY You can see Jim looking up while he's singing. We're in this beautiful square with incredible architecture all around. I know he was just looking at all the cool stuff surrounding us. I wish they had panned around to show where we were, because it was absolutely amazing!

Lippmann + Rau and
SBA open and present
728
The Doors
Stadtsteueramt Frankfurt am Main
Samstag 14. September 1968 21 Uhr
Kongreßhalle
Messegelände
DM 16,–
inklusive 5,5 % Mehrwertsteuer
Balkon Mitte
Reihe Nr. 2
Platz Nr. 269
Druckerei Merkur Frankfurt

4A
5
5A

10A
11

12A

16
16A

17
17A

18
18A
KODAK SAFETY FILM

28

29
29A

30

Backstage and on stage at Kongresshalle, Frankfurt, Germany, 14 September 1968

CONCERTGEBOUW

Concertgebouwplein 10, Amsterdam

JOHN IT WAS LIKE JIM WAS CARRYING THE WEIGHT OF EVERYTHING AROUND.

Above: The Doors playing without Jim, Concertgebouw, Amsterdam, Netherlands, 15 September 1968
Opposite top: TV appearance, Copenhagen, Denmark, 18 September 1968
Opposite, bottom right: Teenbeat *article on the Amsterdam incident, published November 1968*

PAUL KANTNER *We were opening in Amsterdam and Jim came on during our set somewhat drug-abused and started doing almost Sufi dancing to 'Plastic Fantastic Lover', which is a pretty fast song for us. He started spinning and we, in our perverse manner, started playing faster just because he had sort of invaded our turf without asking. We didn't consult among ourselves, it just occurred and it was amusing and he just kept going faster and faster. But then backstage he collapsed and couldn't do the show.*

ROBBY He was breathing but he was out cold. An ambulance took him to the hospital and we were faced with the difficult decision of whether or not to play without him. Other than one set at the Whisky, Jim had never missed a show before. At the Whisky we were an opening band playing a small club. This was a headlining show in a foreign country in front of 2,000 people. We deliberated over what to do and we ultimately figured we'd let the crowd decide. We sent out Vince to explain the situation and offer the crowd a choice between a refund and a Doors concert without Jim Morrison. They chose the concert.

JIM I've never thought that an audience should be as passive as they've become. I think they should be an active participant in what's happening.

GRACE SLICK *That's where Ray Manzarek comes in and the man is amazing. I've watched him and heard stories about him having to do things that were just incredible. I don't know another band member who can just take over and do the rest of the show. Sing, and play the piano and get all the phrasing right, probably never having done it before. I don't know of another band where the lead singer was that erratic. We were sort of erratic but Marty and I were generally on stage.*

ROBBY Having grown weary of the expectations of American audiences based on our image, we found it a breath of fresh air to finally play in front of an audience that was genuinely interested in the music. It's a shame Jim missed it.

ROBBY In the dressing room before our Amsterdam show, we thought Jim had drunk too much, as usual. He was barely able to stand, so Bill Siddons's wife, Cheri, was using all her strength to prop him up over the bathroom sink while Bill splashed water on his face. Jim gradually went limp and then (as the song goes) he slipped into unconsciousness.

JOHN I couldn't understand why Jim was always so down, or stoned or crazy. But I can see that he was troubled about lots of things. When I read his poems, I just wish he was alive. He was self-destructive.

ROBBY Bill and Vince tried to revive him but we were getting nowhere. Jefferson Airplane were touring with us as an opening act and one of their roadies told me someone had handed Jim a block of hash earlier in the day, which he immediately gulped down. I also found out that while the Airplane were playing and we were backstage preparing to go on, Jim had wandered on to the stage and done some sort of flailing dance. Who knows what else he had taken?

GRACE SLICK *Amsterdam was like San Francisco was at the time. The buildings were painted the same way, in the psychedelic sense – the business of having the door frame red, the door yellow, window frames blue, walls purple with bongs in all four corners of the room. And, of course, drugs were legal.*

There was one street where they had psychedelic stuff and both bands were walking down the street and the kids were offering us drugs of all kinds. You wouldn't take everything, otherwise you'd be dead. Jim, on the other hand, took everything that was given to him on the spot.

VINCE TREANOR *Shure microphones were used by The Doors during performances beginning in summer of 1967. It is likely they were purchased from Yale Radio in Hollywood by Bill Siddons. They were used by Ray and Jim.*

TV appearance, Copenhagen, Denmark, 18 September 1968
Previous pages: Falkoner Centret, Copenhagen, Denmark, 17 September 1968
Opposite, top left: Yale Radio Electric Company, Los Angeles, CA, circa 1950
Opposite, right: Jim's handwritten lyrics for 'Texas Radio and the Big Beat'

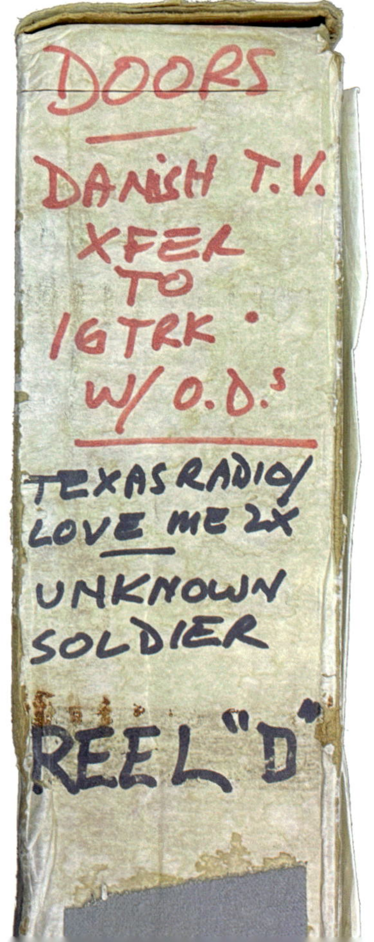

A9

<< Now listen to this:
~~I'll~~ tell you about
Texas Radio & the Big Beat
Soft driven slow & mad
like some new language
Reaching your head
w/ the cold sudden fury
of a divine messenger
Let me tell you about
heartache & the loss
of God
Wandering, wandering
in hopeless night
The negroes in the forest
brightly feathered
let me show you the maiden
w/ wrought-iron soul
Out here on the perimeter
There are no stars
Out here we is stoned
immaculate >>

ROBBY They asked if we wanted to play a TV show while we were in Denmark. We said, 'OK'. Then they told us the bad news, which was we'd have to get there at 6 o'clock in the morning. It was kind of like waking up in a dream. It was tough to pull out a performance in conditions like that. I was really proud of how we did.

RAY My favorite song from this performance is 'Texas Radio and the Big Beat'; Jim's poetry set to music. It's what we tried to do later with *An American Prayer*. The art of poetry and music.

JIM I think music and poetry are a free activity, almost like child's play, and it's a good way to move through life: playing rather than working at it too hard. If there was more music, if more people were playing, I think things would be a lot easier, a lot smoother.

ROBBY WE PLAYED A GOOD SHOW IN STOCKHOLM BUT THE AUDIENCE WERE WEIRD. THEY WOULDN'T CLAP. IT DROVE JIM NUTS.

Los Angeles, CA, 1968

ELEKTRA SOUND STUDIOS

962 La Cienega Blvd, LA

RAY We began the lengthy recording process of The Doors' fourth album, *The Soft Parade*. It was to be a sonic extravaganza, with horns and strings augmenting our basic guitar, keyboards and drums sound. We were going to bring in jazz cats, country and western pickers and classical players.

JOHN *The Soft Parade* cost around $200,000 to make, which was a lot at the time. Ray and I talked about jazz from the beginning and we talked about getting that into *The Soft Parade* with some horns and strings. Then *Sgt. Pepper* gets released. We're like, 'Oh my God'. So we try to make ours and we went for this big thing. If we hadn't gone through that, we wouldn't have realised we needed to get back to the garage. *Morrison Hotel*, *L.A.Woman* was in the rehearsal room. Back to our roots as a garage band. It was a wonderful arc.

ROBBY When Paul suggested bringing in an orchestra to fill out some of the songs, I wasn't a fan of the idea. But writing such complex and grandiose arrangements turned out to be a stimulating challenge, and when you're in the studio listening live to all those strings and horns, the power of it washes over you. Still, it felt like we were copying The Beatles. Or worse: copying The Rolling Stones when they were copying The Beatles.

JOHN George Harrison was in town and dropped by to see Elektra's new studio and we got to meet a Beatle. Alluding to the extra musicians that we had play on the record, he commented that our session looked like the one for *Sgt. Pepper*. I guess that's what we were trying to do. It was a thrill meeting him, although I found myself tongue-tied. George Harrison dropping by or not, the press killed us for changing our precious 'Doors' sound. This didn't stop 'Touch Me' from going to number one.

ROBBY **IN THIS CASE THE LESSON WAS CLEAR: NEVER TRY TO COPY THE BEATLES.**

ROBBY *The Soft Parade* marked a break with tradition because Jim suggested we credit ourselves as individuals instead of sharing credit as a group. This had allegedly been traced back to an argument Jim and I had about the lyric 'Can't you see me growing, get your guns' in 'Tell All the People'. But I was never so precious about my words that I'd argue fiercely against Jim wanting to change them. And if I tried, do you think I'd win? Whenever Jim wanted to change a lyric, he just did it. He was the poet. I was the guitarist.

JIM In the beginning, I wrote most of the songs. On each successive album, Robby contributed more songs until finally on this album it's almost split between us.

ROBBY I think I was getting better at writing by that stage. Other than 'Light My Fire' and 'Love Me Two Times' I hadn't written much but Jim had run out of songs and so I started writing more. It wasn't easy – words for Jim were easy – but for me I would always do the music first and try to fit the words around it. The ones Jim wrote were more avant-garde.

JIM We have a very different vision of reality, different points to make. So I felt it was time. We're a partnership, artistically and financially. We share equally. In the beginning, a lot of it was in the interest of unity, to keep it together. Now that the unity's not that much in jeopardy, I thought it was time people knew who was saying what. So this will be the first album when we'll be giving writer credits and I think we'll just keep doing that.

ROBBY It's funny, people say I sound like Bob Dylan on 'Runnin' Blue'. I was writing more songs at the time because Jim was all messed up.

RAY I enjoyed the hell out of the production of the album. John didn't. He said Rothchild was pushing too hard, demanding too many takes, becoming too much of a perfectionist. Maybe he was ... but it worked. I especially enjoyed working with Paul Harris on the arrangements for the tunes that were going to get a sonic wash of horns and strings.

Incorporated under the Laws of the State of California

NUMBER 4

SHARES -25-

DOORS PRODUCTIONS CORP.

CAPITAL STOCK $25,000.00

500 SHARES

PAR VALUE $50.00

This Certifies that RAYMOND D. MANZAREK is the registered holder of -TWENTY-FIVE- Shares

DOORS PRODUCTIONS CORP.

transferable only on the books of the Corporation by the holder hereof in person or by Attorney upon surrender of this Certificate properly endorsed.

In Witness Whereof, the said Corporation has caused this Certificate to be signed by its duly authorized officers and its Corporate Seal to be hereunto affixed this 21st day of January A.D. 19 69

John P. Densmore SECRETARY

James D. Morrison PRESIDENT

This page and opposite: The Soft Parade *recording sessions, Elektra Sound Studios, Los Angeles, CA, 1968*
Bottom right: When The Doors' production company was officially incorporated on 21 January 1969, the four band members, who were the sole and equal shareholders, were each issued with a stock certificate. This one, for Ray Manzarek, was signed by John Densmore and Jim Morrison

PAUL ROTHCHILD *The sessions were very difficult. Jim decided around this time that he was going to be really rebellious. I think he was trying to test us. He tested us all every minute of every day. He tested people's limits to see where their level of infuriation was.*

JIM It got out of control and took too long. It was spread over nine months.

RAY Perhaps it was too much of a 'quest for perfection'.

ROBBY Paul Rothchild had earned the nickname Little Hitler for his rigid, torturous producing style. His perfectionist drive had been validated by the success of *Waiting for the Sun*, so we were again subjected to endless takes and infinite tweaks, and again Jim drank to cope with the drudgery.

RAY **THE SOFT PARADE WAS ONE OF OUR MOST INNOVATIVE ALBUMS, EVEN IF IT DID TAKE AN UNGODLY LONG TIME TO COMPLETE.**

ROBBY *The Soft Parade* was dismissed as self-indulgent by a lot of critics and fans due to the fanciful instrumentation, but the strings and horns only appear on half the songs. If we had rearranged the sequence of the tracks, I wonder if it would have been as distracting. For the 50th anniversary of the album, we released a remixed, orchestra-less version of the songs, but the problem is, they were specifically written to accommodate the orchestral arrangement, so they sounded empty. I added a few guitar parts to fill things out, but I'll always wonder how different the album would have been if we'd just written it as a four-piece. I don't regret going out on a limb and trying something new, though. It was an experiment and experiments teach you valuable lessons.

Above: Advertisement for The Soft Parade, *released 18 July 1969*
Right: Advertisements for singles 'Wishful Sinful' and 'Runnin' Blue', taken from The Soft Parade

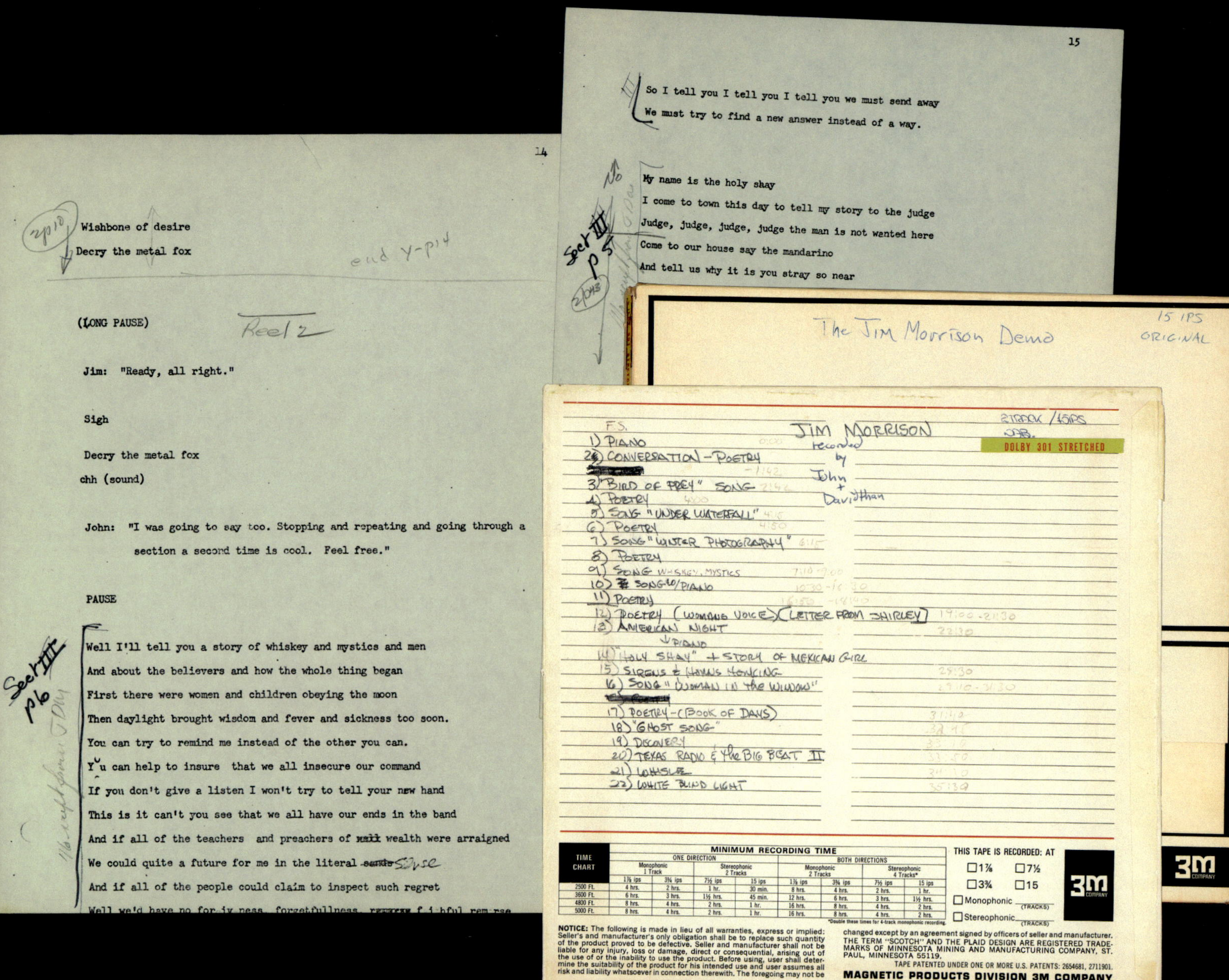

JAC HOLZMAN *Jim wanted to record his poetry. And I agreed, so we entered into a separate non-Doors agreement. Some people thought that we did this as a sop to Jim. I don't think it was that. There was a willingness to accommodate him.*

We went in on a Sunday and recorded several hours of his poetry. Then I couldn't get him back into the studio to do any more. I think he was unsure of himself.

ROBBY A lot of Jim's songs came from his little poetry notebooks that he wrote in high school. It wasn't until later that he actually recorded some of his poetry, which we ended up putting music to on *American Prayer*.

FRANK LISCIANDRO *When Jim walked into the West Coast offices and recording studio of Elektra Records that day in February 1969, he was carrying a file folder holding 14 pages of neatly typed poetry and lyrics. His readings for a performance or a recording were never random or haphazard; he knew what he was going to read and in what order.*

Producer John Haeny had the studio mixing board and tape machines lit up and ready to record. He got Jim set up in front of a microphone and asked him to say a few words so that he could adjust sound levels. Finally satisfied with the sound quality, John said, '... and you've got about 40 minutes of tape.'

Jim said, 'OK. I'll try and get as much as I can.' And he began to read from the typed pages.

Above: Recording transcripts and tape box from Jim's poetry sessions at Elektra Studios

JIM As long as there are people, they can remember words and combinations of words. Nothing else can survive a holocaust, but poetry and songs. No one can remember an entire novel. No one can describe a film, a piece of sculpture, a painting. But so long as there are human beings, songs and poetry can continue.

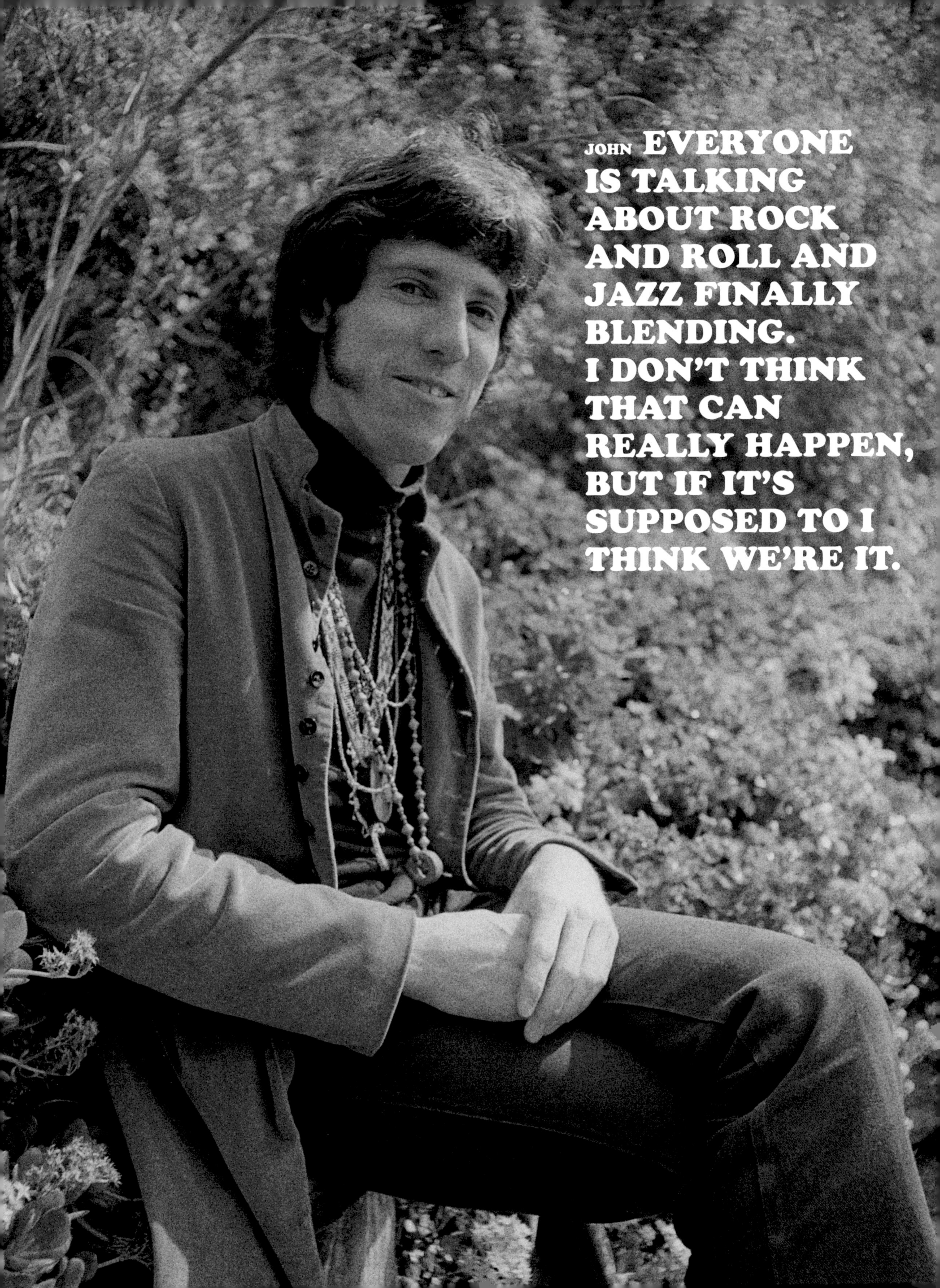
JOHN EVERYONE IS TALKING ABOUT ROCK AND ROLL AND JAZZ FINALLY BLENDING. I DON'T THINK THAT CAN REALLY HAPPEN, BUT IF IT'S SUPPOSED TO I THINK WE'RE IT.

MADISON SQUARE GARDEN
4 Pennsylvania Plaza, NYC

RAY In between recording sessions for *The Soft Parade* we played some monster gigs. Our first basketball arenas. The LA Forum, home of the Lakers, and Madison Square Garden, home of the New York Knicks. We took the horns and the strings from the sessions with us. It was quite the spectacle. Very untypical for The Doors, but what the hell. At the Forum we had a Chinese classical musician play a pipa for the audience. They didn't get it. And we had Jerry Lee Lewis play his country set for the audience. They didn't get it. When we took the stage with the horns and strings – Curtis Amy on sax, George Bohanon on trombone and two jazz friends of theirs on trumpet and baritone sax plus violins, viola and cello – they didn't get it.

ROBBY Despite Madison Square Garden's size and reputation, it wasn't originally intended to host rock concerts. Their PA system was built to announce sports. We had our own PA, but it was hardly powerful enough for a venue that size. The sound was slapping back from the rear walls, and Jim had to sing with no monitors. The crowd forgave the technical limitations and seemed to enjoy the set, even though the sound of our grand, dulcet orchestra was pumped at them through the same loudspeakers that blasted the end-of-period horn at hockey games.

Wild child
Full of grace
Savior of
The human race
your cool face

KIEL AUDITORIUM
14th and Market Sts. St. Louis, Missouri
RIGHT CENT'R
SEC. ROW SEAT
S 118
NOV. 9 1968
SATURDAY 8:30 P.M.
K. X. O. K. PRESENTS
THE DOORS
ORCHESTRA $5.50
Est. Price 5.34 — Sales Tax 16
THE ARCUS TICKET CO CHICAGO
EVG. NOV. 9 1968
8:30 P.M. SATURDAY
KIEL AUDITORIUM
ORCHESTRA $5.50

MINNEAPOLIS AUDITORIUM
ENTER ON GRANT ST.
UPPER BALCONY
5 11 11
SUN. NOV. 10
8:00 P.M. 1968
TRIANGLE THEATRICAL PRODUCTIONS, Inc.
PRESENTS
THE DOORS
UPPER BALCONY
EST. PRICE $3.40
SALES TAX .10
$3.50
ANSELL-SIMPLEX TICKET CO. CHICAGO, ILL.
MINNEAPOLIS AUDITORIUM
SUN. EVE. 8:00 P.M. NOV. 10
SEC. ROW SEAT
UPPER BALCONY

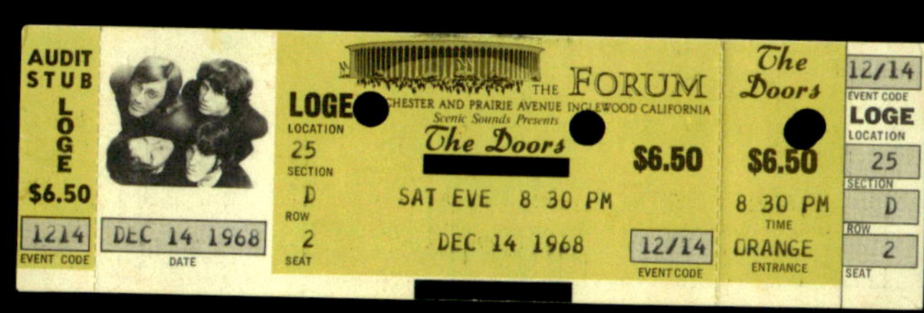

AUDIT STUB
LOGE
$6.50
1214
EVENT CODE
DEC 14 1968
DATE
LOGE
LOCATION
25
SECTION
D
ROW
2
SEAT
THE FORUM
MANCHESTER AND PRAIRIE AVENUE INGLEWOOD CALIFORNIA
Scenic Sounds Presents
The Doors
$6.50
SAT EVE 8 30 PM
DEC 14 1968
12/14
EVENT CODE
The Doors
$6.50
8 30 PM
TIME
ORANGE
ENTRANCE
12/14
EVENT CODE
LOGE
LOCATION
25
SECTION
D
ROW
2
SEAT

AUDIT STUB
COLN
$4.50
EVENT CODE
DATE
COLN
LOCATION
SECTION
ROW
SEAT
THE FORUM
MANCHESTER AND PRAIRIE AVENUE INGLEWOOD CALIFORNIA
Scenic Sounds Presents
The Doors
Guest Star SWEETWATER
$4.50
EVENT CODE
Also Pacific Gas & Electric
The Doors
$4.50
TIME
ENTRANCE
EVENT CODE
COLN
LOCATION
SECTION
ROW
SEAT

RAY The Smothers Brothers were great guys, and very controversial. They wouldn't bow to the powers-that-be and were always poking fun at the establishment. Eventually, the establishment decided to poke back and they were kicked off the air.

JIM I think the new heroes will probably be political activists. In the Twenties it was sports figures, in the Thirties and Forties it was movie stars, World War II aces and that kind of thing, then the music figures became the heroes. I think the next heroes will be the intellectual sort, perhaps scientists and computer experts. People that have an intellectual understanding and knowledge of how things run in society.

Hero = someone who gets away w/it.

JOHN THEIR POLITICS WERE OUR POLITICS, PLUS THEY WERE AGAINST THE VIETNAM WAR. WE WERE REALLY PROUD TO BE ON THEIR SHOW.

THE DOORS
AND
ELEKTRA RECORDS
WISH TO
THANK
YOU FOR
ANOTHER
MILLION-SELLER.

The Smothers Brothers Comedy Hour, *recorded 6 December 1968. The band performs two songs, 'Wild Child' and their recently released single 'Touch Me', alongside the Smothers Brothers Orchestra*

Robby Krieger, for my money one of the top four or five guitarists in rock, was brilliant; his guitar work was effortlessly smooth, his phrasing perfectly suited to everything they played. He also served to synchronize the group behind Morrison's unpredictable excursions into the minds and genitals of the audience.

John Densmore on drums was very good, and tremendously improvisational If you were watching him closely you noticed how every move seemed well placed and carefully thought out. I would much rather watch a jazz influenced drummer such as Densmore than one like Ginger Baker (don't get uptight I dig Baker too, but not as much as a less violent, less flashey cat.)

Morrison instrumented the effect this time. He didn't give the audience what they expected. He gave them what they wanted. He gave them the Doors.

As an organist, Manzarak is very tasty. He seems very classical in his chord structuring and variations and I suppose that's one of the things that makes the Doors the Doors. He seemed very much into the keys, and for the first time in my life I dug the key bass as a substitute for a string bass.

ROBBY After the recording of *The Soft Parade* I went on a fishing trip to Mexico with my friend Donna and her boyfriend. We could have easily driven a few hours down to Baja, or we could have stayed right where we were – we lived on the California coast – but for some reason Donna wanted to make the drive to Guaymas, a small port city on the Mexican mainland over 800 miles away. The only problem was I had to be back in LA a few days later to appear on *The Smothers Brothers Comedy Hour.* We figured out that if we drove in shifts through the night the whole way there and the whole way back, we'd end up with one full day fishing. It was an insane plan.

Once we crossed into Mexico the speed limits vanished and I took over the driving. Night fell and our visibility was limited to the scope of our headlights, which for a couple of hours illuminated nothing but a long, straight, empty stretch of boring blacktop, which slowly lulled us into complacency.

And then the road curved. I hit the brakes and yanked the wheel to the left but it was too late. We skidded off a small cliff and my aborted turn sent the van into a roll. We slammed into the ground. Blackness.

I awoke to some local villagers pulling us from the wreck. My knee ached and I had some cuts and bruises but it didn't seem like any bones were broken. Donna's boyfriend Milton had hurt his foot but seemed relatively fine. We were grateful that we had worn our seatbelts. Donna, however, had been lying in the back seat and was rushed to hospital by ambulance. The doctors kept an eye on Donna while the rest of us returned to LA. I barely made it back in time for *Smothers Brothers*. I walked into the studio with a bulging black eye and played down the seriousness of the incident. The make-up people wanted to cover up my black shiner but I resisted.

Thankfully, we only had to mime our songs; Jim's vocals were the only element that wasn't pre-recorded. But I still had to stand there and pretend to play, and pretend like I hadn't almost died recently. The truth is, though, I never really dwelled on how bad things might've gone for me. My bigger concern was Donna. Her spinal cord had been injured. She would never walk again without help. As she struggled to piece her life together, I struggled with survivor's guilt. Why her and not me? Was this my fault? Whether I was responsible or not, I told Donna I'd always take care of her. I was lucky enough to have the money to be able to help her, and she was unlucky enough to be in the back seat that night. I try to balance things out where I can.

To this day, Doors fans will approach me and ask me about my black eye on the *Smothers Brothers* show. It's the single most common question I get, even though everyone seems to think they're the first one to ever ask me about it. I usually say Jim and I got in a fight before the show. Sometimes I'll say we were attacked by rednecks who didn't like long hair; other times I'll say I hit my eye on a desk. Part of the reason I do that is just to be mischievous. I used to love it when Jim gave conflicting stories to the press to keep people guessing about us, and I like to carry on that tradition. But part of it is that it's just easier to offer a phony answer than to constantly relive one of the most difficult experiences of my life.

ROBBY MY BLACK EYE SHOULD SERVE AS A REMINDER THAT NO MATTER HOW MUCH A PERSON THINKS THEY KNOW ABOUT THE DOORS, THERE'S ALWAYS MORE TO THE STORY. MUCH MORE.

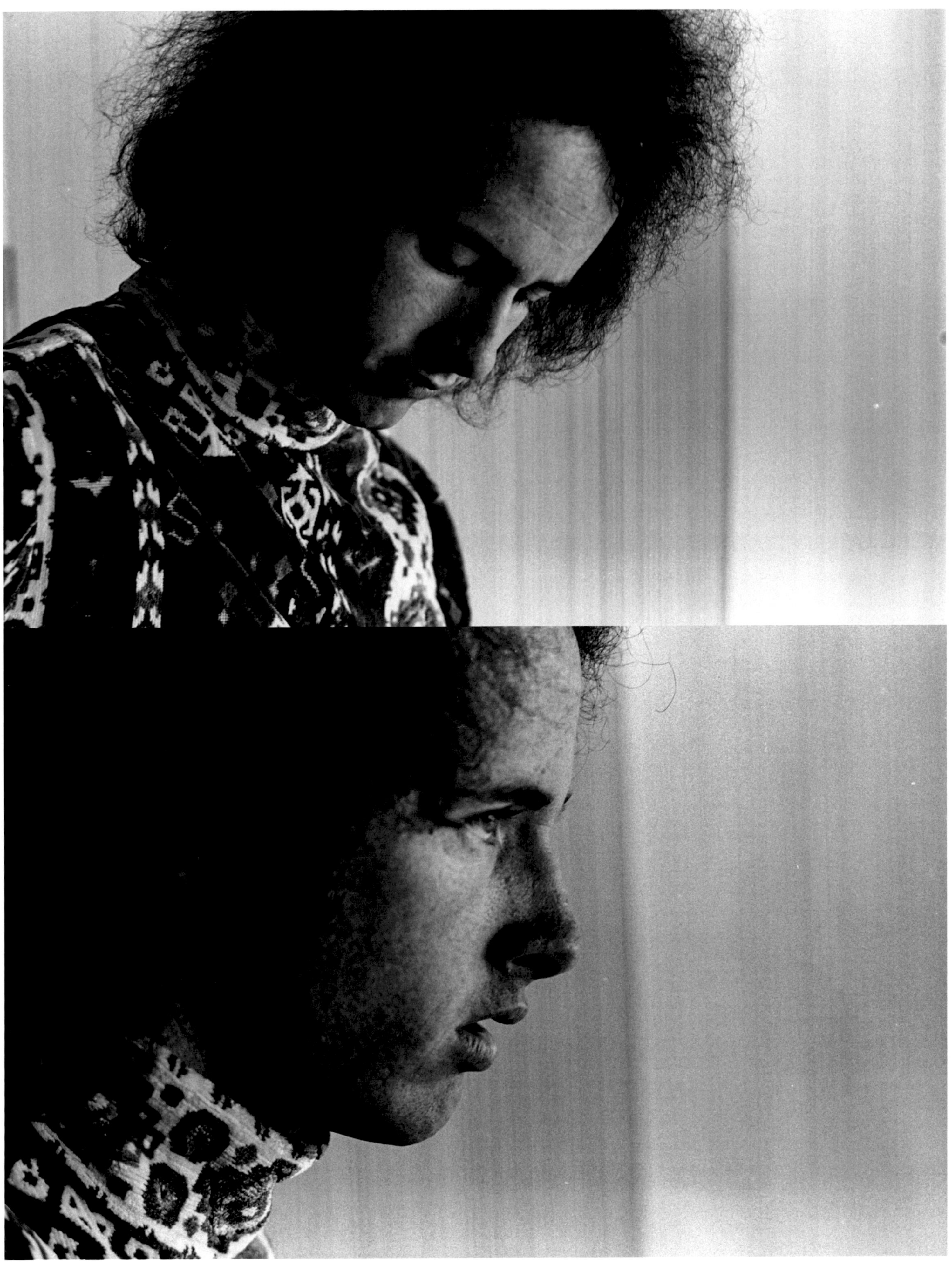

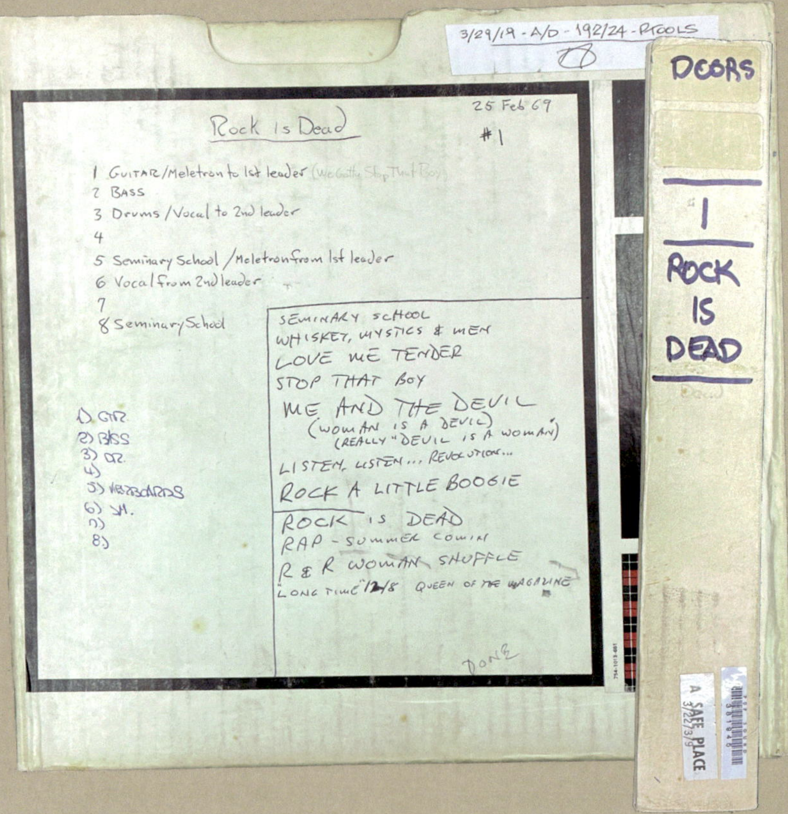

One night, in late February 1969, after the band had dinner and drinks at a local Mexican restaurant, they decided to go into the studio and jam. As they played and improvised, they progressed through rock history, starting with Chuck Berry and Elvis and ending with 'the death of rock and roll'. As they got closer to the end of the session, Jim started reciting some of the provocative lines he had heard at a recent play by avant-garde performance artists the Living Theatre: 'Hey, I'm not talking about no revolution! There's just one thing I want to see. I want to see some dancing. We're gonna have some fun. We're gonna have a good time. Are you ready? Are you ready? Let's roll!' Jim would use those exact same words on stage a week later in Miami.

RAY Four Doors drunk as skunks. Dinner at the Blue Boar just down the street from the Elektra Studio on La Cienega Boulevard. Too many beers and glasses of wine. Too many toasts by Paul Ferrara and Babe Hill. It was friends and it was fun and it was a good time to be alive. We went back to the studio and Jim said, 'Let's jam.' ['Rock Is Dead'] is the result of the Night of the Blue Boar.

JOHN After a large meal in a mediocre Mexican restaurant complete with several bottles of Dos Equis, this opus was possible. Wouldn't have happened without pork fat.

RAY It was just a bunch of drunks jamming in the studio and then we started to get into something.

JIM We needed another song for the album. We were racking our brains ... We were in the studio and so we started throwing out all these old songs. Blues trips. Rock classics. Finally we just started playing and we played for about an hour, and we went through the whole history of rock music – starting with blues, going through rock and roll, surf music, Latin, the whole thing. I call it 'Rock Is Dead'.

RAY It came out towards the tail end of the sessions. It was Jim at his prescient best. Predicting the death of rock and roll. The usurpation of rock by the corporate mind, the co-opting of the revolution by the power of the dollar.

We just snapped it out of the limbo state it was dwelling in and made it ours. We put it on tape. Jammed it into existence. And had one hell of a good time creating it.

ROBBY We came back and turned on the mics. The rest is history. It's kind of amazing how Jim was ahead of his time. Soon after this Cream broke up and Janis and Jimi died. Rock did die.

JIM I was saying rock is dead years ago. For example, in one period jazz was the kind of music people went to and large crowds danced to. Rock and roll replaced that and then another generation came along and they called it rock. A new generation of kids will come along in a few years, swarm together and have a new name for it. It'll be the kind of music that people like to go out and get it on to. Years ago the music didn't become a symbol of a whole new culture or subculture. But each generation wants new symbols, new people, new names. They want to divorce themselves from the preceding generation; they won't call it rock.

RAY Before the madness [of Miami] came the Buick fiasco. They wanted 'Light My Fire' for a television commercial. At the time, there was not a lot of rock and roll on television, so to be asked to use a rock song over a commercial for a new sharp little machine was at once lucrative and subversive. We could make a few inroads in the changeover of consciousness. Or so I thought.

ROBBY General Motors offered The Doors $75,000 to use 'Light My Fire'. The car looked cool and was fuel efficient and we couldn't see any reason not to accept the offer. We had already provided music for a Ford Motor Company training film; why would we view this any differently?

RAY I approved the request posthaste. So did Robby and John. Jim was nowhere to be found. When he finally did show up a few days later, the Buick commercial was a fait accompli. They needed a yes or a no immediately. We said yes and signed the paper. Jim freaked.

JOHN The greed gene was flowing through my veins back then when Jim's outrageous burst of passion against our selling a song to an ad agency became etched on my brain, never to be forgotten.

ROBBY The story most people like to retell is that he was livid about the idea of our music appearing in a commercial because it sullied our art. But in reality he was mainly upset about us making a decision without consulting him.

JOHN I think Jim calling up Buick and saying that if they aired the ad he would smash an Opel on television with a sledgehammer was fantastic. I guess that's one of the reasons why I miss the guy.

ROBBY In the end, the deal was cancelled and the commercial never aired (although Buick still ran print ads with the tagline 'light your fire'). It was never as big an issue as Doors historians make it out to be.

RAY We were hard and heavy into recording and playing gigs around the country. We were being creative and productive. Everything seemed to be going smoothly. And then the Living Theatre came to town.

Julian Beck and Judith Malina led a very avant-garde troupe that engaged in 'confrontational' theatre. A form of in-your-face, antagonistic, urgent and angry performance art. They wanted to shake their audience awake. They wanted freedom. Liberation. And their new play was called *Paradise Now*.

Jim was hooked immediately. The Living Theatre was in town for six performances and he bought tickets for all of them. He saw young New York theatre people who looked like him, confronting the audience just as he did on stage. But they went further. They took their clothes off. They were stark naked in most cities. However, the police in LA let them know ahead of time that they would be busted if anyone went nude. So the young players stripped down to jock-straps and bras and panties as they ranted their pleas for freedom.

JIM Police are different in every town and every country. I suppose the greatest police, unless you get on the wrong side of them, are the English bobbies. They seem to me to be very civil, gentlemanly kind of cats. The cops in LA are different than in most towns. They are idealists and they're almost fanatical in believing in the rightness of the cause of their profession. They have a whole philosophy behind their tyranny, whereas in most places the police are doing a job.

RAY Jim was mesmerised. He even joined them on stage for the last performance. Ranting and raving himself. He was exhilarated. He loved this confrontational theatre. And then the idea struck him. He was going to do the same thing! And he was going to do it at our next gig. Miami.

Top: The Buick print ad that used the 'light your fire' tagline
Above: Original Paradise Now *programme from the Living Theatre's European shows*
Opposite: The tape box from the 'Rock is Dead' session, 25 February 1969

DINNER KEY AUDITORIUM

2700 S Bayshore Drive, Miami

Public Reacts to Rock Show

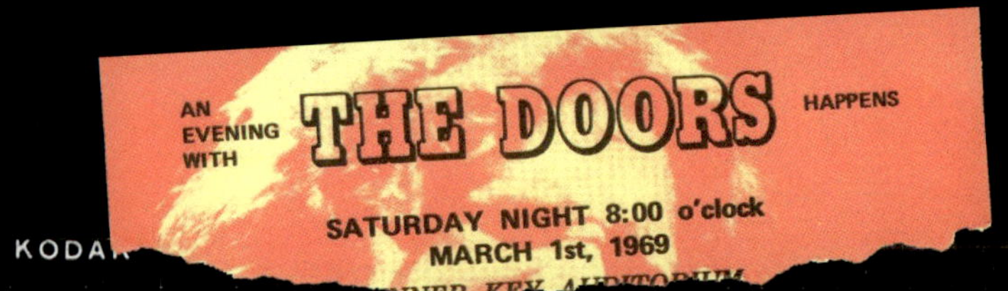

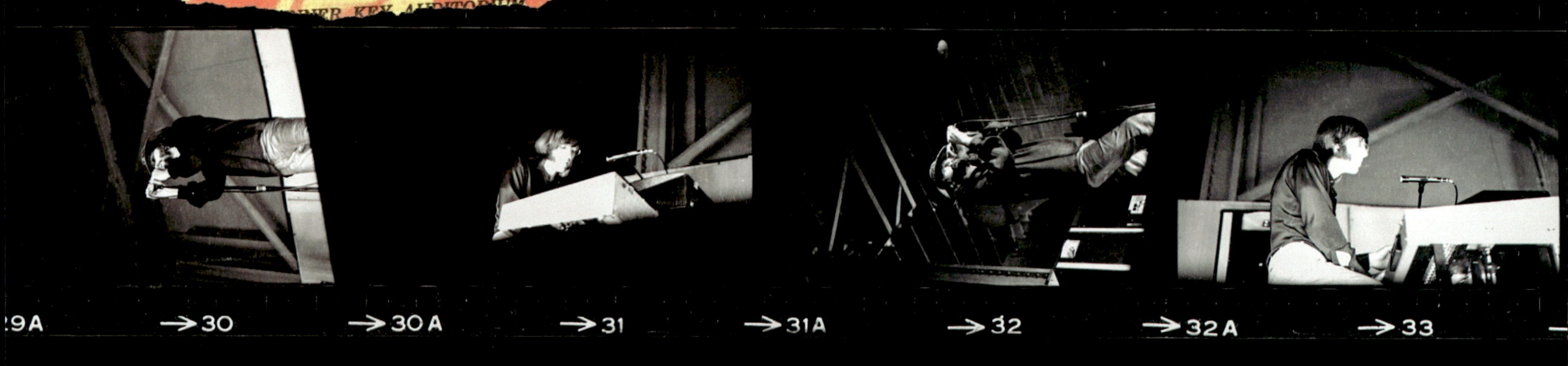

JIM I don't know why the South has such a reputation. Maybe these cliches are really true but I never noticed that the South is any worse than any other part of the United States. Of course, I'm from there so I might be prejudiced but I think it's a gross caricature. However, it is a strange territory.

JAC HOLZMAN *Bill Siddons said that the venue in Miami was supposed to hold about 8,000, and that was the agreed-upon limit negotiated with the promoter, but there were close to double that number. And no seats. It was hot, stinking, overcrowded, packed to the rafters and beyond. The promoter was ripping off the band and the audience.*

An audience of dummies

Will Doors Open In Jacksonville On Sunday Night?

What happened Saturday night is still the talk of Miami. Jim Morrison, The Doors specialist in obscene words and crowd incitement, apparently unzipped his pants onstage, exposed himself and disgusted his youthful audience.

With The Doors' bad reputation — and it was publicized in Life Magazine several months ago — how did City of Miami property become available to The Doors?

Dinner Key Auditorium, Miami, FL, 1 March 1969

RAY HE WAS GOING TO SHOW THESE FLORIDA PEOPLE WHAT PSYCHEDELIC, WEST COAST SHAMANISM AND CONFRONTATION WAS ALL ABOUT.

VINCE TREANOR *There was another problem brewing. Jim was late. The previous evening Jim had attended a performance by the Living Theatre troupe. At parties following the theatrical performance Jim had gotten drunk. He woke up late that morning and then had an argument with Pam in Los Angeles. As a result, he had missed his scheduled flight. He had to reschedule his passage to Miami but many of the early flights were fully booked. Finally he was able to get a seat, but the plane would land about one hour before the performance. He would still have to get from the airport to the venue. It would be a close thing.*

JOHN The Dinner Key Auditorium in Miami was sweltering with all those extra people they stuffed in by taking out the seats. It was 8.15 p.m. We were supposed to go on 15 minutes earlier, and there was still no sight of Jim. I busied myself with a drummer's stretching exercise.

Finally, Vince came running up the stairs to the dressing room shouting, 'He's here!' I turned my back in order not to have eye contact as I felt the presence of someone coming into the room with an entirely different vibration from everyone else. You could literally feel the chaos. It's what the press people called 'charisma'. I call it psychosis.

RAY We were in Miami and it was hot and sweaty, a swamp, a horrible venue with 14,000 people packed in there. Jim had just seen the Living Theatre and he was going to do his version in front of what was virtually his home crowd. He was drunk as a skunk.

JOHN As we descended the stairs, it felt like entering a sauna. Dante's Inferno. As we stepped onto the stage, Vince warned us that it was poorly constructed. We started 'Back Door Man', and Jim sang a few lines and suddenly stopped. We vamped for a while but soon petered out. Then Jim went into a drunken rap: 'You're all a bunch of fuckin' idiots. You let people tell you what you're gonna do. Let people push you around. You love it, don't ya? Maybe you love gettin' your face shoved in shit ... you're all a bunch of slaves. What are you going to do about it? What are you gonna do?'

JIM I don't like it when people in the audience start trying to be the performers, I've always disliked that. That has its place at a party or something but if people come to see you perform a work of art I think they should let you do what you're supposed to do. I've felt for a long time that somehow we're all afflicted these days with the psychology of the voyeur and not in a strictly clinical or criminal sense but in our whole emotional and moral stance before the world. Anytime we try to break out of that bound of passivity our actions usually seem awkward and obscene like an invalid who has forgotten how to walk. I don't like a separation between actors and spectators – I'm against that – but you find in reality that if a person in the audience jumps up, or just sits in their seat, and shouts something out and it's not good, if it's stupid, if you affect them but what they come out with is petty, then I think they should be put down. Or if someone jumped up on stage and tried to take away the microphone, if they were good at it, and looked good and had something to say with style I think I'd let them do it. But if it's some drunk, or some idiot just trying to expose himself without anything to say, I'd shove him back into the pit.

RAY He told the crowd, 'You didn't come here to hear a rock and roll band play some really good songs, you came to see something didn't you? What did you come to see? You came to see something you've never seen before, something greater than you've ever seen. What do you want? OK, how about if I show you my cock?' The audience went crazy. It was madness. Jim took his shirt off and put it in front of himself and the audience was screaming wild. He whips the shirt to the side and asks them, 'Did you see it?' And they saw what they wanted to see. It was like one of those 'Jesus on a tortilla' events, a mass hallucination. I swear to God he never did it.

ROBBY It was the logical place for Jim to do that because he was from the South and it was his hometown if he had one. But, of course, he didn't do it. It was total chaos. He was wasted drunk and he was storming around the stage screaming and yelling and we were trying to play and keep it together as we often did. The audience were yelling and screaming and he was screaming back.

JOHN Miami was one of Jim's last attempts to get a new creative spark going and to quell the demons that had had him off-centre from birth. Jim had intensified his quest with existential reading, psychedelics and alcohol. Like his romantic idols Nietzsche and Rimbaud, he had glamorised death. Writing and performing seemed to be the only things that abated Jim's angst. Of course, neither the band nor the audience knew what Jim was up to. He hadn't told us about taking acid right before the Hollywood Bowl, and he hadn't mentioned how this night he was going to try to inject confrontational theatre into our performance.

JIM Lewis Marvin happened to be down there. He travelled around spreading his philosophy of non-violence and vegetarianism and carried this little lamb around to demonstrate his principles. In other words, if you eat meat, you're killing this little lamb. He gave it to me during the middle of the show and I just held it for a little while. There was a lot of noise and a lot of commotion. It was almost deafening, but the lamb was breathing normally, almost purring like a cat, totally relaxed. I guess what they say about lambs to the slaughter is true, they don't feel a thing.

ROBBY It was total chaos but I think most people had a good time. Not much music, you couldn't really call it a concert.

RAY Jim invited the audience on stage, and they started, but the rickety little stage collapsed. John and Robby left the stage and I continued to play a screaming, crunching organ. There was part of me that was thinking we're going to get in big trouble, but it was too late to stop it, so why not treat it as a theatrical event?

Result of Miami Performance

Rock Singer Charged

Six warrants, including one for a felony, were sworn out Wednesday on singer Jim Morrison of The Doors, four days after his chaotic appearance before 12,000 young rock music fans at the city's Dinner Key Auditorium.

The felony charge, as worded by the Dade State Attorney's Office, is "lewd and lascirious behavior in public by exposing his private parts and by simulating masturbation and oral copulation."

Dinner Key Auditorium, Miami, FL, 1 March 1969

JIM I was just fed up with the image that had been created around me, which I had sometimes consciously, most of the time unconsciously, cooperated with. It got too much for me to stomach so I kind of just put an end to it in one glorious evening.

JOHN Scared shitless, Robby and I ran up the stairs to get out of the madness. Jim was now in the middle of the auditorium, leading a snake dance with 10,000 people following him. I looked down from the balcony, and the audience looked like a giant whirlpool with Jim at the centre. As I went into the dressing room, Bill came racing out. 'Get him out of there!' I warned. 'He could get hurt!' 'That's what I'm going to do!' Bill screamed.

Ten minutes later the Lizard King strolled in with a group of people laughing and talking. He was sober now; a concert being a better cure for a hangover than drinking several cups of coffee. My anger over the performance was subsiding as Ray and I looked out the window at the crowd driving away. There was one thought that I couldn't get out of my mind, though. How long were we going to get away with this? The ledge at the top of our pedestal was getting narrower.

JIM A journalist heard about the concert and went, and the next day he wrote a front-page sensationalist story about the concert, about inciting a riot. The citizens began getting irate and calling the police station and asking why this had been allowed to go on and why I hadn't been arrested. About three or four days after the whole thing they had a warrant out for my arrest.

RAY Sure enough, within a week, Jim had been arrested and charged with indecent exposure, open profanity, public drunkenness and simulation of oral copulation.

JIM WE'RE A PRETTY SEDATE GROUP, NO DOPERS OR SEX MANIACS OR ANYTHING LIKE THAT.

Dinner Key Rock Show Backer Slams The Doors

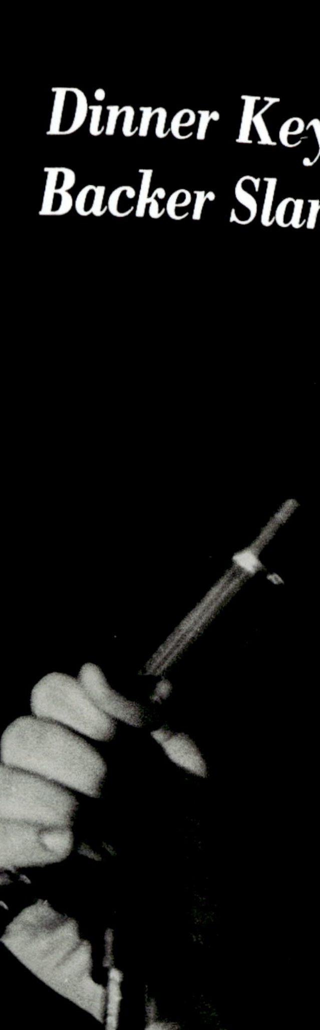

ROBBY It was totally ridiculous but it totally ruined our career for about a year. Nobody would hire us in anywhere decent and they banned our records on the Top 40 stations.

JIM I think it was the lifestyle that they were going after, I don't think it was me personally. I just kind of stepped into a hornet's nest. I had no idea that the sentiment down there was so tender. The audience that was there really enjoyed it but I think people reading about it in the paper had this distorted version, creating a climate of hysteria. A few weeks later they had an anti-indecency rally at the Orange Bowl.

JOHN If he had whipped it out, why hadn't they arrested him on the spot, and why had the police been so friendly after the concert? The long and short of it is: a) The warrant wasn't issued for nine days; b) It was a fugitive warrant – despite public knowledge of our planned vacation, the warrant claimed that Morrison left Miami to avoid prosecution. Political? You bet.

Dinner Key Auditorium, Miami, FL, 1 March 1969
Opposite: Report on the Miami incident
Opposite, bottom left: Jim's speech during the show

50
r Service

Sullivan Investigators
1 NORTH 13th STREET
Suite 211
Philadelphia, Penna.
"Your Problem Is Our Business"

Licensed & Bonded
Detective

e:
L. Sullivan

Confidential Report

To: Bill Siddon: Manager of Doors
Concerning incident of March 9,1969 at the Dinner Keys Auditorium. "MIAMI"

Acting on information received, I was to look in the matter immediately concerning the actions of one, Jim Morrison, singer of the Doors. I made three confidential phone calls to Miami to asceratain if there was anything could be done to stop the arrest of one Jim Morrison. I inturn received information that it could be slowed up or stopped or dropped to a lesser charge, I sent one of my agents to Miami to make the contacts and the transactions. I took a later flight to Miami.

I arrived in Miami Beach at 8:30pm. After we were given the assurance they would do this, I then proceeded from the airport to locate one Ken Collier one of the owners of the Imiage. Acting on information received, Mr. Collier was the main complainant to the police dept. I wanted to receive from Mr. Collier 2 tapes recordings, still photo"s , motion pictures of the show. I was able to ascertain them but the source destroyed them in my presence and would rather stay annonymous because of his police record. At this time I learned from the news announcer on the radio, they were asking the public if they had any pictures of the show to contact that station and they would receive a reward for each photo and they would remain annonymous.

At this time I proceeded to the police dept. were I was told there were no warrants issued for one Jim Morrison, because what evidence they had on city level would consist of a very small charge, which would be a misdeamor handled in lower courts which would consist of a fine. On Wed. March 5,1969, I had received information that warrants had been issued for disorderly conduct and drunk and recklessness. There were no warrant issued for inciting riot, abusive language or exposure

C-O-N-F-I-D-E-N-T-I-A-L R-E-P-O-R-T

MIAMI INCIDENT

of personal private parts. I went back to the hotel to wait for a call from 3 different informers. I received a call telling me that they had no complaints from the police dept. because they had information that I had in my posession, facts concerning the show, that would implicate 28 police officers, 2 sergeants and 1 captain. They were willing to cooperate with me as long as I didnt expose this to the crime commission, who are opening up an investigation about this matter. The commision is concerned with why the city of Miami let Mr. Collier hold ashow at the Municipal Auditorium. The police dept. informed me they knew the where abouts of Jim Morrison on the isle of Jamaice and could arrest him at anytime. At this time I was able to ascertain the location of Jim Morrison by phone.

I talked to approximately four witnesses who the police had spoken to and they had stated that they did not tell the police anything. and said they did not see that part of the performace. They told me they did see it but they were not going to tell the police.

At 9:30 am Thursday I had information that one Michael Brumer, attorney-at-law, suite 402 aimsley building could be able to get photos of the performace and also zerox copies of the warrant. I had the attorney talk to someone in California.

I had the understanding that this part of the matter would be taken care of by the attorney.

Opinion of the investigator:

THis investigation will inflat further than anyone can imagine. (You know what I mean King A Sabe) It is just as hard to kill a rock as to stop this now because of public opinion. It is a known fact that Ken Collier has political ideas and his opponents would like to see him in hell with his back broke. From the time I arrived in Miami until now I have not been able to see or communicate with him and his associates. The reason I left the investigation as it was because the attorney general's office was gathering all information for the grand jury. Iam sending all the news paper clippings and a confidential letter.

Respectively submitted

George Sullivan

George Sullivan

JIM I think it was more of a political than a sexual scandal. They picked upon the erotica aspect because there would really have been no political charge they could have brought against me. Really it was a lifestyle that was on trial more than any specific incident. It boils down to that I told the audience that they were a bunch of fucking idiots to be a member of an audience. The basic message was to realise that you're not really here to listen to a bunch of songs by some fairly good musicians but you're here for something else and won't admit it.

You're all a bunch of fucking idiots! Letting people tell you what you're gonna do, letting people push you around. How much longer do you think it's gonna last? How much longer are you gonna let it go on? How much longer are you gonna let them push you around?

Maybe you like it. Maybe you like being pushed around. Maybe you love it! Maybe you love getting your face stuck in the shit, come on! Maybe you love getting pushed around. You love it, you're all a bunch of slaves, bunch of slaves, you're all a bunch of slaves. Letting people push you around.

What are you gonna do about it? What are you gonna do about it? What are you gonna do about it? What are you gonna do about it? What are you gonna do? What are you gonna do about it? What are you gonna do about it?

JOHN Jim was very subdued on *Critique* because of the trial and he was sobered by all that, but personally I think he was still one foot in the wine vat.

JIM I wasted a lot of time and energy with the whole thing. I had about a year and a half of this gnawing disquiet about it. But I guess it was a valuable experience, because I think before the trial I had an unrealistic schoolboy attitude about the American judicial system and my eyes were opened up a little bit. There were black guys that would go in before me, they'd have five minutes in the court room and then they would end up with 20 or 30 years in jail. If I hadn't had unlimited funds to continue fighting my case I'd be in jail now, for three years. If you've got money, you generally don't go to jail.

JOHN The Hall Owners Association had a little newsletter that they passed to each other all around the country. It said, 'Don't hire the dirty Doors.' Convicted until proven innocent.

RAY Jim was feeling the pressures of Miami when we did this show called *Critique*. He hadn't even gone to trial yet, and all the charges were pending. If he were to be convicted on the four charges filed against him, he would be spending up to three and a half years in Raiford Penitentiary in Bradford County, Florida. Jim was scared.

ROBBY It was another tough show to do because there was no audience. It was a cold studio with nobody to play off of. It's so funny now listening to that panel discussion. There's this one guy who is so sure that we're going to be a flash in the pan and that no one will ever hear about us after another year. He was convinced that we would never influence anyone.

In April of 1969, The Doors were still dealing with the consequences of the Miami incident and the subsequent FBI charges against Jim. Some 17 concerts had been cancelled since Miami, and they were essentially blacklisted from performing at that point. Even though this gave them an opportunity to get back into the recording studio to work on their next album, they wanted to get out and play live. This is why they jumped at the chance to play, uncensored, on a New York PBS television show called Critique.

They would be allowed to play an entire set of songs, and also be interviewed by Richard Goldstein of the Village Voice. *The Doors decided to play a bluesy set of their standards plus songs from* The Soft Parade. *This is possibly the only time you'll get to hear what* The Soft Parade *might have sounded like without the strings and horns.*

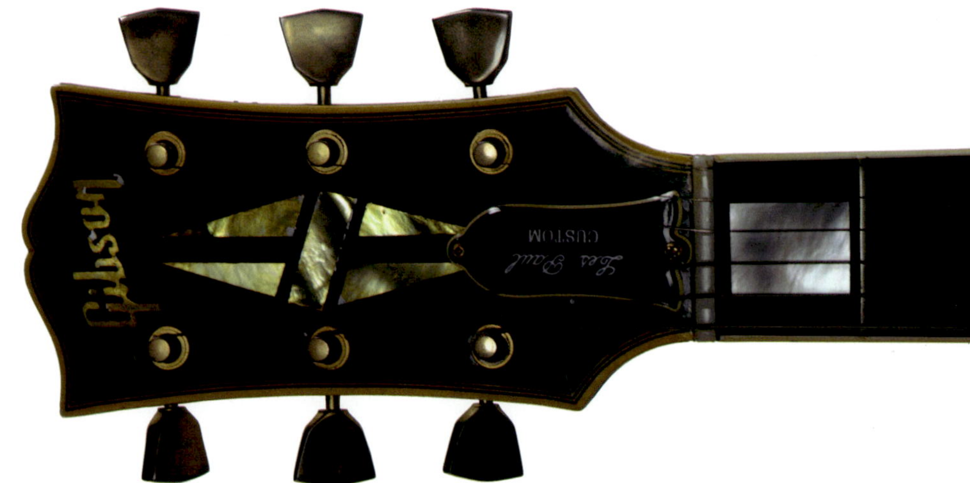

ROBBY I used the Les Paul on most of the slide songs. I didn't use it in the studio. You can see it on the stage here, and I also used it at the Hollywood Bowl.

VINCE TREANOR *All Robby's guitars were from Gibson. He liked the feel and sound of their guitars. Gibson liked Robby as well. They provided him with some new models.*

Robby Krieger acquired a 1954 Gibson Les Paul Custom Black Beauty in mid-1968 for bottleneck playing. Gibson's replica of this guitar, shown here, is missing the gold Bigsby tailpiece and has a Seymour Duncan mini-humbucker in the neck in place of the stock Alnico V pick-up (modifications Robby made in later years). This is the guitar Robby used in the studio to record 'Wild Child'. He can also be seen playing it at the Hollywood Bowl, in the group's Critique *television appearance, and during the post-Morrison Doors tours*

fri & Sat 30 - 31

fri and sat may 30-31./

NORMAN MAILER CAMPAIGN BENEFIT: Presented by Cinematheque 16 & Tom Baker. Super Films & Super Stars. Andy Warhol's "I, A Man", and "Feast of Friends," featring "The Doors." Norman Mailer's works will be read by Tom Baker author of "The Beard" Mike McClure; Jim Morrison of "The Doors"; Mary Woronov ie. Hanoi Hanna in "Chelsia Girls" Seymore Cassle star of "Faces"; and Jamie Sanchez starred in "The Pawnbroker." All proceeds go directly to Mailer's campaign headquarters. Cinematheque-16, 8816 1/2 Sunset Blvs. 657-8914 after 7 pm. $5.

JIM BOOKS OF POETRY DON'T USUALLY REACH A LOT OF PEOPLE.

FRANK LISCIANDRO *To raise money for Norman Mailer's campaign to become mayor of New York City, a multimedia event was held at the Cinematheque 16 movie theatre in Los Angeles on 30 and 31 May 1969. There were screenings of the Andy Warhol film* I, a Man *and the Doors documentary* Feast of Friends*, as well as readings by Jim Morrison (accompanied by Robby Krieger), Michael C. Ford, Michael McClure and other poets and actors.*

ROBBY As this was a poetry reading, Jim couldn't drag the whole band up there, so I just brought an acoustic guitar and played a little. We also played a few songs, including 'Back Door Man' and 'Heartbreak Hotel'. I remember we got the most applause. I'm sure Jim would have been satisfied doing that forever. The whole rock and roll thing, I don't think he really planned that.

FRANK LISCIANDRO *I helped set up the event at the Cinematheque 16. I made sure they got a print of* Feast of Friends. *My wife at the time, Katherine, and I decided that we'd go early and get good seats, which was unnecessary because there were probably as few as 50 people in the whole theatre.*

Jim came in a little late with Michael McClure. They had been out eating a late dinner, and probably doing some drinking. Michael read first, and then Jim followed. Robby was noodling on his guitar. Jim would look over at him and they would laugh. Jim didn't really get nervous about anything, but he seemed a lot more comfortable reading poetry than singing live. There wasn't any music to keep up with, or a set list to follow.

RAY Jim, in his poetry, has always had a rhythmic sort of quality. I've always felt him to be in the tradition of the Greek poet ... who gets on the stage and recites his poetry to handclapping or a drum beating, or to an implied beat. Jim always had that sense of implied rhythm in his poems, so it was easy for us as musicians to lock into a rhythm.

Opposite, top: Auditorium Theatre, Chicago, IL, 14 June 1969
Opposite, bottom: Jim's notebook

AUDITORIUM THEATRE

50 East Ida B. Wells Drive, Chicago

Motives for performing
Plays as child
competition for the goods
of the world: women

Dream on returning from Jamaica
Dream of the sexual outlaw

VINCE TREANOR *Finally for the first time in three months we were on the road again. Jim was in good form. They began with 'When the Music's Over'. The performance was good. Jim was as animated as in the early days. Everything went smoothly and the audience was responsive. The set ended with the first public performance of 'The Soft Parade'. The audience was delighted and the applause seemed to never end. This was one of the rare times the boys played an encore. What else but 'Light My Fire'? They brought a standing ovation and thunderous applause. The boys were excited and happy to be back. There was a second encore – 'Maggie M'Gill' – and, with that, the show ended.*

The second show started at about midnight. It lasted for about two hours. Jim was full of energy. It was like the typical show of 1967. During this show Jim was talking to the audience – making a lot of quips and jokes. The audience loved it. As in the first set, they ended with 'Light My Fire'. This performance was a smash success. Jim was back to his old self.

ROBBY People always say Jim had gotten sick of being a rock star after the Miami incident. He was sick of certain aspects of it, for sure. He was sick of the expectations from audiences and critics. He was sick of the scrutiny from law enforcement. But he wasn't sick of performing.

THE FORUM

866 Avenida de los Insurgentes, Mexico City

After the fiasco in Miami and the concert cancellations that followed, The Doors were excited to get back on the road. One of their first large-scale gigs was to be at Mexico City's Plaza Monumental, a giant bullring that could hold 48,000 fans.

Unfortunately, the promoters could not secure the necessary permits. They were also wary of having so many young people in one spot due to the civil unrest occurring in Mexico at the time, so they moved the concert to a small, exclusive venue called The Forum.

In the process, they also bumped up the ticket prices so only Mexico's elite could afford to attend. The Doors were extremely unhappy about the prices, but were locked into a contract, so they reluctantly performed four consecutive nights of sold-out shows at The Forum.

Those dirty Doors are back in the news again. But, for a change, the news concerns music!

The Doors will present the first live rock concert in the history of Mexico on June 28.

Mexico City, June 1969

JIM In Mexico City they were rather boisterous. It was a unique problem because it was a hotbed of political unrest. I read some stories down there that would curl your hair. They let us sign up for a concert and then about two days before we showed up, the mayor or the sheriff wanted to get his name in the paper and tried to cancel the show. It's a political football. We're the band you love to hate.

JOHN I couldn't stand the upper-class Vegas-type club we had been suckered into. But the deal we had made with the Mexican government was four nights in that sleazy hole in exchange for playing one night in the bullring for the masses at a price they could afford. I should have known from the Mexican press it wasn't going to happen. Too much danger of a riot … Bullshit. *El Heraldo* called us 'hippies' and 'undesirables'.

JIM **WE NEVER REALLY HAD ANY RIOTS. A RIOT IS AN OUT OF CONTROL, VIOLENT THING.**

RAY The bullring concert never happened. The government pulled the plug. So we wound up playing a sit-down supper club for the rich kids. They liked Ford Mustangs and the Oedipal Doors. 'Father … Yes, son … I want to kill you … Mother, I want to …' They loved it. They shouted it out in unison from their tables. From behind their fancy place settings. At the top of their lungs.

JOHN 'The End' is not quite dinner-club Muzak, and watching people eat roast beef in a red velvet lizard lounge while we were on stage seemed surreal. In his black leather pants, Jim looked like he was from another planet. I could even hear the clanking of silverware right in the middle of the Oedipal section where it was usually pin-drop time. Those homicidal lines stopped the diners in mid-chew. Jaws dropped. Mouths full of food gaped open. It must have driven Jim crazy because he hated people who chewed gum, let alone crunched on dinner.

VINCE TREANOR **WE WERE THE POLLUTED, WE WERE THE UNTOUCHABLES, CONTAGIOUS.**

Mexican parachute
Blue green pink
Invented of silk
& Stretched on grass
Draped in the trees
of a Mexican Park
T-shirt boys in their
slumbering art

On 13 September 1969, The Doors headlined the Toronto Rock and Roll Revival concert. The entire band was looking forward to this show, as it featured many of their heroes, including Little Richard, Gene Vincent, Jerry Lee Lewis, Chuck Berry and Bo Diddley. When the band started their set, Jim commented what an honour it was to perform on the same stage as so many 'illustrious musical geniuses'.

ROBBY We had to follow Little Richard at a festival in Toronto. Unfortunately for us, he just blew the place away; he did most of the show standing on his grand piano with his crazy clothes. Jim didn't know what to do. How do you top that? So he gave this little speech, an ode to all the people that were there – Chuck Berry, Alice Cooper, Little Richard.

JIM Adolescents and early youth – the fires are burning fastest and your energy level is probably at its highest so it demands a kind of rock, screaming type of music. At 26, I'm getting more interested in jazz. I can't even listen to the radio anymore. I like old blues, early rock and roll, but frankly I find most of it really boring. Young people are being programmed by the radios. The major rock stations only play 30 songs over and over, 24 hours a day. It's been proven that what you hear the most is what you like the most so there's really no choice involved. Someone is programming it. What everyone should say is that the medium is the message and the message is me. That's the answer: for everyone to stand up and say, 'I'm me,' and be fully aware of that fact. That you are yourself and express it.

ROBBY Alice Cooper famously threw a live chicken into the audience, and the crowd tore it to pieces.

ALICE COOPER *The chicken incident was an accident that could not have happened at a better time. We were just a new band and we were there with John and Yoko, The Doors and everybody you could imagine. We went on between John Lennon and The Doors at the prime time. At the end of the show we would open up these feather pillows and use CO_2 cartridges to make it look like a blizzard. Then, I looked down on the stage and there was a chicken.*

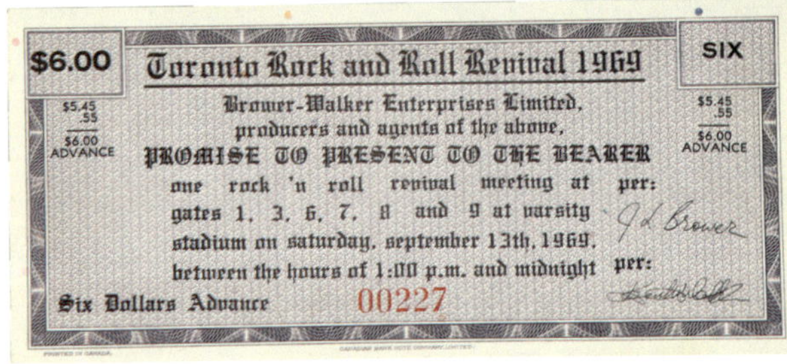

$6.00 — Toronto Rock and Roll Revival 1969 — SIX

$5.45 / .55 / $6.00 ADVANCE

Brower-Walker Enterprises Limited, producers and agents of the above,
PROMISE TO PRESENT TO THE BEARER
one rock 'n roll revival meeting at gates 1, 3, 6, 7, 8 and 9 at varsity stadium on saturday, september 13th, 1969, between the hours of 1:00 p.m. and midnight

per: J. L. Brower
per:

Six Dollars Advance 00227

ALICE COOPER *I didn't bring the chicken. I'm picturing this guy in the audience thinking, 'I've got my keys, my wallet, my tickets and my chicken and I'm ready to see Alice.' I'm from Detroit, I've never been on a farm. In my mind, a chicken has feathers and it has wings, so it should fly. It's a bird! So I picked up the chicken and flung it into the audience. Turns out that chickens don't so much fly as plummet. The audience tore it to pieces and threw it back on stage. There was blood everywhere. Next day in the papers: 'Alice Cooper kills chicken on stage.' The audience was the culprit in killing the chicken.*

Frank Zappa called me up and said, 'Did you kill a chicken last night?' I said, 'No,' and he said, 'Well, don't tell anybody because they love it!'

ROBBY The Doors never did anything that terrible, but everywhere we went that year we were the band the cops had their eyes on.

Jim backstage at the Toronto Rock and Roll Revival, Varsity Stadium, Toronto, ON, 13 September 1969
Opposite: John, circa 1970

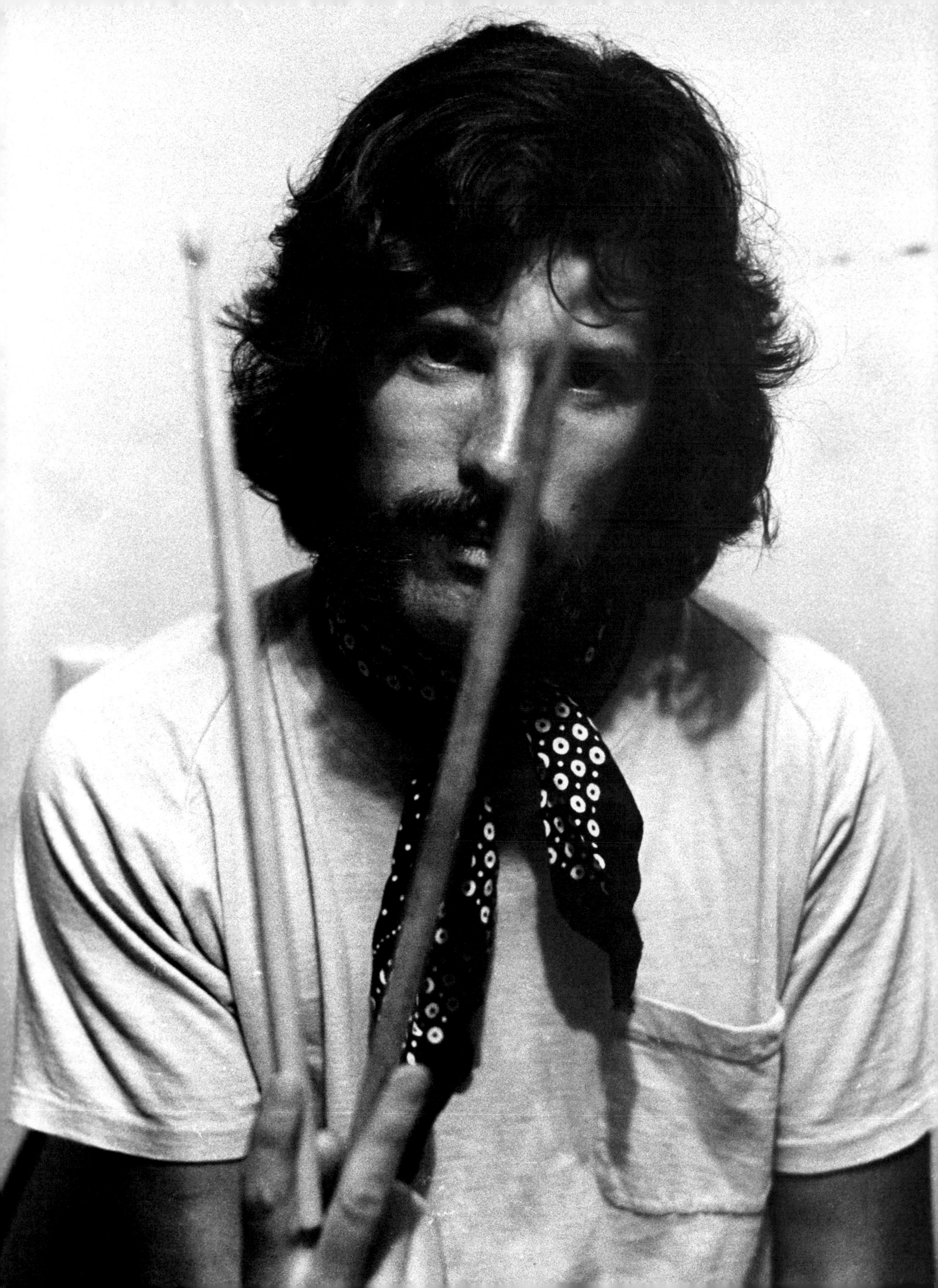

ROBBY Towards the end of the year, while awaiting trial for the Miami incident, Jim and his friend Tom Baker caused another incident, this time on a flight from LA to Phoenix. They were on their way to see The Rolling Stones play, but they got drunk on the plane and harassed the cabin crew. Jim and Tom were taken into custody when they landed. There was bail and fines and Max Fink had to go to Phoenix and deal with all of it. The trial and legal mess would play out over the following seven months, running parallel to the trial and legal mess following Miami.

RAY Between Miami and Phoenix, Jim was facing a maximum of over 13 years in prison. Three and a half in Raiford Penitentiary in the 'County of the Dead', and ten in a federal hoosegow because 'interference with a flight crew' was an offence under a new skyjacking law. He would probably get off but it weighed on Jim's psyche. His soul was heavy.

JOHN The whole country was polarised, like today. It was for the war or against the war. Getting Jim would put a dent in the movement and that's what was going on.

This trial is really a trial.
It's an education in human nature
Funky old human nature.
Your basic human being.

Death-night in Jamaica
Shakespeare was some help
in the dark hours.

Frisbee by the pool
Games (rediscovery of)

Cross-examination style

a drunken goof

ROBBY It was a year and a half of motions and filings and adjournments and everything else before we actually ended up in a courtroom. In September 1970, Ray, John and I flew to Miami to testify. Max Fink was handling Jim's defence. He didn't tell us to prep much in terms of what to say. All we had to do was tell the truth: that nothing happened. Most of the questions were answerable with a simple yes or no. The only real highlight was when the prosecution were trying to suggest that Jim had simulated oral copulation on me and Jim was explaining that he only kneeled down to admire my guitar playing.

JIM We never knew from one day to the next when the court would be in session and it would change every day. I really needed the weekends to rest up; it was really an ordeal.

RAY The State of Florida vs. James Douglas Morrison. 150 photos were offered in evidence but there was not a single photo of Jim's schlong. There were photos of Jim with a skull-and-crossbones hat, Jim with a lamb, Jim kneeling in front of Robby, Jim leading a snake line in the audience, the stage collapsing, all of it. But not a single photo of Jim's member. And yet they were convinced he did it.

JIM I felt like a spectator. I wouldn't have wanted to defend myself, it's not as easy as it looks. I didn't have to testify but we decided it might be a good thing for the jury to see what I was like. So I testified for a couple of days. I don't think it meant anything one way or the other. I saw half of it but I couldn't sit through all of it, not that I don't appreciate satire.

JIM I MIGHT EVEN BUY A SUIT TO MAKE A GOOD IMPRESSION ON THE JUDGE AND JURY. A CONSERVATIVE DARK BLUE SUIT.

Top left: Jim, accompanied by his attorney Max Fink, arriving at the Los Angeles Federal Building to appear before the US Commissioner for proceedings to extradite him to Florida, 14 April 1969
Top right: Jim's notes on the Miami trial. Jim's several notebooks written over the course of the trial include journalistic observations, general notes, as well as entries written during his time spent away from the trial
Opposite: Jim being interviewed, 1969

ELEKTRA SOUND STUDIOS

962 La Cienega Blvd, LA

Above: Ray at Elektra Sound Studios, Los Angeles, CA, 1969
Opposite: Backstage at the Auditorium Theatre, Chicago, IL, 14 June 1969
This page and opposite: Tapes from Morrison Hotel *recording and resmastering sessions*

JOHN After the first round of trials was over, we were back on Santa Monica Boulevard in our rehearsal room, where we wrote another album's worth of songs. I always got inspired when I thought of going into the studio and polishing new songs into gems. I didn't hear any hits, but it was another group of tightly arranged numbers with Ray's dependable trademark sound and Robby's risky guitar flights into failure and magic. The rehearsals weren't totally free of tension, though.

RAY The forced layoff caused by Miami resulted in a burst of creativity for Jim and Robby. We were loaded with hot new songs. The rehearsals were very productive. We were having fun again. Jimbo was nowhere to be seen. Jim was relaxed and as happy as a man facing possibly 13 years in the slammer could be. He simply put it out of his mind, as we all did – we never spoke of it. Instead, he threw himself into creativity. And the songs were hot!

JIM Besides the live album, my favourite album is *Morrison Hotel*, in the respect that we didn't use any other musicians, except for the bass player.

BRUCE BOTNICK *The first song out of the box was destined to become the all-time American bar band song, 'Roadhouse Blues'. It took two days to realise Paul Rothchild's vision of recorded perfection. Through this, Jim was mostly out of it and going into blues-singer mode, repeating the line 'Ladies and gentlemen, money beats soul every time,' and then Robby kicked it off. On the first day Ray was on a Wurlitzer electric piano. On the second he moved to a tack piano, which happens to be the very same piano that Brian Wilson used on 'Good Vibrations'.*

RAY It was all good stuff. And all to be played within our basic Doors format. No horns, no strings, just pure Doors. Pure rock and blues and jazz and soul and love. We were going to lay it down, hard and fat. John Sebastian sat in on harp on 'Roadhouse Blues', as did Lonnie Mack on bass. Ray Neapolitan played bass on all the other cuts.

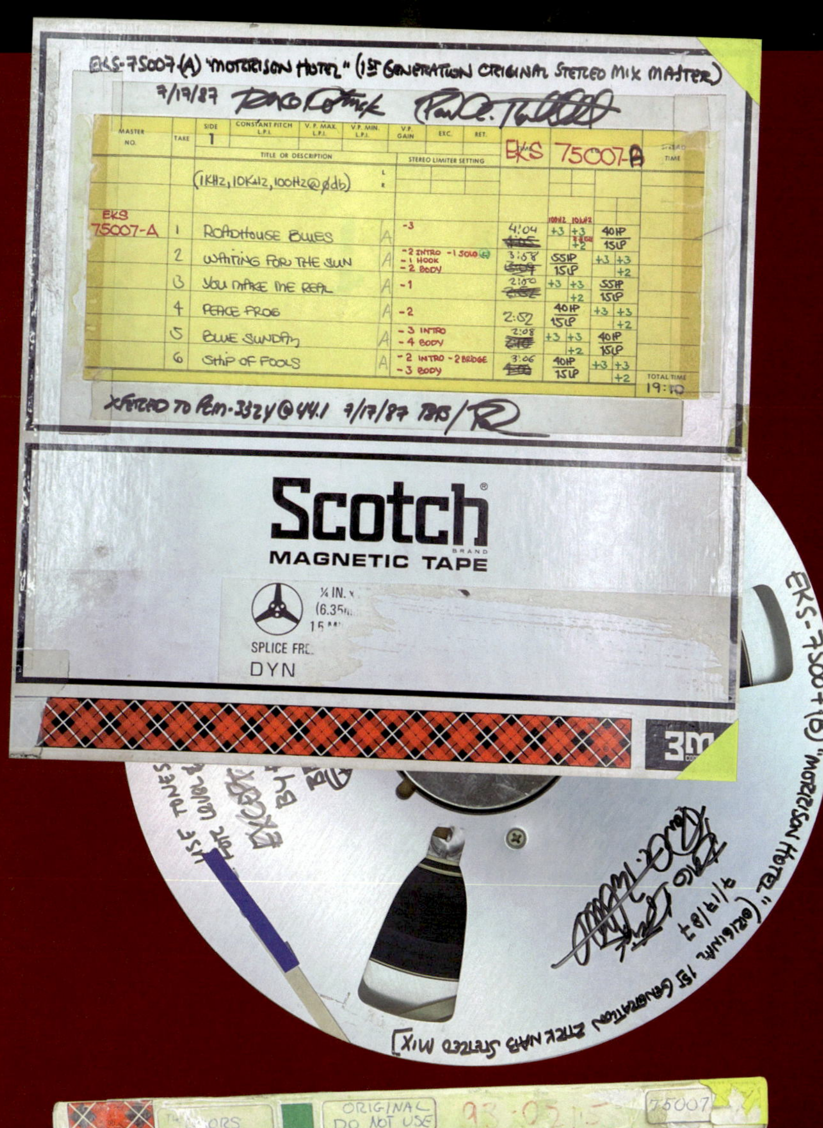

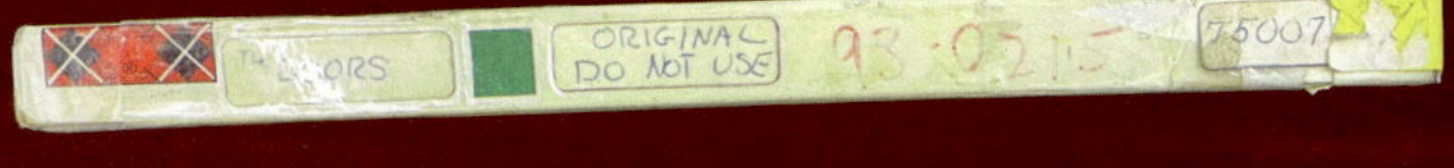

JIM Every time we make a choice for a single it usually turns out wrong and so what we're going to do for *Morrison Hotel* is put out the album and let the public decide which one they like the best and then we'll release that as a single. It seems like the most realistic way of doing it. I don't think we have the key to the pulse of the nation because we make more mistakes than doing things right.

ROBBY I had some ideas for the music for 'Peace Frog' but I didn't have any words so I took it to Jim but he couldn't figure out any words for it. So we looked through his poetry books and we found a poem called 'Abortion Stories' and it had some interesting stuff in it. We recorded some stuff in the studio first and then Jim went away to work on the poetry.

JOHN 'Peace Frog' was frustrating. Robby had this great rhythm guitar lick, but Jim wasn't coming up with anything lyrically to complement it. One day, when he was around the corner at the Palms Bar with Frank and Babe, we went ahead and recorded an instrumental based on Robby's lick. The track smoked! Jim finally came in to do some vocals and Rothchild asked him to bring his poetry notebooks the next day.

Not having enough material to fill out the album, like in the old days, we took a listen to 'Indian Summer', the first song we ever recorded. It had been kept in the can because of a couple of bad notes from Robby and Jim, but among the *Morrison Hotel* songs it felt like a breath of fresh air. Raga tuning with California lyrics.

ROBBY I wrote the music for 'Indian Summer' during our Whisky residency, inspired by my Indian music class at UCLA.

JOHN Mr Rothchild was the fifth Door behind some of the most beloved releases by the band, from *The Doors* to *Morrison Hotel*. Rothchild was right about getting a grittier sound than *Soft Parade* – a blues-based record. I thought 12 to 15 takes was still too many, though. It was better than *The Soft Parade*'s absurd 30 and above.

BRUCE BOTNICK *Paul Rothchild felt after* The Soft Parade *that he had to save the band. He got into the idea of perfection rather than performance. You can really hear that on* Morrison Hotel.

RAY It was a great album to record. The sessions were super. Many friends and guests dropped in for moral and vibrational support. Babe Hill, Frank Lisciandro and Paul Ferrara all came by. Pure fun.

JOHN 'The Spy' was fun for me because I got the chance to show off my jazz brush technique. We tried to create a mood for the song to complement Jim's words. Putting heavy echo on Jim's vocals enhanced his lyrics.

There's blood in the streets
& it's up to my ankles
Blood in the streets
& it's up to my knee
Blood in the streets
of the town of Chicago
Blood on the rise
& its following me –
Blood in the streets
runs a river of sadness
Blood in the streets
& its up to my thigh
The river runs red
down the legs of the city
The women are crying
red rivers of weeping

Elektra Sound Studios, Los Angeles, CA, 1969

ROBBY In this photo you can see Jim at my house up in Benedict Canyon, where we wrote a couple of songs including 'Hyacinth House'. The song makes a reference to some hyacinth flowers right outside the window.

JIM IT WAS A CREATIVE SUMMER FOR ME.

MASTERS — NOV 17, 1969

SPY IN THE HOUSE OF LOVE — 4:15
2. LAND HO 4:06
PEACE FROG — 2:52 > 5:02
BLUE SUNDAY — 2:10
YOU MAKE ME REAL — 2:52
6. QUEEN OF THE HIGHWAY 2:49
ROAD HOUSE BLUES #2 — 4:05
~~8. ROAD HOUSE BLUES #1 4:05~~
8. WAITING FOR THE SUN 4:00

821
502
1323
2 52
16:15

Jim at Robby's Benedict Canyon house, CA
Opposite, top: Morrison Hotel *cover shoot, Los Angeles, CA, 17 December 1969*
Opposite, bottom: Tape boxes from the Morrison Hotel *sessions*

MORRISON HOTEL

PASSENGER LOADING ONLY

ROOMS
FROM $2.50 UP

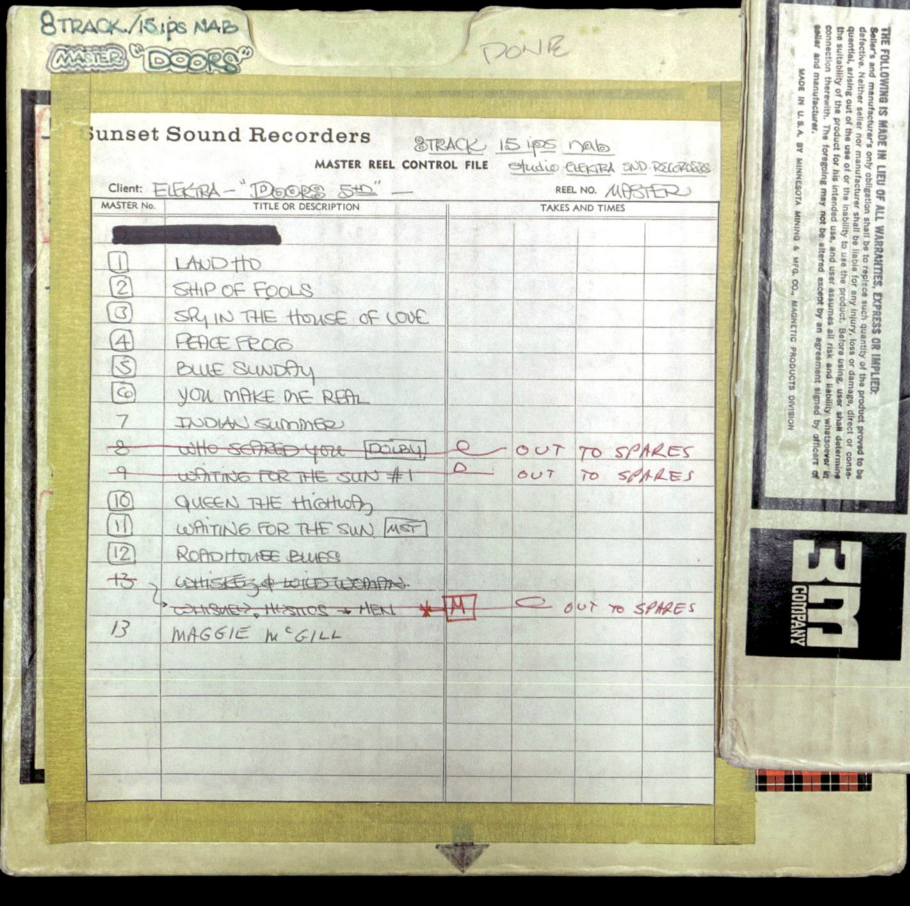

8 TRACK/15 ips NAB
MASTER "DOORS"
DONE

Sunset Sound Recorders
MASTER REEL CONTROL FILE
8 TRACK 15 ips nab
Studio ELEKTRA SND RECORDERS
Client: ELEKTRA – "DOORS 5th" —
REEL NO. MASTER

MASTER No.	TITLE OR DESCRIPTION	TAKES AND TIMES
1	LAND HO	
2	SHIP OF FOOLS	
3	SPY IN THE HOUSE OF LOVE	
4	PEACE FROG	
5	BLUE SUNDAY	
6	YOU MAKE ME REAL	
7	INDIAN SUMMER	
~~8~~	~~WHO SCARED YOU~~ DOLBY	OUT TO SPARES
~~9~~	~~WAITING FOR THE SUN #1~~	OUT TO SPARES
10	QUEEN THE HIGHWAY	
11	WAITING FOR THE SUN MST	
12	ROADHOUSE BLUES	
~~13~~	~~WHISKEY & WILD WOMEN~~	
	~~WHISKEY, MYSTICS & MEN~~ M	OUT TO SPARES
13	MAGGIE M^cGILL	

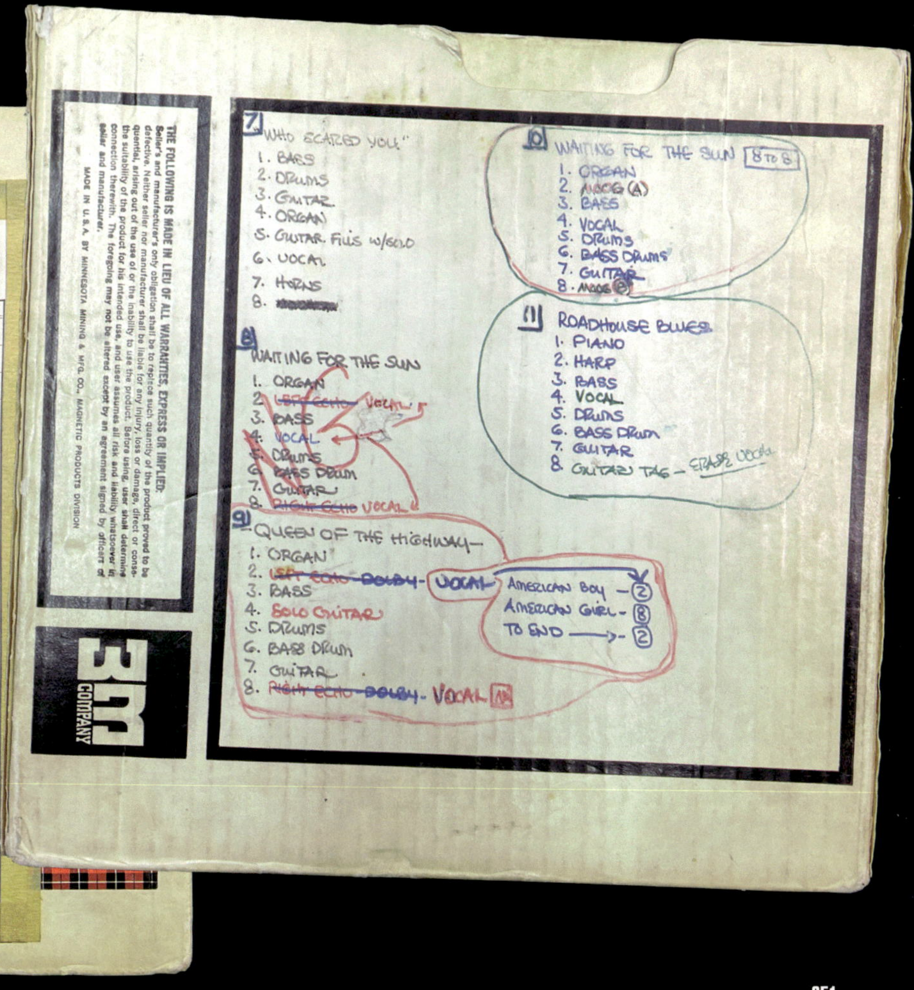

THE FOLLOWING IS MADE IN LIEU OF ALL WARRANTIES, EXPRESS OR IMPLIED: Seller's and manufacturer's only obligation shall be to replace such quantity of the product proved to be defective. Neither seller nor manufacturer shall be liable for any injury, loss or damage, direct or consequential, arising out of the use of or the inability to use the product. Before using, user shall determine the suitability of the product for his intended use, and user assumes all risk and liability whatsoever in connection therewith. The foregoing may not be altered, except by an agreement signed by officers of seller and manufacturer.

MADE IN U.S.A. BY MINNESOTA MINING & MFG. CO. MAGNETIC PRODUCTS DIVISION

3M COMPANY

7 "WHO SCARED YOU"
1. BASS
2. DRUMS
3. GUITAR
4. ORGAN
5. GUITAR FILLS w/ECHO
6. VOCAL
7. HORNS
8. ~~[crossed out]~~

8 WAITING FOR THE SUN
1. ORGAN
2. ~~LEFT ECHO~~ VOCAL
3. BASS
4. ~~VOCAL~~
5. DRUMS
6. BASS DRUM
7. GUITAR
8. ~~RIGHT ECHO~~ VOCAL

9 QUEEN OF THE HIGHWAY
1. ORGAN
2. ~~LEFT ECHO DOLBY~~ - VOCAL
3. BASS
4. SOLO GUITAR
5. DRUMS
6. BASS DRUM
7. GUITAR
8. ~~RIGHT ECHO DOLBY~~ - VOCAL M

AMERICAN BOY – 2
AMERICAN GIRL – 8
TO END → 2

10 WAITING FOR THE SUN 8 TO 8
1. ORGAN
2. MOOG (A)
3. BASS
4. VOCAL
5. DRUMS
6. BASS DRUMS
7. GUITAR
8. MOOG (B)

11 ROADHOUSE BLUES
1. PIANO
2. HARP
3. BASS
4. VOCAL
5. DRUMS
6. BASS DRUM
7. GUITAR
8. GUITAR TAG – ERASE VOCAL

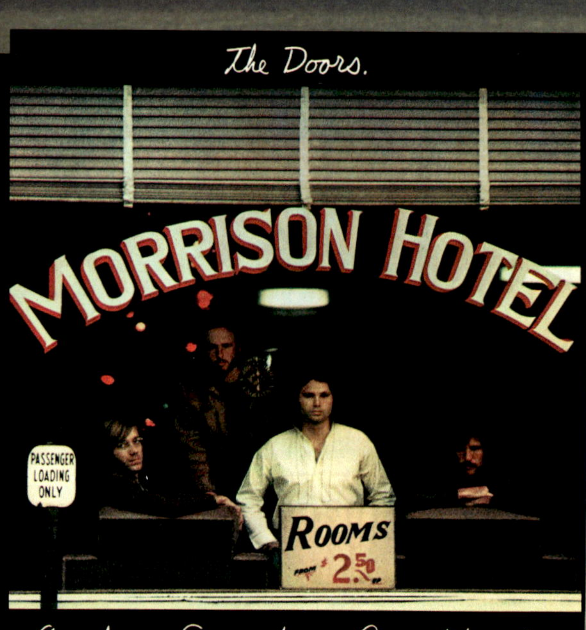

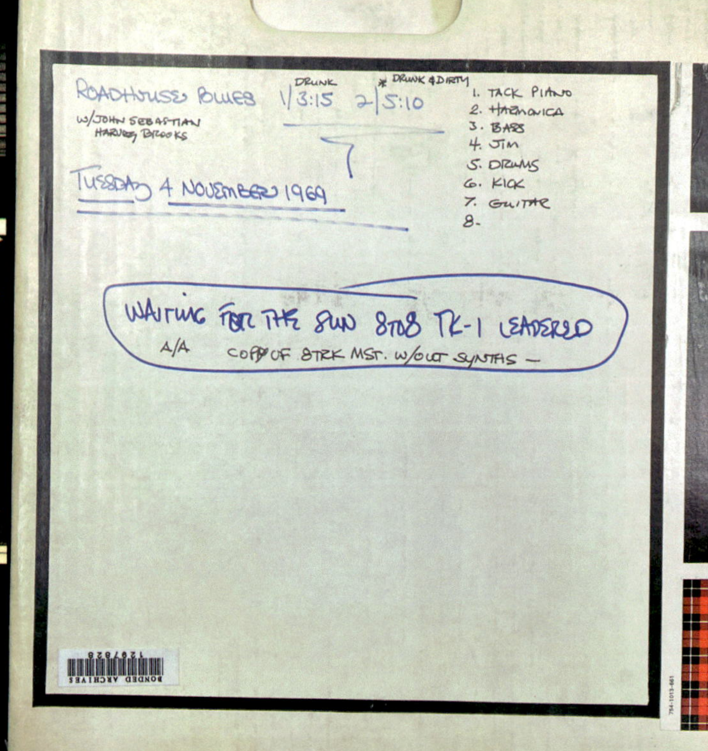

This page and opposite, top: Morrison Hotel *cover shoot, Los Angeles, CA, 17 December 1969*
Bottom right: Tape box for the Morrison Hotel *session outtakes, 4 November 1969*

1. TACK PIANO
2. HARMONICA
3. BASS
4. JIM
5. DRUMS
5. DRUMS
6. KICK
7. GUITAR
8.

* DRUNK & DIRTY

JOHN On one of Ray's drives around obscure parts of LA, he found a dingy hotel downtown called Morrison Hotel. Henry Diltz, our new photographer, said there was another great location near the hotel, a funky bar called the Hard Rock Cafe. We went down to these two locations to do a photo session for the cover of our fifth album. Unfortunately, the manager of the hotel wouldn't give us permission to shoot in the lobby. We went across the street and Henry suggested we quickly run into the lobby, look out the window, and he would shoot us from across the street with his telephoto lens. We did just that, and before the manager caught on and started walking over to throw us out, we had our shot.

ROBBY I don't know if we were thinking of it as an album cover. I tried not to talk to the guys in there. They were pretty hardcore bums and it was very much their place. I didn't want to disrupt the flow at that point. Nobody was belligerent or anything like that. It was kind of fun. What I remember most about that situation was the guy out on the street with the whistle. As we were getting out of the car, this guy said, 'Can I have a dollar? If you give me some money, I'll whistle for ya, 'cause the Lord has made me the loudest whistler in the world.' So we were like 'Yeah. Go for it, man.'

ROBBY **IT'S THE ANTITHESIS OF MOST ROCK COVERS.**

JOHN The reviews of *Morrison Hotel* were very good. Bruce Harris of *Jazz & Pop* wrote, 'A return to the tight fury of early Doors music, abounding with funk and guts and earth-energy. *Morrison Hotel* is one of the major musical events of Rock '70.' I felt that there were a couple of mediocre cuts on the record, though. 'Queen of the Highway' had some nice autobiographical lyrics from Jim, but the track never settled into a good groove. It was the first time I ever thought we let Jim down in supporting his words.

She was a Princess
Queen of the Highway
Sign on the road said
Take us to Madre

MORRISON HOTEL
PASSENGER LOADING ONLY
ROOMS
2.50

MORRISON HOTEL
PASSENGER LOADING ONLY
ROOMS
2.50

MORRISON HOTEL
ROOMS
ROOMS

MORRISON HOTEL
ROOMS
2.50

MORRISON HOTEL

MORRISON HOTEL
ROOMS
1246

MORRISON HOTEL
ROOMS

MORRISON HOTEL
ROOMS

WED 12/19

(P) Doors on Skid Row

Hard Rock Cafe & Morrison Hotel.

PHOTOGRAPHER'S PASS

THE DOOR'S

DATE: 5-1-70 №: 0427

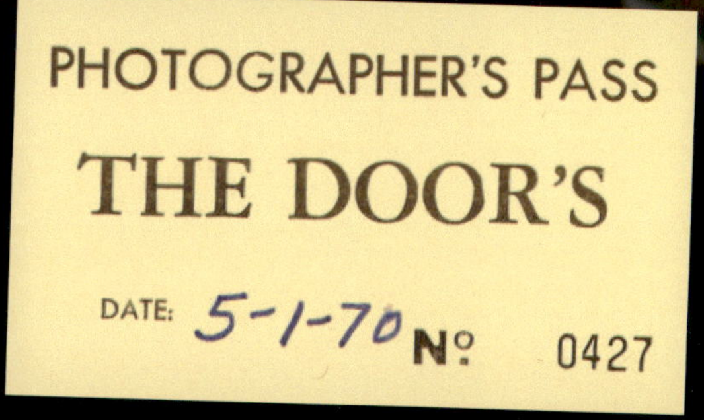

HENRY DILTZ *The winos thought of Jim as their new friend – they all thought he was a great guy because he really was interested in them. Jim loved to hear people talk about life. People ask me what Jim Morrison was really like and although there are a lot of stories about him getting drunk and behaving antagonistically, whenever I was with him taking photos he was very well-behaved. The word I usually use to describe him is bemused; he was not a guy who would hold forth on anything. He was more of a listener. He had a way of nodding his head with a little smile on his face, encouraging you to keep talking. And that's what he did with these winos in there. In fact, he and I walked down the street to another bar after the Hard Rock Cafe and he bought beers for a couple of guys so that he could sit at a booth and just get them to talk about their lives.*

JOHN We ordered beers, and the bartender said it was OK to shoot all the pictures we wanted as long as we kept ordering drinks.

ROBBY I don't know why the *Morrison Hotel* album cover became so iconic. I think it's because it's so funky looking – it's a crummy hotel, it's so real. There are no props and nothing's staged. At that point in our career we were trying to get real. We had just done *The Soft Parade*, which had a lot of add-ons – horns and strings and all kinds of fancy production stuff. There wasn't a band – that album was more like Jim Morrison and an orchestra. I think the *Morrison Hotel* album cover reflects our return to simplicity.

HENRY DILTZ *Shortly after the* Morrison Hotel *shoot, when the album was about to come out, they needed publicity pictures and so we spent a really great day at Venice Beach shooting pictures. I always carried* Time *magazine with me because if there was ever an idle moment when I had to wait around I would have something to keep me entertained. What often happened is that there would be an opportunity to read it and just before I picked it up someone else would pinch it and be reading it for 20 minutes! Well, the exact thing happened with Jim. We were in the van and I was about to read it and he said, 'Let me see that* Time *magazine.'*

In this one shot where he's reading it, he's looking up at me as if to say, 'What the heck are you doing?' He's not really angry but he is giving me a kind of a look that says, 'Hey! I'm busy reading' – and he's reading my magazine! So I felt justified in taking this picture. God darn it!

JIM I always liked all the things I read. Of course, it was [often] all about me and so usually you're most interested in yourself and people you know. They were concentrating on my progenitive organ too much though.

Your ticket
to
THE DOORS ABSOLUTELY LIVE
at
the Felt Forum in New York City
the Aquarius Theater in Los Angeles
the Cobo Arena in Detroit
the Arena in Boston
the Spectrum in Philadelphia
the Civic Center in Pittsburgh

Released on 20 July 1970, Absolutely Live *was The Doors' first live album. Among several other previously unreleased tracks on the record, there was a performance of* The Celebration of the Lizard, *recorded in full at the Aquarius Theatre in Los Angeles in July 1969, incorporating some additional lines from Jim. The band would go on to release three further live albums with Elektra:* Alive, She Cried, Live at the Hollywood Bowl *and* In Concert, *as well as numerous live albums on their own Bright Midnight label. The Bright Midnight releases include* Live at the Aquarius Theatre, Live at the Matrix *1967 and* The Lost Interview Tapes. *(A full discography can be found on pages 327–332.)*

Audience Hears a New Jim Morrison

VINCE TREANOR *The Doors, Paul Rothchild and Elektra all agreed that an album of live performance would be appropriate. Certainly recording live performances would capture the raw sounds of the hall, the audience reaction to each song and Jim's introduction or commentary during the progress of the song. It would be a real taste of what The Doors sounded like on stage.*

JIM The live album was condensed from about 24 hours of taped concerts that we did over approximately a year, starting with the Aquarius Theatre in July 1969. We thought we might have one that night. We did two sets but when we listened to it in the studio it didn't really add up to a very good album. It was a good evening but on tape it didn't sound that good. So we recorded seven or eight other concerts, and listened to all of it and cut it down. I think that it is a fairly true document of what the band sounds like on a fairly good night. It's not the best that we can do, and it's certainly not the worst. I think it's a true document of an above average evening.

JOHN I like *Absolutely Live* very much. There's a few things in there that we couldn't do in the studio. I thought it was a real good document of our live show.

JIM I think most of it is pretty professional. There are a few cuts that were done for the first time on stage that we hadn't really worked with that much that had flaws in, but I don't think they're that significant.

ROBBY One thing that I could say is that Morrison was one of the few performers that really believed what he was saying. He lived that life. He wasn't just up there doing his trip and then going home to watch TV with a beer and laughing all the way to the bank. He lived that life that he lived on stage. When he went home it was to some cheap motel and he just hung out until the next show.

JIM I like *Celebration of the Lizard*. It's not a great version of that piece but I went ahead and put it out because I doubted if we would have put it out otherwise. We did it at the time of *Waiting for the Sun* and it just didn't seem to make it in the studio, so we used one piece out of it, 'Not to Touch the Earth'. I think if we didn't put it on the live album we would have shelved it forever, so I'm glad we did it even in the imperfect form that it exists.

PAUL ROTHCHILD *I made that album at one of the hottest points in their career. You wouldn't believe what we had to do to make it, how many centuries of tape we had to glean to make that fairly skinny double record set. I couldn't get complete takes of a lot of songs so I'd find myself suddenly cutting from Detroit to Philadelphia in mid-song. There must be 2,000 edits on that album.*

ROBBY It was amazing how in tune Jim always was. He never hit a wrong note.

For me, *Live at the Matrix* is a better representation of a Doors live show than *Absolutely Live.* The Matrix was a small club, with probably only around 20 people there, and the album is just one show all the way through.

JIM I believe [albums have] replaced books and movies. They're better than movies, because a movie you see once or twice, then later on television maybe. But an album, man, it's more influential than any art form going. Everybody digs them. They've got about 40 of them in their houses and some of them you listen to 50 times, like the Stones' albums or Dylan's.

***Opposite:** Felt Forum, New York, NY, January 1970. The four shows that the band played at the Felt Forum on 17 and 18 January 1970 were recorded and used for the* Absolutely Live *album. In 2009, these recordings were released in full as the six-CD box set* Live in New York

The Doors Stumble Through a Concert

A small audience at the Coliseum last night slammed the door on what was once the nation's most popular rock group.

Despite a dynamic buildup by Albert King, impressive blues singer who has been touring with The Doors on this concert swing, when Jim Morrison, lead singer, sauntered on stage he got the coldest reception this town has ever accorded a superstar.

Audience unrest flared as Morrison, in simple blue tee shirt and black pants, dwadled inexcusably between selections. There were periods of no music, no talk, no action for up to 9 minutes each.

The young crowd took over.

First the shouts were for Doors favorites, like "Light My Fire," which brought the California group to the music scene in 1967. As Morrison refused to respond, a cat-call suggested "Sugar, Sugar' . . . anything!"

"Remember Miami!" a bitter member of the audience shouted. Obscene explitives bounced from many parts of the stadium. A concert in Miami brought a sudden dip in the group's popularity when Morrison was accused of an obscene performance on stage.

As cat-calls increased, Morrison grew more remote. Ray Manzarek, organist, Robbie Kreiger, guitar, and John Densmore, drums, competant musicians, were left leaderless.

West Coast Promotions, a Los Angeles firm which arranged this concert, one and one which follows in Vancouver, B. C., were hoping for a revival of interest in The Doors.

This is a new wholesome show, one of the promoters explained, before the concert.

"Give the singer a chance," Morrison mumbled. "I haven't been to Seattle in two years."

The audience rebutted: "You were here tast summer!"

Morrison made a tasteless pun on the Latin phrase. Tempus Fuget, and described Seattle as a 1930 version of 20 years in the future. Most understood the first joke, only half understood the second.

Morrison was piqued enough at one point to simulate an act, which back in the 1950's even a Seattle audience would have called self abuse.

Equipment failures complicated matters. During one selection Manzarek's electric organ was dismantled and replaced.

The morose finale, "The End," was stopped three minutes from its climax. Houselights were turned on. The sound was cut. A dazzled Morrison was led off the stage by one of his staff members. It was 12:05 a. m., time for the Coliseum to close.

The Doors had begun at 10:20; in the 1¾ hours Morrison had managed to mangle only nine selections—all old hits—only one of which managed to set off sparks.

The disappointed promoters said afterward it was not a typical concert. In the 14,000 seat Coliseum, they drew what was estimated as just over 4,000.

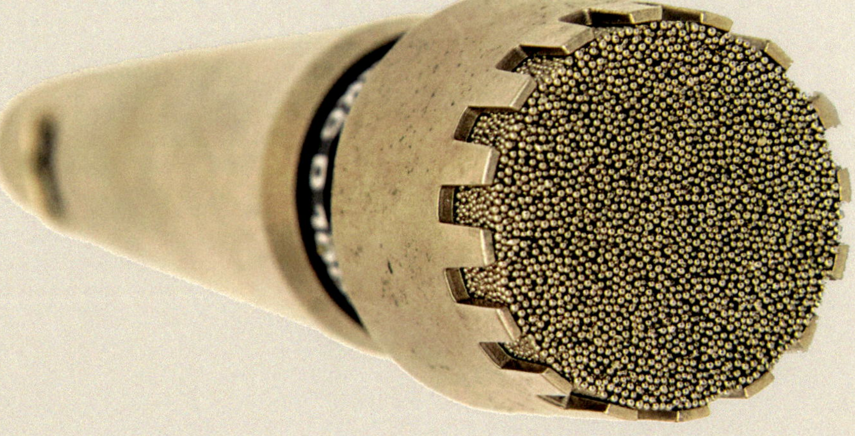

Above: A bad review from The Doors' show at the Seattle Center Coliseum, Seattle, WA, 5 June 1970
Opposite, bottom: Jim at the Seattle Space Needle, Seattle, WA, June 1970

VINCE TREANOR *[In Seattle,] wondering if I could successfully record without all the equipment, baffles and splitters that often ruined the sound, I set up my Sony recorder for the show. I recorded using two AKG-D1000 microphones placed beside – but not in front of – the two columns of the four vocal amplifiers at the corners of the stage. Of course, the tape ran out towards the end of the performance, which ran from about 10.30 p.m. until midnight when the power was cut off. This was the second location where this was done. Unfortunately, the reviews were scathing.*

JIM **I WAS A FAIRLY HEALTHY, YOUNG, MALE SPECIMEN WHO ALSO HAD, OTHER THAN YOUR USUAL ARMS AND LEGS, AND RIBS AND THORAX, EYES AND NOSE, A CEREBELLUM.**

Monday, August 24, 1970

Swingin' Doors Really Open Up During Concert

By LEE GRANT

Right there in front of the stage she was, this girl in skin-tight pants and striped T-shirt, no more than 16.

The next instant she was on stage, hugging and kissing the thin, long-haired, full-bearded singer.

Jim Morrison stood there as the girl hugged and hung on. He kept singing, "Break on through to the other side, yeah, break on through to the other side."

From the wings, a burly bodyguard sped onstage and tore the girl off Morrison. The girl cried.

She was the first of a half-dozen who jumped up to kiss this dynamic lead singer of The Doors.

It was Saturday night at the International Sports Arena, and it was a typical rock concert Saturday night.

The band on vacation, Kona Village, Hawaii, April 1970
Opposite, bottom right: Elektra Records end-of-year 'Thank You' ad featured in Cash Box magazine

the doors
Another great year gone—
And a better year on the way
Thanks
Available through Bill Siddons 8512 Santa Monica Blvd. Los Angeles 90069 (213) 659-1667
elektra

ROBBY When *Feast of Friends* wrapped, Jim and his crew wanted to make a feature film called *HWY*. Jim put up the money himself but as a loan from the band against future royalties. He rented a separate production space near the band's office and went to work with Frank, Paul and Babe.

JIM I completed a short feature movie called *HWY* with a few friends. I think it's quite good. Essentially there's no plot or story in the traditional sense. A person, played by me, comes down out of the mountains and hitchhikes his way to a modern city, which happened to be LA and that's where it ends. It's a very beautiful film. I had an idea about a hitchhiker that becomes a mass murderer, the kind of thing that happens every year or so, like the Zodiac character. So we went out into the desert to start shooting it and while we were out there the film took over and went in its own direction and became something a little different. The only thing that was left from the original idea was the hitchhiker. The only reason I did it was because I couldn't think of anyone else to do it and it was just as easy for me to do it. I'm not that crazy about being an actor, I'd rather be a director or a writer. But if I had the chance I'd probably do a few films, why not? Shakespeare was an actor when he first came to London.

PAUL FERRARA *It was clear it wasn't going to be your normal Hollywood film. It had art house written all over it.*

FRANK LISCIANDRO *We were raised on the sacred text of* On the Road. *That book inspired Jim and me to be on the road. It sent him hitchhiking around the country and his poetry was filled with ideas about the hitchhiker.*

JIM It's a lyrical piece that lasts half an hour. There's no plot. It's essentially a silent movie. It has a non-rock music track. A friend of mine, a classical composer named Fred Myrow, plays keyboard on the track and then we mixed in tapes, records and stuff from the radio to give a kind of portrait of Los Angeles.

PAUL FERRARA *Jim wrote about the film, thought about the film, talked about the film. He had been a film student and we had come up with something unique. There was no pigeonhole it fit in. We took the print of* HWY *to every festival that would have him. He was proud of the film. [Today] it still struggles to be seen. It has become a huge bootleg favourite, mostly in Europe. Every Doors fan has seen it. There is a constant dialogue as to its meaning and people have focused on its every detail.*

JIM The trial went on for two months. During that time the only thing I did was fly to the Isle of Wight and come back. I flew over there from Miami, arrived in London and then drove to a little airport where we got a small plane to the Isle of Wight where we drove to the concert. By the time we went on I don't think I'd slept in about 36 hours so I wasn't at my best. I wasn't at my peak of physical perfection. Put it this way: we were not the highlight of the festivities but we weren't shitty by any means.

ROBBY We had been playing 'Crossroads' a bit just for fun but Jim took us by surprise when he started doing it at the festival. It kind of threw me for a loop because we started playing 'The End', which is in a total different tuning. When he went into 'Crossroads' it took me five minutes to get it right but that's what it was like playing with The Doors.

JIM It seemed pretty well organised for such a huge event. I can see why people like it. People that say these huge festivals are over or dead are wrong. I think they're going to become increasingly significant in the next three, four or five years.

RAY I remember the Isle of Wight Festival vividly and with great fondness. Three quarters of a million hippies! My God, what a sight. Cool and fine vibrations, peace and love.

DOORS OPEN ISLE OF WIGHT

THE Doors, America's most controversial progressive rock group, have definitely been signed for this year's Isle of Wight Festival!

The Doors booking has been clinched by promoters Ron and Ray Foulk after negotiations spread over the last six months.

This page and overleaf: Isle of Wight Festival, UK, 30 August 1970

JIM I didn't let myself think about what the outcome would be. One thing that came out of it was that I had a chance to get out of LA for an extended period for the first time in five years. Florida is a beautiful place, unpolluted more or less. I even got a chance to go down to Nassau for a while and learn how to scuba dive. The Caribbean is one of the most beautiful places I've ever visited. The water is perfectly clear and the sand is pure white. The sand in LA is a kind of brownish hue. Out there it looks like white seashells that were ground really finely.

JOHN Things happen in waves. We had the darkness that was Miami but then there was Woodstock. If we didn't have eight years of George Bush we wouldn't have had the courage to elect Obama. So life goes on. It's not the Apocalypse.

JAC HOLZMAN *While Jim was going through his ordeal by trial, Jimi Hendrix overdosed in London, aged 27. In October, Janis Joplin overdosed in the Landmark Hotel in Los Angeles, also 27. Jim was approaching his 27th birthday. He began to refer to himself as 'number three'.*

JIM I guess that great creative burst of energy that happened was hard to sustain. For sensitive people they might be dissatisfied with anything except the heights and when reality stops fulfilling their inner vision I guess they get depressed. But that's not my theory on why people die. Sometimes it could be an accident, sometimes it could be suicide, sometimes it could be murder.

RAY We weren't able to change the obscenity laws of America as we had set out to do. We had seen it as a grand noble cause for artistic freedom, for the rights of free speech; another battle against the encrusted, entrenched establishment. But it wasn't enough; we lost.

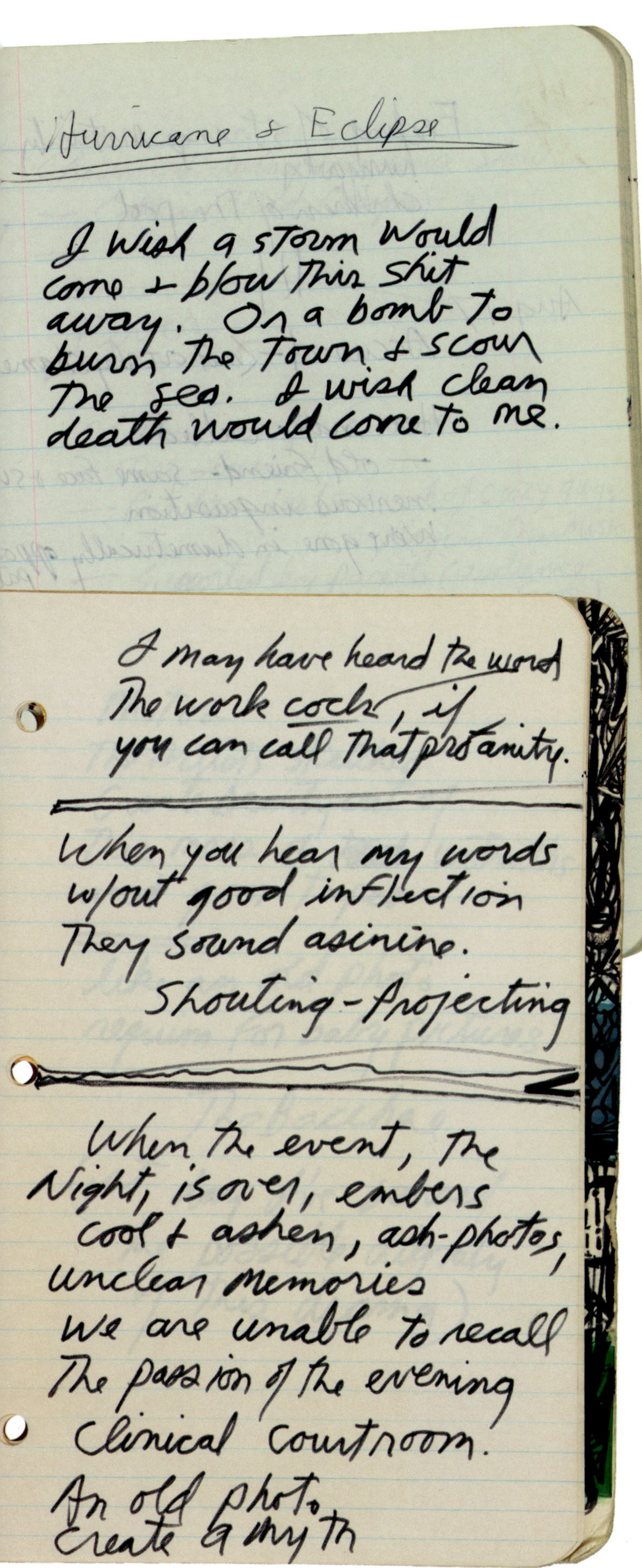

Jim's notes on the Miami trial

Police
State vs. James Morrison
Depositions

JIM I was hoping – or I thought – there might be a possibility of it becoming a major, ground-breaking kind of case, but it didn't turn out that way.

I thought it might become just a basic American issue involving freedom of speech and the right of anyone with a personal viewpoint to state their ideas in public and receive a hearing without legal pressure being put on them. In fact, my lawyer made a speech part way through the trial in which he traced the origin of freedom of speech, which goes side by side with the origin of drama, actually. The right of the dramatist or artist to state his views.

It was a brilliant summary of that historical process, but it didn't have any effect on the outcome at all. The First Amendment provides supposedly for the freedom of expression. There's a clause which states that any dramatic or public artistic performance comes under this amendment.

Basically, the prosecution refused to listen to any testimony which would come under that clause. They were prosecuting totally on a criminal case. My defence counsel was prepared to put the whole case on the fact that even if this alleged event did occur, it did not violate contemporary community standards ... but the judge anticipated that, and he threw out the proceedings. He refused to allow any testimony regarding community standards.

FRANK LISCIANDRO *Ultimately, Jim Morrison was charged with three misdemeanours, indecent exposure, public drunkenness and profanity, and a felony, lewd and lascivious behaviour, for his 1 March 1969 performance at Dinner Key Auditorium in Miami.*

A year and a half after the concert, in October 1970, Jim was acquitted of the felony charge and, incredibly, the public drunkenness charge – something that Jim actually admitted during the trial. He was found guilty of the indecent exposure and profanity charges and was given a sentence of six months in jail and a $500 fine. He was released on bail pending his appeal, which was still underway when Jim died in Paris on 3 July 1971.

On 9 December 2010 – one day after what would have been his 67th birthday – Jim Morrison was granted a posthumous pardon by Florida Governor, Charlie Crist, who expressed personal doubts that Morrison had exposed himself at the concert.

LIVE DOORS

As comment on the Doors as a musical group is often overshadowed by comment on Jim Morrison's public parts, I didn't know for sure what we were going to the concert to see. As it was, Morrison had a beard and a mustashe on his face, extra pounds on his body, and his sex trip (represented Friday night by a few "squeeze my lemon"--style phrases) was subordianted to the group's music.

Morrison has a vocal style similar to John Kay's. Subtly aggressive, insinuating, it drones on, weaving itself around the band's rock/blues progressions. They can be soft or hard; they can mold the texture of a song smooth as glass only to smash it with one tremendous downbeat--"We want the world and we want it...NOW!" Final chords crash upon the keyboard, across guitar strings, overstressing the instruments into electronic freakout. And it's satisfying, an outgrowth of what's gone before, rather than jarring, out of context.

Their performance was casual, informal. Morrison asked the audience what they wanted to hear and they told him. "Not all at once," and they took turns calling out numbers: "Land Ho!" "Turn Off the Light"...No "Light My Fire" and no encore was played, but the set was a satisfying one that rounded out their music, giving it an electronic blues dimension that doesn't come through as strongly on record.

Courtship opened with a stage show that had the appeal of a Saturday afternoon magic act between flicks at the local movie house. You went expecting to be taken outside yourself with delight, assaulted with admireable feats, that you knew were all tricks, really. Courtship's act is self-parody (qua Sha-Na-Na), but their rock and roll star posturing is subtle enough to make you wonder if maybe they're serious. Their music is fast, funky, exuberant, in a word, fun.

--Pat Pope

VINCE TREANOR *Based on Jim's solemn promise of good behaviour and a more or less 'traditional' performance, a couple of dates were arranged. Dallas would be the first and consist of two performances on the same night. An afternoon performance in New Orleans would be the next day. It would be in December to allow plenty of time for advertisements to let people know that The Doors was still a group to be reckoned with. This would also give them time to make serious progress on the last album for Elektra under their existing contract.*

JOHN I'd had high hopes that we still had a future playing live, despite the steady decline in our stage ability. In Texas we played 'Riders on the Storm' for the first time in public and it was received quite well. The song hadn't been released yet so it was a pure response. That night I thought our live performances could evolve into a subtler jazz format. Maybe we could recapture the magic in a different way, a more mature way. There are smaller peaks and valleys along the big career trajectory, and although we were on the down side, Dallas felt like a peak.

ROBBY It wasn't flashy or crazy or historic, but Jim sang well and we got to play some of the songs that would be on *L.A. Woman* publicly for the first time. In a way, it was nice to finally play some shows where the focus was on our music rather than our antics.

JOHN In Dallas we thought, wow, maybe we could be a jazz rock thing, maybe it's going to be different. But then the next night Jim was drunk, sat on the drum riser with his head down. Ray said he saw Jim's spirit leave his body at that gig.

Top: A review of The Doors' second to last show with Jim at State Fair Music Hall, Dallas, TX, 11 December 1970
Opposite: The Doors' last show with Jim Morrison, A Warehouse, New Orleans, LA, 12 December 1970

RAY He was standing stage centre, holding on to the microphone, but his energy, his psyche, had dissolved. It had gone. In one song he started smashing the microphone stand into this old, splintered, wooden stage. It was like his energy was making one last statement. Vince came out and put his arm around Jim's shoulder and led him off the stage. That was our last show. It was an experiment to see if Jim could still go out there and play and he just couldn't.

ROBBY Jim had no energy for our last show. It was over.

JOHN I lobbied with Ray and Robby to get off the road for a year just to back off. In the studio we had control – if Jim was too loaded, we'd go home. We were really good live and I hated seeing that eroded and it got eroded from Jim's substance abuse. It was sad.

RAY When we got back to Los Angeles, Robby, John and I had a short meeting and unanimously agreed to stop performing in public; Jim wasn't up to it anymore. It was too much of a strain on him. We couldn't risk his health, both physical and psychological.

JIM When you're creating well, when the music is going well, everyone is well. It's only when your creativity dies off a bit that everyone starts feeling the strain.

JOHN Jim was just trying to change. It was the thing that I hated about him but that I also loved about him. He gained a few pounds and grew a beard and in retrospect I can see he was just trying to grow.

JIM What's wrong with being fat? That's what I want to know. Why is it so onerous to be fat? I don't see anything wrong with fat. It's terrible to be thin and wispy because you could get knocked over by a strong wind. Fat is beautiful.

DOORS WORKSHOP

8512 Santa Monica Blvd, LA

JOHN We had done *The Soft Parade*, which was our attempt at a *Sgt. Pepper*, and then we did *Morrison Hotel* and finally *L.A. Woman* took us back to our roots. Back to the blues, back to the garage. And it was done quickly – we did it in a few weeks. We spoke about doing a couple of takes on each song and if there were mistakes it didn't matter. We were getting back to the essence of what we were about and no extra.

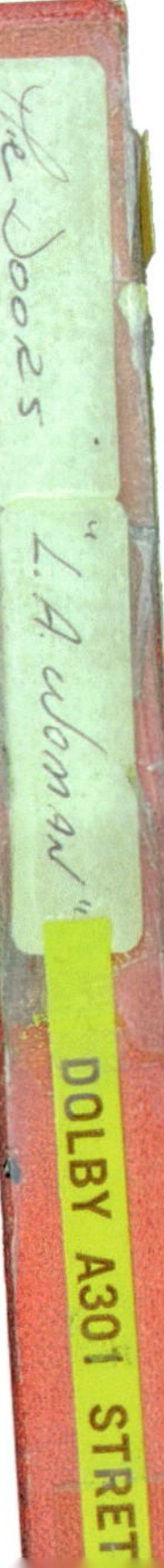

ROBBY We did *L.A. Woman* in our rehearsal studio. There were no time constraints and it really was a group effort, more so than any of the other albums before it.

BRUCE BOTNICK *I asked The Doors where they felt most comfortable and they said their rehearsal room. I thought, 'Great, I'll get some remote gear and we'll do it there.' About two weeks later we recorded the album and, like the first album, it took only five days to record.*

We brought in Jerry Scheff, Elvis Presley's bass player, and also a second guitarist, Marc Benno of The Asylum Choir, to allow Robby to play freely without having to worry about overdubbing.

RAY After we decided to record it in our own studio, Bruce Botnick told us that he could get the control room board from Sunset Sound, which we used when we made the first two Doors records. It was an old tube board and it had a great sound. It was antiquated but we recorded most of the album live. It was like being on stage but we had space for overdubs. So he brought it over from Elektra Records, who had bought it, as well as the tack piano which you can hear on 'L.A. Woman'.

Jim Morrison during the recording of L.A.Woman, *Doors Workshop, Los Angeles, CA, circa 1970*

JIM I'VE ALWAYS SEEN LOS ANGELES AS A MICROCOSM OF THE STATES, A GENETIC BLUEPRINT.

JIM The songs have a lot to do with America and what it's like to live these years in LA.

PAUL ROTHCHILD *I felt things had been going downhill for some time when we started* L.A.Woman. *There had been a couple of peaks, but basically, things had been sliding since Miami. Jim was really not interested after the third album. He wanted to do other things. He wanted to write. Wanted to be an actor. Being lead singer of The Doors was really not his idea of a good time. It became very difficult to get him involved with the records. When we made* The Soft Parade *it was like pulling teeth to get Jim into it.*

JOHN We had been recording new songs for Paul Rothchild and there was a tense silence in the air, the same silence we encountered when Paul dropped in on our rehearsals. True, we didn't have enough songs, but Paul had a 'show-me' attitude. He realised it would be another 'pulling-teeth' album like *Waiting for the Sun*.

BRUCE BOTNICK *When Paul arrived at Sunset Sound for* L.A.Woman, *the band didn't want to go through the negative experience of* The Soft Parade *and* Morrison Hotel *again. They felt that they didn't need to be produced anymore. Paul sat there listening to 'Riders on the Storm' and said, 'This is cocktail jazz. I'm out of here, I can't do this anymore.'*

PAUL ROTHCHILD *They only had four or five ideas that were defined enough to play as songs by this point. The most complete were 'L.A. Woman' and 'Riders on the Storm', both of which I thought were great songs. My problem was I couldn't get them to play either of them decently. Their heart wasn't in it and it was easy to see why: Jim's heart wasn't in it. We rehearsed and rehearsed but it didn't get any better. I finally turned to Bruce Botnick and said, 'I know another producer would stick with this because it's a quarter of a million dollars for the producer, but I can't do it.' I went into the studio finally and said, 'Guys, I think the best thing that could happen is for me to leave. The only way you'll survive is if you make the record yourself. You'll have to generate the enthusiasm and brilliance.'*

Top and opposite: Doors Workshop, Los Angeles, CA, circa 1970
Above: L.A.Woman master tape box

Album 6-7

Night & a Day
LAmerica
The Changeling
The Cars hiss by my window
Deja Vu
Some day Soon
Away in India
'Push-Push'
Rock is Dead
The Lizard
I will never be Untrue

JOHN Bruce's idea to do a couple of takes on everything was the right one. It was perfect that we did it with Bruce and it's amazing that, even with Jim's demise, the last album is excellent. His drinking never affected the work in the studio and I think he was empowered by us producing *L.A.Woman* ourselves. We all were. So, although Paul Rothchild taught us how to make records, it was good to say goodbye to him.

PAUL ROTHCHILD *We said a very warm and tender and loving goodbye and I left but we continued to be friends.*

JAC HOLZMAN *I wasn't a bit worried about Bruce. He had contributed brilliantly to every note The Doors had recorded. Robby's point about the band making its own choices was fair. They had more than earned the right.*

Jim sitting on a Doors flight case (shown opposite) during the L.A.Woman sessions, with Robby and Paul Rothchild, Doors Workshop, Los Angeles, CA, circa 1970

THE DOORS FRAGILE

VINCE TREANOR *People who go to concerts don't think about the incredible logistics required to put on a performance. In this case it was one guy. Bill Siddons took on an enormous task and managed to make it work.*

The doors

To whom it may concern:

This is the Doors property. It was the case for an old, broken tape recorder. Jim Morrison used to sit on this case and smoke a joint now and then,

Congradulations!

Ray Manzarek

Doors Keyboardist

9000 Sunset Blvd., Suite 1410, West Hollywood, CA 90069 (310) 274-8471 FAX (310) 274-9856 E-mail: dsugerman@aol.com

KING RECORD CO.
JAMES BROWN
'LIVE' AT THE APOLLO

BRUCE BOTNICK ON A SLATE CHALKBOARD, JIM WROTE THE WORDS 'A CLEAN SLATE', AS IF TO DEFINE THE MOMENT.

ROBBY I'd use the Twin Reverb amp in the studio and in a live setting. It was OK but it was kind of noisy.

Previous pages: L.A.Woman *recording sessions, Doors Workshop, Los Angeles, CA, circa 1970*
Jim's 'a clean slate' chalkboard can be seen behind him
Above and oppposite: Robby's Fender Twin Reverb amplifier (seen in the studio on p.279)

Fender
NORMAL
VIBRATO
TWIN REVERB
-AMP

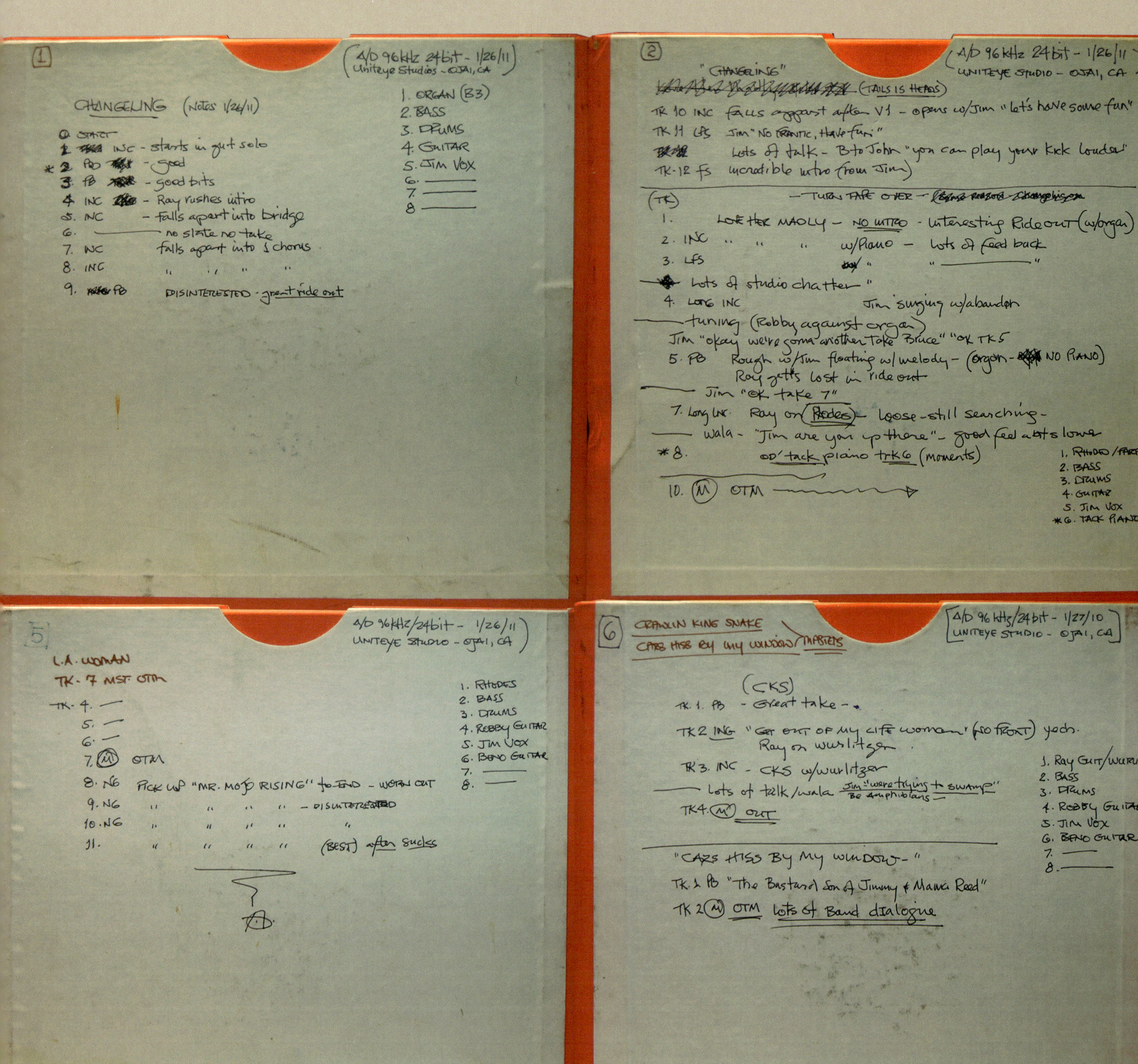

1
A/D 96kHz 24bit - 1/26/11
Uniteye Studios - OJAI, CA
CHANGELING (Notes 1/26/11)
1. ORGAN (B3)
2. BASS
3. DRUMS
4. GUITAR
5. JIM VOX
0 START
1 INC - starts in gut solo
* 2 PB - good
3 PB - good bits
4 INC - Ray rushes intro
5. INC - falls apart into bridge
6. no slate no take
7. INC falls apart into 1 chorus
8. INC
9. PB DISINTERESTED - great ride out
2
A/D 96kHz 24bit - 1/26/11
UNITEYE STUDIO - OJAI, CA
"CHANGELING"
(TAILS IS HEADS)
TK 10 INC falls apart after V1 - opens w/Jim "let's have some fun"
TK 11 LFS Jim "NO FRANTIC, Have fun"
Lots of talk - B to John "you can play your kick louder"
TK-12 FS incredible intro (from Jim)
- TURN TAPE OVER -
(TK)
1. LOVE HER MADLY - NO INTRO - interesting Rideout (w/organ)
2. INC w/Piano - lots of feed back
3. LFS
Lots of studio chatter
4. LONG INC Jim singing w/abandon
tuning (Robby against organ)
Jim "okay we're gonna another Take Bruce" "OK TK5
5. PB Rough w/Jim floating w/ melody - (organ - NO PIANO)
Ray gets lost in ride out
Jim "OK take 7"
7. Long INC. Ray on Rhodes - Loose - still searching -
wala - "Jim are you up there" - good feel a lots lower
* 8. OD' tack piano TRK6 (moments)
10. (M) OTM
1. RHODES / FARFISA
2. BASS
3. DRUMS
4. GUITAR
5. JIM VOX
* 6. TACK PIANO
A/D 96kHz/24bit - 1/26/11
UNITEYE STUDIO - OJAI, CA
L.A. WOMAN
TK - 7 MST OTM
TK - 4.
5.
6.
7. (M) OTM
8. NG PICK UP "MR. MOJO RISING" to END - WORN OUT
9. NG - DISINTERESTED
10. NG
11. (BEST) after sucks
1. RHODES
2. BASS
3. DRUMS
4. ROBBY GUITAR
5. JIM VOX
6. BENO GUITAR
6
CRAWLIN KING SNAKE
CARS HISS BY MY WINDOW / MASTERS
A/D 96 kHz/24bit - 1/27/10
UNITEYE STUDIO - OJAI, CA
(CKS)
TK 1. PB - Great take -
TK 2 INC "Get out of my life woman" (no FRONT) yeah.
Ray on wurlitzer
TK 3. INC - CKS w/wurlitzer
Lots of talk / wala
TK 4. (M) OUT
1. Ray Gut/Wurlitzer
2. BASS
3. DRUMS
4. ROBBY GUITAR
5. JIM VOX
6. BENO GUITAR
"CARS HISS BY MY WINDOW"
TK 1 PB "The Bastard Son of Jimmy & Mama Reed"
TK 2 (M) OTM Lots of Band dialogue

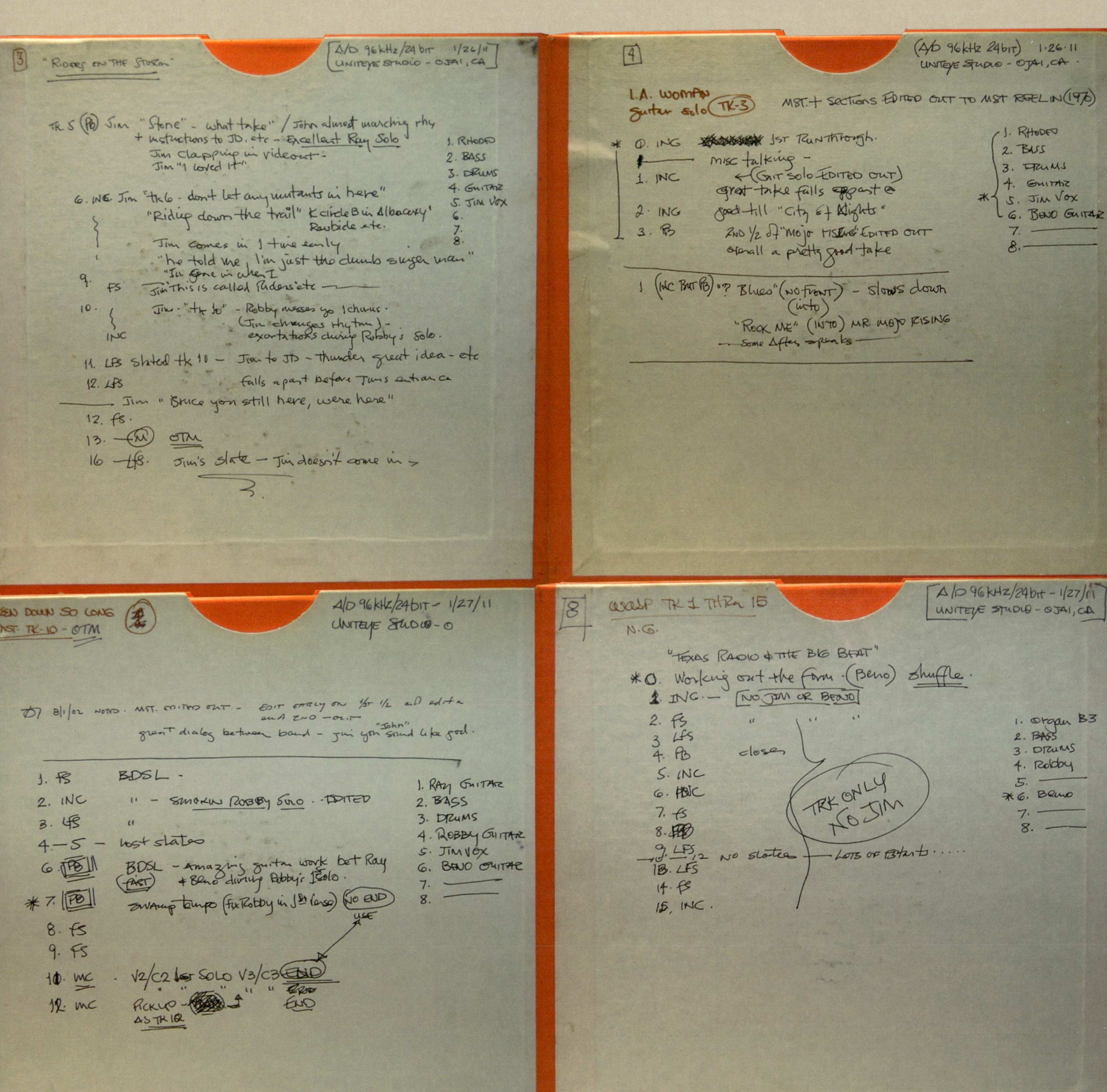

JOHN 'L.A. Woman' is the most difficult Doors song, rhythmically. The tempo is just perfect for a 60mph LA freeway ride.

RAY It was an homage to women, all women. And not just LA women. It was also an homage to LA as a woman, the city itself.

Original L.A.Woman *tape boxes*
Overleaf: L.A.Woman *sessions, Doors Workshop, Los Angeles, CA, circa 1970*

doors

The Mod Orange Ludwig Downbeat drum kit has become known as John Densmore's signature set-up. He first used it on 9 September 1967 at the Village Theatre in New York. In 1968, he acquired a bass drum cover with The Doors' logo on it, but, with the exception of the band's January 1969 Madison Square Garden concert, only used it for TV appearances.

The floor tom shown here is the last known piece of John's Mod Orange Downbeat kit.

He also had a White Marine Pearl Ludwig set, which he alternated with the Mod Orange set, and he is seen playing a White Marine Pearl Gretsch set in some photo and video shoots.

JOHN Billy Cobham and Art Blakey were big influences for me. I started with Gretsch drums and then switched to Ludwig. It was a pretty standard set-up. One tom-tom on the bass drum and a floor tom. Real spectacular! I never went for the two bass drum routine; there are lots of people who can do more with one than most guys can do with two. I liked to take the bottom heads off my toms to make them bark and growl. I hated new skins – I loved the sound of them after they'd been beaten to death for months. Snarling as hell – that was my sound.

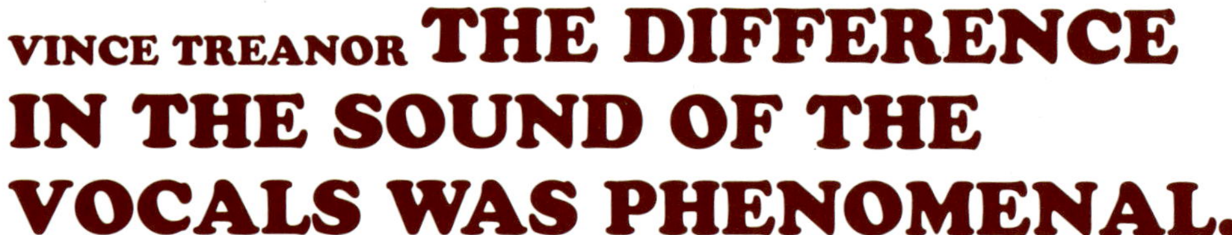

VINCE TREANOR THE DIFFERENCE IN THE SOUND OF THE VOCALS WAS PHENOMENAL.

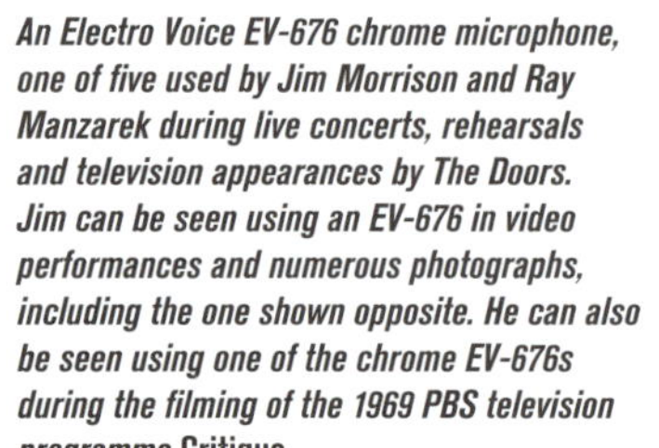

An Electro Voice EV-676 chrome microphone, one of five used by Jim Morrison and Ray Manzarek during live concerts, rehearsals and television appearances by The Doors. Jim can be seen using an EV-676 in video performances and numerous photographs, including the one shown opposite. He can also be seen using one of the chrome EV-676s during the filming of the 1969 PBS television programme Critique.

VINCE TREANOR *During 1967 and possibly before, the group had used Shure ball microphones. There was one for Jim and one for Ray, who sang harmony or back-up for Jim. These were inexpensive, high impedance microphones, which could be plugged into any instrument amplifier and used to serve the lead and back-up singers for a group. They were in common use by most groups because they were inexpensive. But they were also fragile, cheaply made and were subject to interference from instrument amplifiers.*

All this changed when I took over. The Shure microphones were replaced by Electro Voice EV-676 microphones, which were low impedance, required three pin connectors, were extremely durable and had a high rejection cardioid pattern.

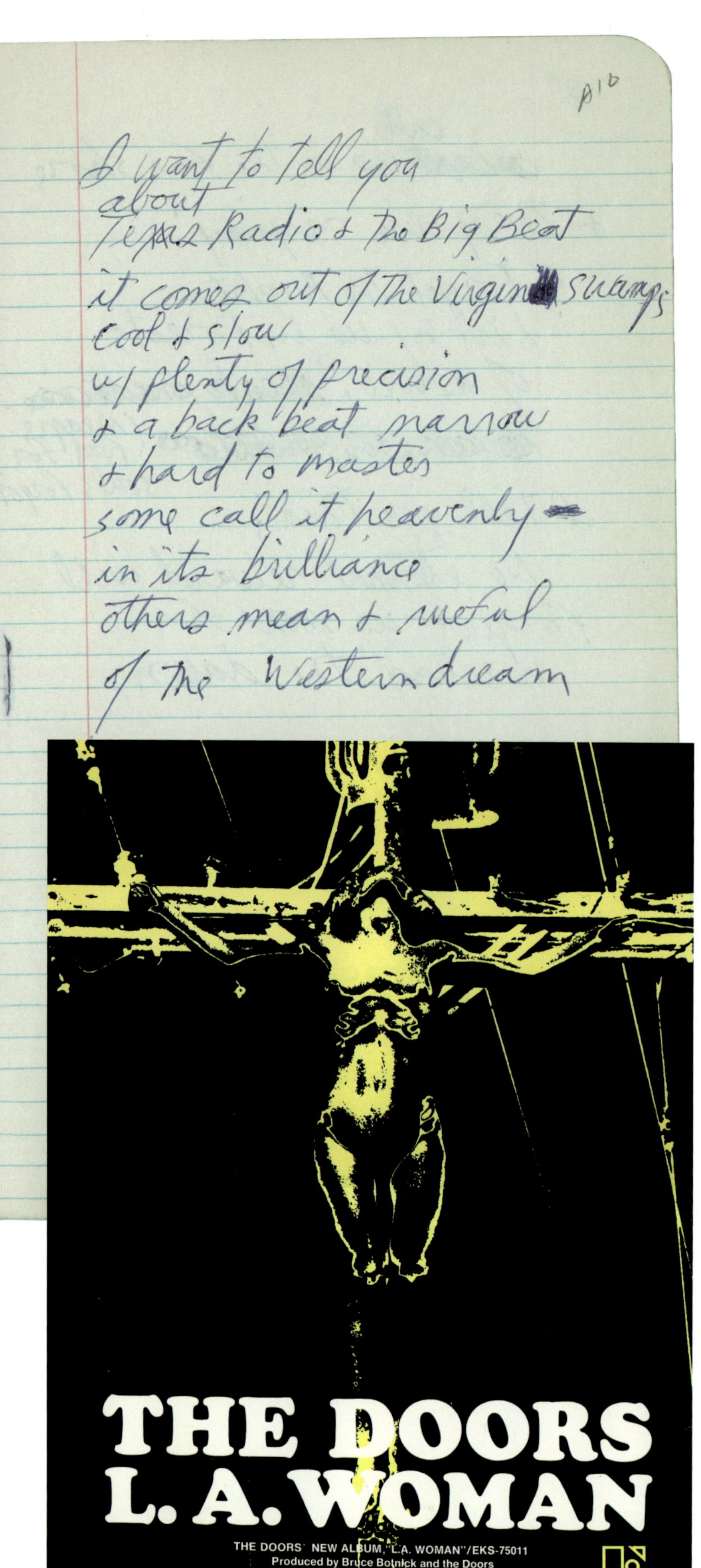

BRUCE BOTNICK *Doors songs were rarely created in the studio, but 'The WASP (Texas Radio and the Big Beat)' was. Ray was looking through one of Jim's notebooks and said, 'You know, it's about time we put some music to this.' So Robby, Ray and John, with Jerry Scheff, created an arrangement, while Jim was across the street having some beers. Then Jim came back with a six pack, loved the arrangement and we recorded.*

ROBBY We always loved doing 'Crawling King Snake'. It was one of our favourite John Lee Hooker songs. We'd meant to record it years before, but never got around to it until *L.A.Woman*. With *L.A.Woman* being a more bluesy album, it was a perfect fit.

JIM When you look at history, it seems to be cyclical. There have been many periods where women were the major controlling influence in life – matriarchal societies. I think women are becoming increasingly important. It's a ridiculous thing to talk about in such simple terms but I think the influence of women is becoming more and more felt. Life is becoming more and more feminine. There's no frontier to conquer, hunting and fishing is a basic survival thing and I think life is becoming more feminised. It's good because women have the right idea. Who makes all the films? Who runs the projection booth? It's somehow a masculine desire to dominate life rather than just accept it. I think women have less need to re-establish a connection to life because they are life.

JOHN It was Jim's genius to write about the city as a woman. I thought that was really something. Referencing the California wildfires, Manson, the guy was so gifted.

JIM I discovered blues in college. Blues is the music I enjoy doing the most, it's the most fun to sing. I like jazz also, but you don't need a singer for jazz. Our later recordings get back to the blues, which is what we do best.

JOHN The whole album was blues based and it was an answer to perfection. Our middle period with *The Soft Parade* took hundreds of takes. The idea of strings and horns was something Ray and I talked about before we even made our first album because we both liked jazz and it was something that we wanted to experiment with. The critics dissed us for changing our sound but if we hadn't gone through that we wouldn't have got back to our roots with *Morrison Hotel* and *L.A.Woman* which is the masterpiece.

Opposite and overleaf: L.A.Woman *sessions, Doors Workshop, Los Angeles, CA, circa 1970*
Top: Jim's handwritten lyrics to 'The WASP (Texas Radio & The Big Beat)'
Bottom: Trade magazine ad for L.A Woman

a
American Woman
a2

ROBBY We all came together on *L.A. Woman*. We would go in there and start jamming and just see what happened. And some cool stuff happened. That's the thing about Doors songs. A lot of the time we weren't perfect. Jim would never come in when we thought he would, which to me made it so much cooler. You could be loose. I think if Jim had lived, we would have continued to record in that way.

BRUCE BOTNICK L.A.Woman *is rich with emotion and great memories. With the guys reconnecting with the original creative force and their almost unconscious attitude about the entire recording and mixing process, we were blessed with an enduring album.*

JOHN In the spring of 1971, the low-budget concept on the *L.A. Woman* album paid off. Our previous record had been a comeback for us, but there'd been no hit singles. Jac Holzman called a meeting to confer with us on picking a song to be released off what was to become our last album.

Jac made his pitch. He had a hunch about 'Love Her Madly'. I did too. 'Nah, it's too commercial,' Robby responded quickly from the corner of the room. It staggered me. Robby had written the song; didn't he want another shot at the big time, 'Light My Fire' being his previous monster? 'Isn't that what a single is supposed to be?' Jac retorted. Jim seemed ambivalent. 'I'd love to release "L.A. Woman",' I added, 'but it would have to be cut down from seven minutes, and I don't know where.' '"Love Her Madly" is a top-five record,' Jac negotiated. 'Let's go with it, and if we get some action, then we can have a second single. "Riders on the Storm" will get more FM airplay than any record in history. If "Love Her Madly" is a hit first, then we release "Riders".'

Song by song, Jac Holzman predicted exactly what happened. On 24 April 1971, 'Love Her Madly' went to number four, and we were back on AM radio, hot and heavy. Meanwhile, 'Riders on the Storm' was also receiving heavy airplay and the pressure was on to put it out. But it was six minutes long and nobody knew how to cut it down. Except me. With my jazz background, I heard several sections in Ray's piano solo that could be lifted out without sacrificing any soul. I called up Botnick, went over to his house, and we did the surgery.

Bruce and I were very proud when Ray couldn't tell where the cuts were in the edited version. The piano solo still built melodically and logically, but it was condensed. Jac released 'Riders' on the heels of 'Love Her Madly'. Despite being our least commercial rock song, it too climbed the charts.

ROBBY I think 'Riders on the Storm' could be one of the best songs we ever did. I'm not saying it was the best song we ever wrote, because it wasn't, but the way it was produced and the sound of it, I really dug it. I think it could have taken us in a new direction.

JIM LOVE IS ONE OF THE HANDFUL OF DEVICES WE HAVE TO AVOID THE VOID.

BRUCE BOTNICK *We mixed* L.A. Woman *at Poppi Studios in West Hollywood. On the second mix day, Tuesday 9 February, we were gifted with a 6.5 magnitude earthquake. The control room had floor-to-ceiling glass walls between it and the studio, so every time there was a tremor, the glass would move and we had to go outside till the tremors passed ... the perfect inspiration for 'Riders'.*

JOHN We were jamming to '(Ghost) Riders in the Sky' and it morphed. For some reason I started playing with my left hand on the snare the same pattern that was on the cymbal which gave it a jazzy feel.

RAY Songs like 'Riders on the Storm' have a repetitive bassline that just keeps on going and it becomes hypnotic. My left hand, 'Lefty', did a very good job. He's not too quick, a bit of a slow-witted fellow, but he's really strong and solid and plays what he knows. Lefty became our bass player. I had a Fender Rhodes keyboard bass sitting on top of my Vox Continental organ. My left hand would play the bass and my right would play the organ.

ROBBY When you listen to Ray's solo on 'Riders on the Storm', it's genius. But playing live, he never played two solos the same.

RAY The album at the end is about death. 'Riders on the Storm' is about death apart from the very last verse: 'Girl, you gotta love your man / Girl, you gotta love your man / Take him by the hand / Make him understand / His world on you depends / Our life will never end / Gotta love your man.' So the last thing Jim recorded was a plea to love and to love one another. It's about a killer on the road but in the end Jim couldn't bring himself to continue with that theme. He turned to love as the saving grace. Love will heal us all and your life will never end. That's the LSD, the mysticism talking.

RAY It was our last album that we were contracted to do with Elektra so we were free to do what we wanted. So Jim decided that he would go to Paris. We were all shocked but it was terrific because he needed a vacation, there was no doubt about that. As the lead singer you have everything, all indulgence is yours, all drugs are available to you, every sin is permitted when you're a rock star. There were too many distractions. He needed to get away to get back to being a writer. He was going to be the next Ernest Hemingway or F. Scott Fitzgerald in Paris.

ROBBY One day while we were mixing the record, Jim came in, handed us all copies of his latest poetry book and said he was moving to Paris. We pointed out the record wasn't fully mixed yet. He said he trusted us to finish it without him. There was no one last drink. There was no one last meal. A few days later he was just gone.

JIM KERR *He was there to run away, run away from himself and his demons. He was feeling the heat, the pressure. Back home he couldn't go anywhere – The Doors were huge. He was in a lot of trouble, due to go to court, possibly prison. The love of his life had already made her way to Paris and this was going to be a new start for him as a poet where he'd always dreamed of making a living.*

April 27, 1971

Dear Ilona,

Thank you for your letter, and your interest in THE DOORS. The album is out, as you already probably know. Sorry this letter is late, but things have been really hettic these last few weeks.

Jim is, in fact in Europe writing a book on the trial. No tour, or concerts is/are planned for quite sometime yet, seeing how Jim probably won't be back for quite some time. The DOORS are NOT breaking, just taking a vacaction. Rest and recuperation.

thanks again.

Sincerely yours,

Danny Sugerman
DOORS PRODUCTIONS

dss

Jim and Pam in Paris, 1971
Above: Letter to a fan by Doors employee Danny Sugerman, 1971

JIM'S APARTMENT
17 Rue Beautreillis, Paris

JIM I can't decide whether to try and be a citizen of the world or to identify with a particular country, but I guess you have no choice. I think whatever happens, America is the arena. It's the centre of the action. It will take a strong, fluid people to survive in a climate like ours, but I'm sure people do. I think for many people, especially city dwellers, it's a state of constant paranoia. As I understand it, paranoia is defined as an irrational fear but what if the paranoia is real? Then you just cope with it second by second.

ROBBY Paris would be a chance for Jim to relax and put the pressures of the world and the band behind him. A chance to centre himself and come back with a renewed passion for making music.

JAC HOLZMAN *When Jim left, I thought we would never see him in a band again. I felt that once he got to Paris, he would be so attracted by the poetry of the city, in all of its aspects, that he would be reluctant to return.*

ROBBY We knew that Jim needed a break, we knew he might be away for a while, but we had no reason to think he wouldn't be back and that we wouldn't pick up where we left off. He asked how *L.A. Woman* was doing and said he'd be back in a few months.

JOHN I personally thought, 'Jim has to clean up his alcoholism, or I don't know what's going to happen.' And he was in Paris, where they have wine for breakfast. But the three of us had developed such a tight musical synchronicity – we didn't want to give that up. So we were in the woodshed and the songs came up.

JIM I guess I see myself as a conscious artist plugging away from day to day, assimilating information. I'd like to get a theatre going of my own. I'm very interested in that. Although I still enjoy singing.

RAY **WHAT COULD BE A BETTER PLACE FOR A POET, AN ARTIST, AN AMERICAN POET TO GO THAN TO PARIS?**

Paris

FRANK LISCIANDRO *I understood that he longed for the freedom of not being recognised, not being harassed, not having to perform rock and roll. There were some French filmmaker friends in Paris and he was carrying* HWY *and* Feast of Friends *under his arm to show them. And he knew that Paris had been a place of comfort and refuge for the poets and writers that came before him.*

I wasn't concerned at all. I thought, 'Well, here's a guy who has shown that he can make it in Los Angeles. He can surely do it in Paris.' Jim would walk out of The Doors' office on Santa Monica Boulevard, go to the corner, put his thumb out and hitch a ride. He enjoyed the expectation and the experience of something different happening. He was a writer and he was writing about his experiences. He could do it in Paris.

KATE SIMON *I spent my sophomore year at George Washington University at the American College in Paris. At the time I was writing a term paper on* Long Day's Journey into Night *by Eugene O'Neill and I was really late with it so I was asking everyone that I ran into if they could help me finish it. One day as I was standing in line at the bank, Jim came over to me and asked if I would teach him French. When I turned around and saw that it was Jim Morrison, I said that I could teach him French but I also asked if he knew* Long Day's Journey into Night. *He knew the play completely and he helped me finish the term paper. He never did mention me teaching him French again.*

He seemed to be stressed out. He had expressed trepidation that he had been arrested for obscenity so it was certainly something that was preying on his mind. He told me that he wanted to go back to filmmaking.

He was completely charismatic, intelligent and likeable. There was something about him that was really special. Although I had never seen anyone drink the way he did, to the extreme, I didn't ever see the Jimbo side. He seemed in his own way to be shy. Maybe he was both an introvert and an extrovert.

I may have given Jim his first copy of L.A. Woman. *I remember he asked me if I would go and buy him a copy because he hadn't seen the record yet. So I went and bought a copy at Lido Musique on the Champs-Élysées.*

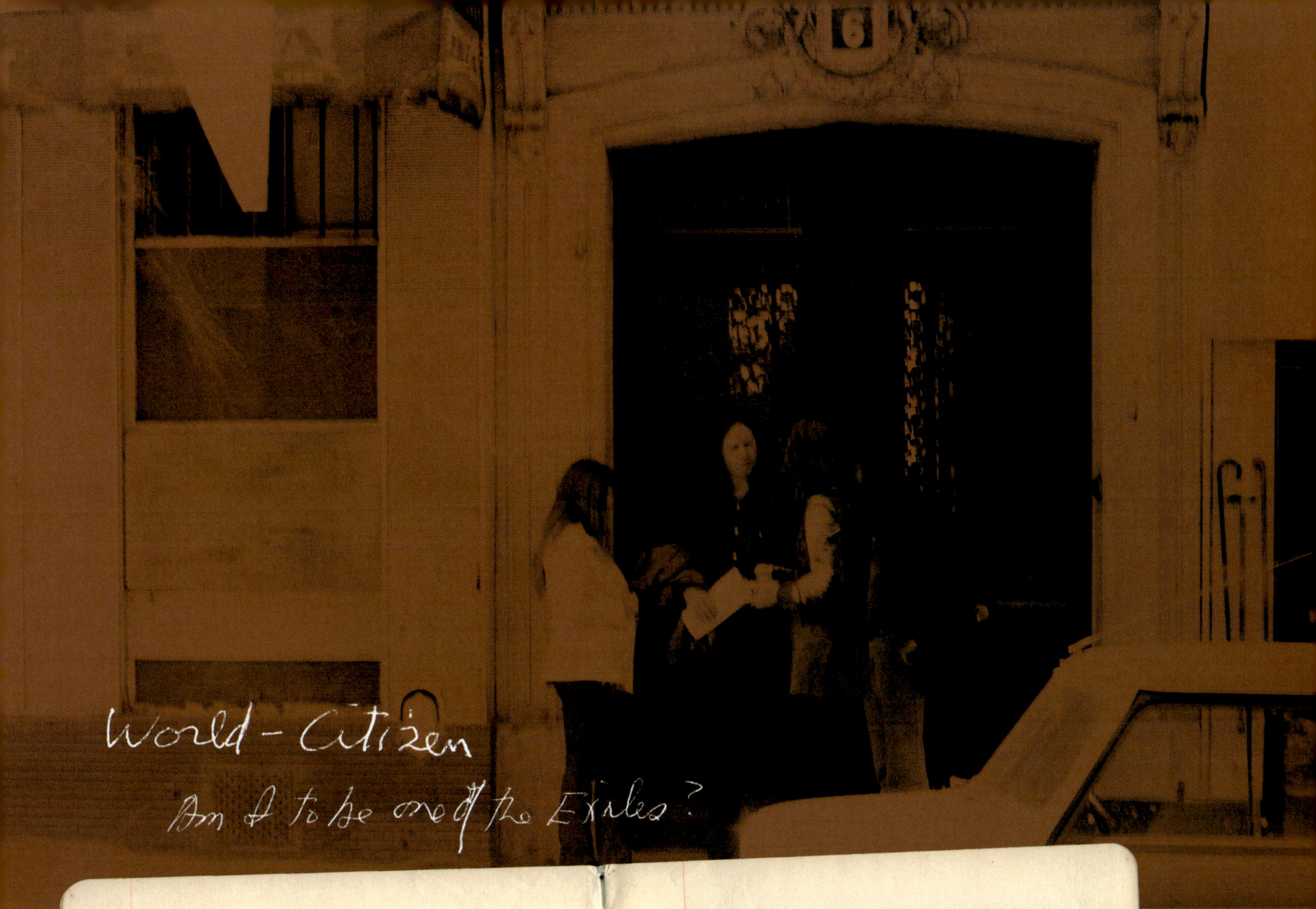

World-Citizen
Am I to be one of the Exiles?

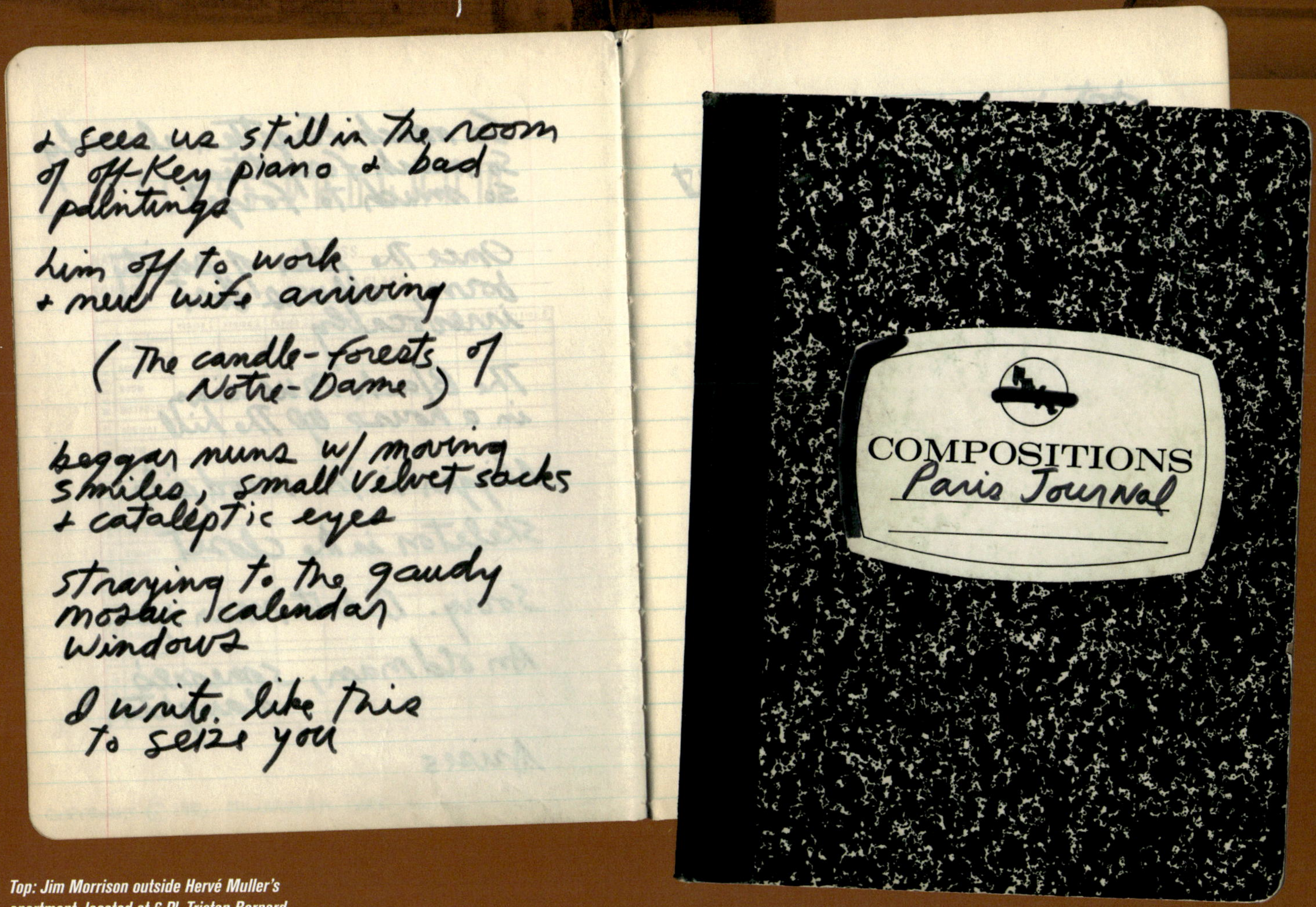

& sees us still in the room
of off-key piano & bad
paintings
him off to work
+ new wife arriving
(The candle-forests of
Notre-Dame)
beggar nuns w/ moving
smiles, small velvet sacks
+ cataleptic eyes
straying to the gaudy
mosaic calendar
windows
I write like this
to seize you
COMPOSITIONS
Paris Journal

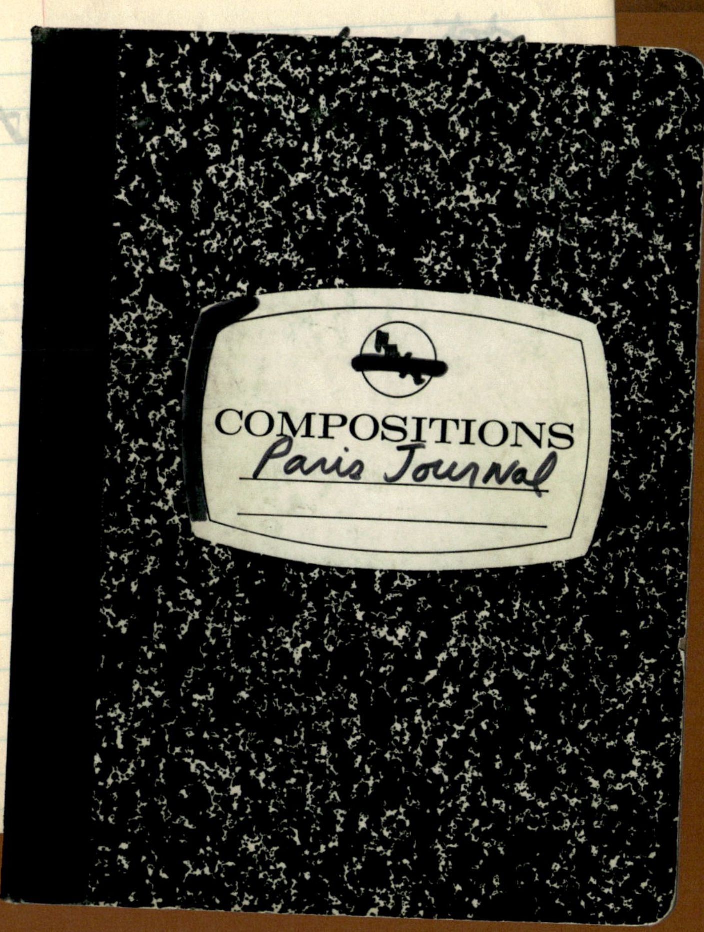

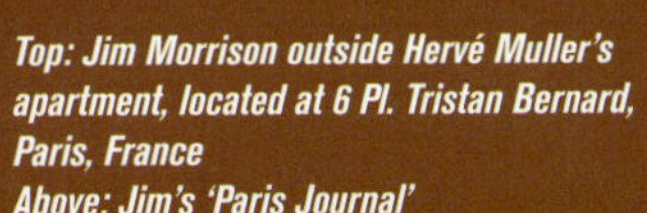

Top: Jim Morrison outside Hervé Muller's apartment, located at 6 Pl. Tristan Bernard, Paris, France
Above: Jim's 'Paris Journal'

Jim Morrison, Lead Singer For Doors, Dies In Paris At 27 Of Natural Causes

LOS ANGELES (AP) — Jim Morrison, propelled to stardom on the acid rock scene as lead singer for The Doors, is dead, his personal manager says.

William Siddons said early Friday that the 27-year-old Morrison died of natural causes in Paris last Saturday and was buried in France Wednesday.

Siddons made the announcement after flying here from Paris with Morrison's wife, Pamela. The Morrisons had no children.

Neither the U.S. Embassy nor music sources in Paris could confirm Morrison's death.

"I can't say the exact cause of death because I didn't see the death certificate before I left." Siddons added.

Max Fink, the singer's personal lawyer, said he had been told that Morrison suffered either a heart attack or died from pneumonia.

Morrison's parents, Adm. and Mrs. Steve Morrison of Arlington, Va., said they had talked Thursday with relatives on the West Coast who had heard nothing unusual about their son.

JIM I hope I die aged 120 with a sense of humour and a comfortable bed. I wouldn't want anybody around. I'd like to just quietly drift off. I think science has a chance in our lifetime to conquer death. I think it's very possible.

JOHN We were fooling around in the studio when we got the news. We didn't take it in. Robby and I were like, 'No, Jim's drunk and he's moved to Haiti.' I don't think I fully assimilated it for many years. After the word came down, we were playing music because that's what felt good. It was our refuge. It was like we were back in Venice.

RAY Jim was on the street with all of us but he was also in the ozone, he was in heaven, he was in hell. He was experiencing as much of life as he could. That's why, in a way, when he was gone at 27, I wasn't too sad because he lived a full life. He just said, 'Take it as it comes but take as much of it as you can. Absorb everything. Live life with great intensity because it's the only one you've got.'

JOHN He just packed it all into 27 years, all the brilliant things he did. When I met him he used to smoke ten joints in the morning and then later acid came in. I saw him take 10,000 micrograms of acid at the Tropicana when we were playing at the Hullaballoo. In retrospect its funny but at the time we were all trying to be together.

JAC HOLZMAN *The same age as Jimi Hendrix and Janis Joplin when they died. I recalled their deaths and what a circus they had become. Elektra had to do better. We were not going to use this as an opportunity to ship records or any kind of that sordid nonsense. It was not our place to tell anyone. That right belonged to Jim's family, or Pamela, or The Doors. Our job was to keep it from turning into a tabloid craze, and in large measure we succeeded.*

Good-bye America
I loved you

JIM **IF I HAD TO DO IT OVER AGAIN, I WOULD HAVE GONE MORE FOR THE QUIET, UNDEMONSTRATIVE LITTLE ARTIST, PLODDING AWAY IN HIS OWN GARDEN.**

RAY We're lucky we had him. They don't come by, those types, often. You get them once in a generation, once every 50 years maybe. I miss him, frankly.

ROBBY Jim should be recognised not just as a rock and roll poet but really as one of the greatest poets of our time.

JIM I'm not denying that I've had a good time. I've met a lot of interesting people and seen a lot of things in a short space of time that I probably wouldn't have run into, so I can't say that I regret it.

GRACE SLICK *He had so much to drink one night that he died. He didn't go into an overdose, he just died. He had probably had that same amount before but it worked out before. I really don't think that when you're 27, you're at the top of your career, you're being written about as a genius, you have all these women, you are having a great time going around the world as a rock and roll star, that you think, 'Gee, I'm gonna kill myself.' I don't think so, folks.*

ALICE COOPER *I believe that some people are natural survivors and they're people that have a will to be somewhere else; on another plane or another planet, whatever death is. Just not being satisfied with the things that are on this planet creatively. Just look at the things Jim wrote. He was so obvious in his lyrics that he was going to be going out pretty soon.*

ROBBY Did Jim die in his bathtub? Did he mistake heroin for cocaine and take too much by accident? Was his body moved to the apartment from a nightclub bathroom? Did Pam lie to the cops? Was the coffin empty? Was the CIA involved? I wasn't there. I haven't investigated. I don't know what's credible. I just know my friend is gone.

JIM KERR *Things certainly fell apart for fans of The Doors on 3 July 1971 when Jim Morrison was found dead in what are still considered to be really mysterious circumstances in Paris. Incredibly, far from being the end of The Doors, today, with 120 million albums sold worldwide and more than 20 million followers on social media, it's obvious that more people than ever are listening to Jim Morrison and The Doors. I'm one of those millions.*

JOHN JIM IS HANGING OUT WITH CHOPIN AND EDITH PIAF. WHAT CAN I SAY? IT'S GOOD COMPANY.

I've always had an affection for death

ROBBY Every time I go to Paris I drop by his grave, check it out. Jim gets some interesting people hanging out there with him. It's kind of cool, all the people that are there. And Jim loved that place. He always said he wanted to be buried there.

JIM KERR *A whole lot of illustrious names are in Père Lachaise cemetery, but probably the most well-known name for people of my generation and subsequent generations is James Douglas Morrison, as it says on his gravestone. [When I visited] in 1979 I would have been 20 years old so Jim Morrison would have been a man to me. Now, it's like looking at the grave of a young boy. I expected a frisson of emotion going there, but the emotion was more than I thought it would be. If you go to the graves of any of the greats, the legends, the biggest cultural names, you're going to feel something. But for people like me, rock and roll music is the lingua franca; nothing can touch rock music. It is more than movies, it is more than literature, and Jim Morrison was up there.*

People talk about The Beatles and The Rolling Stones for obvious reasons, as well as The Who and The Kinks, but The Doors had a peak of their own, so it's not surprising that I felt this great emotion there. I had a feeling of gratitude visiting Jim's grave. But it was a mix: on the one hand I felt the presence of a legend but I also felt the presence of a young lad. I felt privileged because any time you see photos of Jim's grave there's always a crowd of people around but there wasn't on that day. In some ways, although Jim is a long way from home, his stature as an artist makes it appropriate that he's in Paris. He wanted to be buried there – there's obviously a fantastic cachet and grandeur to the place. His own self-reasoning was that he wasn't a rock star, he was a poet.

When it came to redoing Jim's tombstone, his father arranged for an inscription in Greek. He said that the words would sum up Jim's character: 'True to his own spirit'. The fact that he recognised his son's spirit, which at the time he may have despaired of as waywardness, shows that there's love there.

Jim Morrison still has an allure. The people turning up to Père Lachaise, as I did, are too young to have seen him perform and yet we feel he's always there. The reason that young people still relate to the image of Morrison goes back to the essence of what young people want: the joy of existence, discovery, freedom. That never changes and I think Jim more than any other music icon stood for that, and still does.

PATTI SMITH *I visited Jim Morrison's grave in 1975. I stopped at a florist just outside the cemetery walls and bought a small bundle of hyacinths and proceeded to search for Jim's grave. At that time there was no marker, and it was not easy to find, but I followed messages scrawled by well-wishers on neighbouring headstones. It was completely silent, save the rustling of autumn leaves and the rain, which was becoming more pronounced. On the unmarked grave were gifts from pilgrims before me: plastic flowers, cigarette butts, half-empty whiskey bottles, broken rosaries and strange charms. The graffiti surrounding him were words in French from his own songs: 'C'est la fin, mon merveilleux ami,' – 'This is the end, beautiful friend.'*

Jim's burial place evolved over the years. It started as an unmarked grave decorated by fans, before being augmented by a stone bust of Jim by the Croatian sculptor Mladen Mikulin in 1981. After years of being vandalised, the bust was stolen in 1988; the existing gravestone was installed by the Morrison family in 1990.

Patti Smith at the gravesite of Jim Morrison, Paris, 1975

The Music will be other voices
on the line
on down the line
on the line

July 14, 1971

Thank you for your letter. As you have undoubtably heard, Jim Morrison passed away July 3 in Paris. The death was attributed to natural causes.

The other three Doors' while understandably upset about the death of their friend realize that the show must go on. They intend to still make music together, and they have no immediate intention of replacing Jim.

We all loved Jim for what he was, a kind warm hearted, gentle person with the soul of a clown. He always cared about you guys out there and he hired me to take care of you. He enjoyed your presents and cards and he proudly displayed them on the wall near his desk.

There is no going back and undoing what has already been done. We're sure Jim is happy, and his presence will always be felt here up at the office. Jim was a good person, but sometimes he tried too hard. He gave everything he had into what he did, and he did it with total conviction.

I'm sure we'll all miss him, that goes without saying. We all should all know how lucky we were to be a part of life, directly or indirectly.

Thank you for your interest and your support.

~~Sincerely,~~ Best Regards

Danny Sug

DANNY SUGERMAN
DOORS PRODUCTIONS

ROBBY We weren't sure what we were going to do after Jim died. We were going to change the name of the band, but no one could come up with anything that didn't sound really pretentious. We just wanted to keep playing music, so that's what we did for a while.

JOHN We had Ray and Robby try and sing. We avoided the trap of having someone trying to fill Jim's leather pants. No matter how good the singer was, they would have been compared to Jim, which would have been a very difficult situation. Ray and Robby couldn't be compared to Jim, they weren't trying to be lead singers.

ROBBY We wrestled with the idea of bringing in a replacement singer, though we felt like it was still too soon. We considered doing an all-instrumental album, but then decided that would be an overcorrection. We decided it'd be best if we took on the vocal duties ourselves.

RAY It was weird from our point of view, especially when Robby and I sang. We'd fight about whose voice was worse! Jim as a person was impossible to replace, but we thought, 'Well, anyone can be a rock and roll singer.' It turned out to be a little harder than that.

JOHN **ULTIMATELY I THINK WE MADE A REALLY GOOD DECISION TO NOT REPLACE JIM.**

ROBBY After months of jam sessions during *L.A. Woman* we had amassed plenty of material, so we assembled it and set to work on what would become *Other Voices*.

Opposite: A draft letter from Doors manager Danny Sugerman to fans following Jim's death. Danny started working with The Doors when he was 12, answering the band's fan mail. At 17 he replaced Bill Siddons, following the death of Jim

Doors Workshop, 1972

ROBBY We needed some lyrics, but I had been coming up with those since the beginning, so it wasn't new territory for me. Ray and John were excited to try their hand at it as well. Ray ended up writing the first single, a song called 'Tightrope Ride' about what it was like being in a band with Jim. John wrote the lyrics to 'Ships with Sails', which was one of my favourite songs of the post-Jim era. It was a new dynamic, but it wasn't odd for the three of us to write and record together without Jim.

It was exciting to experiment with new sounds and styles, and we genuinely liked the songs we had come up with. Jac Holzman gave us mountains of encouragement. He probably knew how much we needed it. We always liked Jac, but it wasn't until much later that we truly appreciated him. No other label owner would've put up with even half of what Jac did.

JAC HOLZMAN *I think Jim would have encouraged them to go on. And if he did that, I had to as well. I knew that they were good musicians, that they could be exciting, because I had seen it on those occasions when Jim didn't show up. They made it work. I wanted to [sign them as a trio] to show them it wasn't all about Jim.*

MARK VOLMAN *After Jim died, The Doors travelled through Europe with us as our opening act performing the songs from* Other Voices. *They were a bit melancholy, those shows. I always felt a bit sorry for the three guys left with the legacy; they would always be remembered first for Jim's death and not how much they all brought to that experience. I always felt that the band, especially Ray, always took a lot of heat from the hip community, who thought they should have just gone away. They were the most inventive band of the late Sixties.*

ROBBY When it came to playing live, we thought back to Amsterdam, where Jim had missed the show but the crowd still embraced us. Maybe they'd welcome us the same way now? There was only one way to find out, so we set out on tour for the first time in almost a year. To our relief the audiences were enthusiastic and open-minded, and the critics gave us far more credit than we expected. The shows were smaller, but it wasn't like we were playing to half-empty bars. In LA, we filled the Hollywood Palladium. In New York, we played to a packed house at Carnegie Hall. As we stood on the boards of one of the most prestigious stages in the world, it seemed like people still wanted to see us.

ROBBY **WE LEANED MORE INTO OUR JAZZ INFLUENCES SINCE WE DIDN'T HAVE JIM THERE TO INSIST ON THE BLUES.**

SANTA MONICA CIVIC AUDITORIUM
SANTA MONICA, CALIF.
KRLA Presents
"DOORS"
PRODUCED BY CONCERT ASSOCIATES
SEPT'BR
10
1972
SUN. EVE. 8:00 P.M.
$6.50
NO REFUND - NO EXCHANGE
$6.50 — SEPT. 10, 1972
Upper Concourse $6.50
Santa Monica Civic Auditorium
GOOD ONLY
SUNDAY EVE.
SEPT'BR
10
1972
R.U.S.U. SOCIAL COMMITTEE
present
The Doors
IN CONCERT
NEW UNION BUILDINGS, WHITEKNIGHTS
SATURDAY, 13th MAY, 1972 at 8.30 p.m.
Tickets £1 in advance
№ 200
PAC
DOORS
RAY MANZAREK
JOHN DENSMORE
ROBBIE KRIEGER
THE DOORS

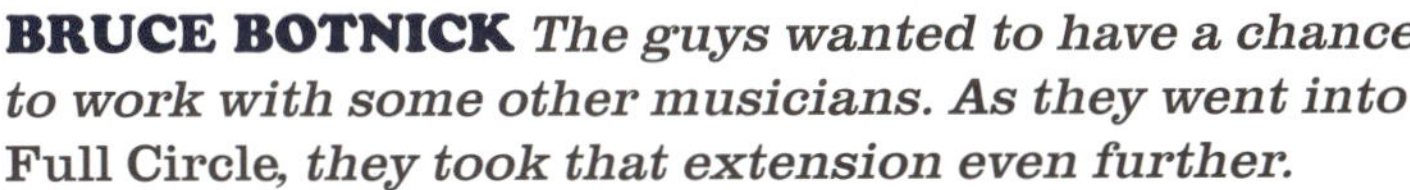

BRUCE BOTNICK *The guys wanted to have a chance to work with some other musicians. As they went into* Full Circle, *they took that extension even further.*

ROBBY When we put out our next album, *Full Circle*, we actually scored a minor hit with 'The Mosquito'. I was on vacation in Mexico, and these three local musicians came down out of the hills. They would sing mariachi stuff, and they had this one song about a mosquito and that inspired me. And I was proud of my tongue-in-cheek lyrics to 'Verdilac', which is a misspelling of a Russian vampire that feeds only on the blood of loved ones. 'The Piano Bird', which was John's song, was probably my favourite after 'The Mosquito'.

The rest of the songs I could do without – and the fans and critics didn't like them any more than I did.

JOHN I played piano when I was eight years old. I was always noodling on the instrument in Doors sessions, during breaks. I had some licks, and I think it was Robby who said, 'That's something. Let's expand on that.'

Opposite: Hollywood Palladium, Los Angeles, CA, 26 November 1971
Above, left: Robby and John 'selfie' taken aboard Ship of Fools, a boat owned by the band
Above right: Robby, Ray and John in London, UK, 27 August 1972
Middle right: A tour pin from The Doors' 1971 tour

JIM ALL THREE OF THEM ARE EXCELLENT MUSICIANS. I WOULD HOPE THAT THEY WOULD GO ON AND CREATE AN INSTRUMENTAL SOUND OF THEIR OWN WHICH DIDN'T DEPEND ON LYRICS.

ROBBY We were a pretty good jazz trio. We could have done that, maybe with various guest stars. We did think about it, but not until it was too late.

JOHN When you're doing it, you hope it's going to last, that it's a continuum. We were a melting pot – Chicago blues, jazz, raga, flamenco. As crazy as Jim was, I knew we were putting magic on tape. If you're interested in the individual ingredients, what created that magic, then you can investigate these albums. You can hear the process.

JAC HOLZMAN *Jim provided an edginess and tension that challenged them to do their very best. The idea of the band is what challenged them afterwards.*

JOHN At the time we had our hearts in it, although halfway through, the songwriting process started to get on everyone's nerves – which song were we going to do? Ray's were turning out this way and Robby's that way, so it got a little touchy. The album didn't turn out all that well.

ROBBY Looking back, I'm glad we did those albums. I don't know what would have happened if we hadn't – maybe something better. But who knows?

DAVID FRICKE *Manzarek, Krieger and Densmore made* Full Circle *with new and more help – away from The Doors Workshop, at LA's AM Studios, with Henry Lewy who had engineered and produced early, defining music by Joni Mitchell and Crosby, Stills & Nash. Lewy was also part of The Doors' LA circle of Transcendental Meditation friends. Musicians included James Taylor's bassist Leland Sklar, percussionist Bobbye Hall and top session vocalists Clydie King and Vanetta Fields.* Full Circle *showed Manzarek, Krieger and Densmore enjoying more of the freedom suddenly dropped on them in July '71, with less of the self-consciousness apparent on* Other Voices.

On 10 September 1972, Manzarek, Krieger and Densmore ended a seven-week US tour, opening for Frank Zappa at the Hollywood Bowl. After that show, they acknowledged the obvious: they could not continue without a new singer. The three went to London, where some remote possibilities – Joe Cocker; Paul Rodgers of the English blues band Free; Kevin Coyne, an eccentric vocal dynamo with the Elektra-related band Siren – quickly fizzled. Manzarek went back to LA, Krieger and Densmore stayed in London, starting a new group, Butts Band, with a new British R&B singer, Jess Roden. Jac Holzman didn't press The Doors for the third album in their contract; he soon left Elektra as well, in late 1973.

RAY ONCE YOU HIT THAT PASSION, IT NEVER CHANGES.

Hollywood Bowl, Los Angeles, CA, 10 September 1972
Opposite, top: Rock Liberation Festival, Balboa Stadium, San Diego, CA, 13 August 1972

RAY After Jim died and we decided to carry on, we signed with Elektra Records for a five album contract. We did two records on the contract and then we decided not to continue any more. It was good music and we had a good time doing it but it just wasn't the same without Jim and to continue on without Morrison just wasn't the right thing to do.

JOHN After *Full Circle* we went over to England to look for a singer. It was ludicrous but the three of us had this musical synchronicity and we didn't want to give it up. We thought of people like Joe Cocker but nothing really worked out. Ray and Dorothy wanted to go home, but Robby and I were tight musically and we wanted to continue. We'd decided that as we'd gone over to start something new we should do just that, so for the next four months we lived there and jammed with different people. It felt good to do something new and to be done with The Doors. It was fresh and exciting to start all over again and scuffle around.

ROBBY We met Jess Roden and we formed a band called Butts Band. One of the guys lived in a place called the Butts. So that's where the name came from. It was like a park area in England. Jess knew Phil Chen and he invited him to come play with us. Phil dug the stuff we were doing and he joined the band.

JOHN Jess was the first guy to join the band. We hadn't heard him in Bronco, because they didn't make any dent in the States, but Davy Harper, our roadie whom we shared with Traffic, mentioned Jess, and that's how we got on to him. We went through a few singers – it's kinda touchy, because you try to seem relaxed and just jam, but then everybody knows you're checking them out. Jess seemed right, though, because he sang Robby's melodies well and he had some of his own stuff, and he brought Phil Chen and Roy Davies.

We recorded the album with Bruce Botnick – half at Olympia in London and half in Jamaica, where Phil Chen was born. We stayed at Chris Blackwell's house up in the hills above Kingston. Kingston was a little daunting but it was great – reggae hadn't really reached the States at this stage. We were in Jimmy Cliff's studio and I'd never heard anything like it. For drummers they turned the beat around – supposedly it came from them hearing American music on the radio. In rock and roll you hit the bass drum on one, two, three and reggae turned it around. When I went back to the States I called Kenny Edwards, who played bass for Linda Ronstadt. I said, 'Wait til you hear this shit. The bass playing is like soloing. It's wild.' A year later Linda Ronstadt covered 'Many Rivers to Cross' and it went to number one. You're welcome.

This page and opposite: Butts Band at the Whisky a Go Go, Los Angeles, CA, 30 November 1974

ROBBY We really liked what Bruce had done with the album. We had a meeting with the head of Elektra and he said, 'Well, this is good but I think you should recut the album.' I must have had a horrible look on my face because he went, 'Wow, you look like you just swallowed a worm!' I didn't want any part of that. Even though he was going to get us this great producer, we'd already done the damn thing and we liked it. I told Phil about what happened and he called me 'The Worm' after that. We all went back to LA to get the band going but it never really got off the ground. The album came out but it didn't do well enough to get gigs.

JOHN Playing music is my path in life but I knew there wasn't going to be a peak like The Doors. I snaked my way downhill rather than straight down from that peak via creative projects. Butts Band was one and I've had many others since. I got into writing and acting as I zigzagged down that steep peak. With each project I want to reach as many people as possible but I'm not going to kvetch too much about it because if I'm getting off on what I'm doing creatively, that's enough. I hope that the projects I do make as much impact as possible. They won't be another 'Light My Fire' but it's the process that excites me.

I did an album with Jac Holzman's son, Adam. I knew he'd played with Miles Davis and one time he came over and we jammed for hours. We couldn't stop and we knew we had to make a record so we went into the studio for two days. I suggested we do an instrumental jazz album – a Doors song or two and a couple of Miles Davis songs. I asked him if he knew 'All Blues' by Miles and he did. It was the first song I ever played with Ray, and I ended up recording it with Jac's son, who played with Miles.

ROBBY It was never going to be like playing with The Doors. Today I play what I like to play, which might not be that commercial but I'm very proud of the albums I've done and I'm lucky that I can do what I do without worrying if it will make money or not.

RAY MY FIRST ALBUM WAS AN OPENING STATEMENT – A COMPLETE, CONCISE AND HEAVILY PERSONAL STATEMENT. I HAD TO DO THAT FIRST.

The first indications of what Ray Manzarek was doing after leaving The Doors came in mid-1973 when the music industry's biggest magazines such as Rolling Stone, Creem, Circus, Billboard *and* Cash Box *all had stories about him being back in LA working on new material for an upcoming solo album with a 'to be announced' guitarist, bassist and drummer.*

All of this press was due to the behind-the-scenes work of Ray's new manager, a 19-year-old named Danny Sugerman, and his newly formed public relations firm, Flackerty Productions. Danny had earlier become a part of The Doors' world when Jim gave him a job answering fan mail.

Ray recruited Bruce Botnick to produce his album at Sunset Sound. The bass player for the project was Jerry Scheff, who had worked on L.A.Woman. *Ray also brought in jazz drummer Tony Williams and guitarist Larry Carlton to complete the foursome. The resulting release,* The Golden Scarab, *was an Egyptian-themed concept album that Ray described as being inspired by acid and seven years of being a Door.*

RAY *The Golden Scarab* tells the story of a psychic journey. A guy waiting for the Messiah, waiting for someone to show him the way. But in the end he finds he can only do it himself. Take life as it is. Don't judge it. Enjoy it. It's life! Musically it plugs back into the first two Doors albums. It's rock and roll plus Chicago blues, Russian classical, African rhythms, Brazilian rhythms and even Oriental music. But with an aggressive hard-rock foundation.

We made the album like we used to record with The Doors. I had the basic framework, showed the band how the song went and said, 'OK, do whatever you want.'

This page and opposite: Ray Manzarek, Whisky a Go Go, Los Angeles, CA, June 1974

RAY Later, my band Nite City represented the dark side of LA. We weren't the Eagles and we weren't Jackson Browne. We were not part of the laid-back country scene. We were a big-city band. LA is a big city and we were part of both its electricity and its strangeness.

Once you've experienced the joy of creating, and how good it is to play music, and what a thrill it is to play it well enough that you think what you're doing is good, that never leaves. For me, that's the whole point: to bring as many other people as I can into that joyous state of creation. Whoa, that is fun! If we can all do that together, not only can we make great music and enjoy listening to records, we can save the planet. We can take that same energy and go into politics with it. We can affect the direction of America and the world. That's what artists can do.

In 1976, Ray founded Nite City, choosing once again a lead singer he aligned with musically. Noah James became Ray's new voice and Ray in turn provided Noah a bizarre soundtrack on which to overdub lyrics. Together they took an unspoken oath to create a new musical expression for an old topic: truth.

RAY We waited and did not want to hype Morrison's death. [Jim] Croce was bigger in death than in life. Hendrix's albums had people playing on them who had never played with Hendrix. The man is dead. The man is gone. Let him rest in peace until the time when that sensational aspect blows over. We figured that the time was right. It's for Jim. Instead of worrying about a tombstone on his grave, let's give the man a living monument, to his poetry and his abilities as a word spinner. We tried to make a nice package of the whole thing. *An American Prayer* is for an evening's entertainment. You go and buy the album, light a candle, sit back, relax, and read and listen. It's like it was in the Sixties when hearing a new album was an exciting event.

Seven years after Jim Morrison died, and five years after the remaining members of the band broke up, Ray Manzarek, Robby Krieger and John Densmore reunited and recorded backing tracks over Morrison's poetry (originally recorded in 1969–1970) and created The Doors' final studio album, An American Prayer.

Above: Outside the Rock Liberation Festival, Balboa Stadium, San Diego, 13 August 1972
Opposite, top: Jim and Pam in the Hollywood Hills, 1969, an outtake from the shoot used on the cover of An American Prayer
Opposite, bottom: Ray and John on Sunset Boulevard, January 1979

FRANK LISCIANDRO *Jim was dedicated to the idea that he was a poet –he worked on his poems constantly – and he wanted to put them down one night, and his birthday seemed like an appropriate kind of celebration evening to put them on tape.*

RAY On Jim's last birthday, 8 December 1970, he went into the recording studio and treated himself to a birthday present of recording some of his poetry. So we had about four or five hours of stuff from that session, and we also had some other outtakes from the live album. We had things from the movie that he was working on too, *HWY*. So, the job was putting it into an album. Jim's words would set off images in your head and those images would call moods to mind. The feeling we got from it was a primal birth kind of sequence and we felt the music had to be a primeval rhythm – the basic rhythms of sex, of humanity, of creation. I was always seeing things when we played and it was the same with this album. It was full of verbal images that would create pictures in your mind and what we tried to do was match our music to the pictures.

ROBBY The general conception of the album is something that stuck in my mind. It seems more for those who were around Jim in some sense yet it was polarising at the same time mainly due to Jim's passing.

RAY It was like the four of us were doing it. We were laying down the tracks and at a certain point I'd nod over to John Haeny and he'd hit the tape that had Jim's voice on it and in would come Jim on the earphones just as if he was in the vocal booth. A couple of times I looked over as if to go, 'Yeah, man!' and I realised he wasn't there but his presence was there.

ROBBY It's one of my favourite albums. I think we had grown as musicians and we still had Jim's wonderful words to work with.

Do you know the warm progress
under the stars?
Do you know we exist?
Have you forgotten the keys to the Kingdom?
Have you been borne yet
& are you alive?

Let's reinvent the gods, all the myths
of the ages
Celebrate symbols from deep elder forests
[Have you forgotten the lessons
of the ancient war]

We need great golden copulations

The fathers are cackling in trees of the fores
Our mother is dead in sea

Do you know we are being led to
slaughters by placid admirals
& that fat slow generals are getting
obscene on young blood

(2)

Do you know we are ruled by T.V.
The moon is a dry blood beast
Guerrilla bands are rolling numbers
in the next block of green vine
amassing for warfare on innocent herdsmen
who are just dying

O great creator of being
grant us one more hour to
perform our art
& perfect our lives

The moths & atheists are doubly divine
& dying
We live, we die
& death not ends it
Journey we more into the
Nightmare
Cling to life
our passion'd flower
Cling to cunts & cocks
of despair
We got our final vision
by clap
Columbus' groin got
filled w/ green death

RAY This is Jim's story told in Jim's own words, from birth to death. You have Jim Morrison the child, Jim Morrison in high school, Jim Morrison the acid poet at the end of side one. Then the public life of Jim Morrison, The Doors, on side two. Then you hear the concert get insane at the end of the song and that's The Doors' career getting crazy, the concerts getting too crazy for any of us, and Jim finally getting out of that and going on the run. Finally in 'An American Prayer', Jim sums it all up. His great statement at the end. That's what we had in mind with the album.

FRANK LISCIANDRO **THE ALBUM INTRODUCED MORE PEOPLE TO JIM THE POET THAN ANYTHING ELSE.**

(3)

(I touched her thigh
& death smiled)
We have assembled inside this ancient
& insane theatre
To propogate our lust for life
& flee the swarming wisdom
of the streets
The barns are stormed
The windows kept
& only one of all the rest
To dance & save us
w/ the divine mockery
of words
Music inflames temperament
(When the true King's murderers
are allowed to roam free
a 1000 Magicians arise
in the land)
Where are the feasts
we were promised
Where is the wine
The New Wine
(dying on the vine)

(4)

resident mockery
give us an hour for magic
We of the purple glove
We of the starling flight
& velvet hour
We of arabic pleasure's breed
We of sundome & the night
Give us a creed
To believe
A night of Lust
Give us trust in
The Night
Give of color
hundred hues
a rich Mandala
for me & you
& for your silky
pillowed house
a head, wisdom
& a bed
Troubled decree
Resident mockery
has claimed thee

We used to believe
in the good old days
We still receive
In little ways
The Things of Kindness
& unsporting brow
Forget & allow

Did you know freedom exists
in a school book
Did you know madmen are
running our prison
w/in a jail, w/in a gaol
w/in a white free protestant
Maelstrom
We're perched headlong
on the edge of boredom
We're reaching for death
on the end of a candle
We're trying for something
That's already found us

Opposite, top: Jim and Pam in the Hollywood Hills, 1969, an outtake from the shoot used on the cover on An American Prayer
Above: A handwritten extract from Jim's long poem 'An American Prayer', 1969

RAY TO SIT BACK IN AN AUDIENCE AND HEAR 'THE END' COME ON AT THE BEGINNING OF *APOCALYPSE NOW* WAS ABSOLUTELY THRILLING.

ROBBY Expectations were high for the release of Francis Ford Coppola's *Apocalypse Now*, but I was already entranced within the first minute. My guitar line for 'The End' danced over rising orange smoke. Jim's echoing voice cued napalm explosions in the trees. John's rattlesnake tambourine ushered helicopters across the frame. And Ray's Vox Continental organ gently awakened Captain Willard. An irrefutable epic of a film played out, bookended by 'The End', which played once more over an intense, bloody finale that I'm sure Jim would have absolutely loved.

JAC HOLZMAN *Doors records continued to sell steadily after the band broke up. But that multiplied many-fold following* Apocalypse Now. *I think one of the reasons was that there was a certain sympathy to Jim in Coppola's approach to making the film. This was inherent in the structure and tension of the film itself, and, most especially, in the courage with which he put up all of his own money to make that film. He put himself at great risk, just like Jim put himself at great risk in what he did. The use of 'The End' in the opening scene was, I thought, one of the very best marriages of a piece of existing music to a scene that was created free-form.*

JIM KERR *I sat down at the cinema, the curtain pulled back and I started to hear this sound. At first, I thought it was a sequencer, a distant sound getting closer and closer, helicopter blades. And then the intro kicks in of arguably The Doors' greatest theatrical piece as a song, 'The End'. Conceptually, it works beautifully. The allegory of the Vietnam War as this Oedipal situation, a conflict between two generations where the younger generation couldn't make sense of the older generation's decision to go to war. Not only could they not make sense of it, they were being offered up.*

Above: Poster for Apocalypse Now, *1979*
Right: A still from the film
Opposite: Four-track mix tape of 'The End' for use on the Apocalypse Now *soundtrack, as well as a contract between the Doors Music Company and American Zoetrope, the production company of the film's producer and director, Francis Ford Coppola*

JOHN It was an extremely powerful combination of visuals and music – *Rolling Stone* writer Anthony DeCurtis said, 'It is to this day one of the classic uses of music in a movie.' The Doors brand was doing fine, even though Jim was no longer with us.

JAC HOLZMAN *I thought it really had an enormous impact on people's recognition that The Doors were not just a band from the late Sixties up until the time that Jim died in 1971. But were a band with relevance today. I think people understood from hearing the material again that that lean, clean, very spare musical line that they had did not put the music into any time zone. The music was itself timeless.*

JIM KERR *It reintroduced the potency of The Doors' music once again. Going into a new decade The Doors were very much getting the credit they deserved.*

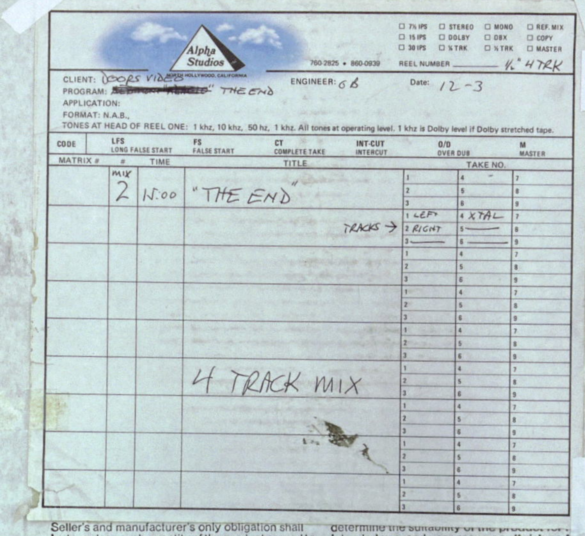

American Zoetrope
July 2, 1979
Page Two

may reduce such royalty to no less than two percent (2%) of suggested retail price of one hundred percent (100%) with regard to a double disc album.

In consideration of the foregoing, you agree that the Album shall be a double disc Album and shall contain two (2) "cuts" (as that term is understood in the record industry) of "The End". You further agree to use your best efforts to cause Elektra/Asylum to sell the Album for a price equivalent to first class double disk albums, and to enforce whatever rights, if any, you may have pursuant to the agreement to cause such first class pricing treatment.

Except as expressly set forth hereinabove, said agreement of 9 January 1978 shall remain in full force and effect.

Sincerely,

RAY MANZAREK

JOHN DENSMORE

ROBERT KRIEGER

COLUMBUS B. COURSON

PEARL M. COURSON

CLARA MORRISON

BY: ADMIRAL GEORGE S. MORRISON

DOORS 1163 THE END MIX #2

efforts to cause Elektra/Asylum to sell the Music Album for a price equivalent to first class single disc albums, and to enforce whatever rights, if any, you may have pursuant to the agreement to cause such first class pricing treatment.

Except as expressly set forth hereinabove, said agreement of 9 January 1978 (as previously amended) shall remain in full force and effect.

Sincerely,

RAY MANZAREK

JOHN DENSMORE

ROBERT KRIEGER

COLUMBUS B. COURSON

PEARL M. COURSON

ROBBY Our *Greatest Hits* album came out in 1980. We decided on fan favourites for the album and most of the time we all agreed. I'm sure a lot of the songs were overlooked – 'Soul Kitchen' for example. *Rolling Stone* put Jim on the cover the following year.

JOHN Our *Greatest Hits* album was so successful, *Rolling Stone* put a photo of Jim on the cover saying: 'HE'S HOT, HE'S SEXY, HE'S DEAD.'

JIM No one is any sexier than anyone else. It's the reporters that create the insanity and make up this stuff and then people start believing it.

The shoot from which Rolling Stone*'s September 1981 Jim Morrison cover photo was taken. The top left image was the one chosen*
Opposite, top: Ray Manzarek, Danny Sugerman and Iggy Pop, Los Angeles, CA, 1974

ROBBY As the Seventies gave way to the Eighties, the release of the *American Prayer* album and *Apocalypse Now* subtly reminded the world of The Doors' existence. Then there was the book.

No One Here Gets Out Alive started with Jerry Hopkins, a *Rolling Stone* writer who had previously covered us. He was a respected journalist and biographer who put together a thoroughly researched manuscript about Jim's life. But every publisher rejected it. Danny Sugerman joined up with Jerry to make the book more appetising.

He was probably one of the biggest Doors fans who ever lived, and Jim was likely the most important and influential figure in his life. But Danny wasn't there. When we met him he wasn't even old enough to get into some of the clubs we were playing. But he claimed to be an insider and punched up Hopkins's manuscript by exaggerating some stories and completely inventing others.

What made things more complicated was that Jerry and Danny had some uncredited help. Bill Siddons would arrive at Danny's house on Doors business to discover Ray sitting behind the typewriter, embellishing the manuscript even further.

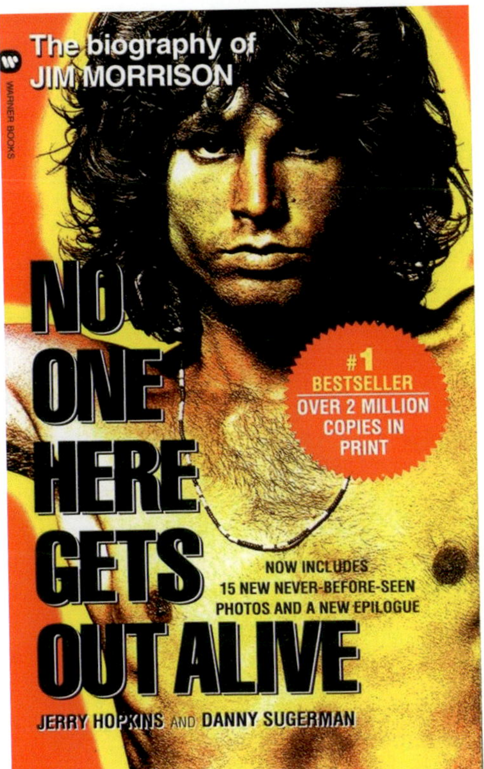

JOHN *No One Here Gets Out Alive* reads as if Jim was a complete asshole, ignoring the genius that went with it. The songs hold up, but Jim's self-destruction has been glamorised.

ROBBY Their plan worked. The book instantly topped the *New York Times* best-seller list.

The source of so many Doors myths can be traced back to Ray. He got the most mileage out of spreading his favourite rumour, the one that had given *No One Here Gets Out Alive* its cliff-hanger ending: maybe Jim's not dead. I used to love talking to Ray, but he would always say, 'I wouldn't be surprised if Jim turned up.' And I used to think, 'Come on, man, you don't really believe that, do you?' It was bullshit.

RAY The French death certificate was signed by only one doctor and claimed Jim's heart stopped. That's all it said. It didn't say what caused his death. I don't know if Jim is dead.

ROBBY Regardless of how noble Ray's intentions may or may not have been, John and I have been sentenced to spending the rest of our days untangling fact from fiction when it comes to our band's history. Long after we're gone, I'm sure some myths will always persist. But thanks to those myths, so will The Doors.

JOHN There was no keyboard player on the planet more appropriate to support Jim Morrison's words. Ray, I felt totally in sync with you musically. It was like we were of one mind, holding down the foundation for Robby and Jim to float on top of. I will miss my musical brother.

ROBBY I'm just glad to have been able to have played Doors songs with him for the last decade. Ray was a huge part of my life and I will always miss him.

ROBBY I think The Doors have remained popular because of the number of great songs. We never let a song on an album unless we all loved it. We weren't really a product of the Sixties. We were more universal than that. When I think of the Sixties, I think of The Mamas & The Papas, Buffalo Springfield, bands like that. The Doors were kind of an anomaly. We didn't really belong in any time frame. I really hope the band is still as popular 50 years from now.

RAY We were just a bunch of psychedelic guys in Venice getting high and making some music. Trying to spread the word and the feel of what it was like to be high in Venice back in the mid-Sixties. And boy was it a good feeling, to watch that sun set into the middle of the ocean and feel that peace, and to feel at one with the universe. It changed my life.

JIM I think some of the ideas and the music were very timely. They seem kind of naive now but I think it was a combination of good musicianship and timeliness. And we may have been one of the first groups to be openly self-conscious about being performers. We were reflecting on our own career as it was happening. It's not that we were trend-conscious, we were doing exactly what we would have been doing anyway, but it came at the right time when you could get away with expressing sentiments like that.

RAY We offered young people an alternative to organised society. It wasn't that we wanted to tear down organised society. It was that we wanted to change it and make it more conducive to human beings.

RAY You don't have to slavishly follow dictates of religion, politics or school. You don't have to slavishly follow the things that adults have told you. You find out what works for you. What you'll find out is that 75 percent of the old dictates, 'Jesus said, "Love thy neighbour as yourself,"' might lead to finding freedom too. It was like what Joseph Campbell the philosopher says: 'Follow your bliss. What you like is what you should be doing.' What an existential leap to dare to be a musician or a writer or an artist.

JOHN We didn't sit down and have a meeting to say, 'Hey, we want to change the minds of people.' We didn't say it but we enjoyed doing it. We could see it happen, we could feel it in concerts – that sociologically, besides musically, it was affecting people. And what a high that is. I'm proud of that.

ROBBY It's an honour to be one of The Doors. The most satisfying thing about being in The Doors is when people tell me that we changed their lives for the better.

JOHN THE DOORS ARE ETCHED ON MY FOREHEAD AND ALWAYS WILL BE.

To the good ones – Thanks
to the rest – you can all
go to Hell.

El DUENDE
Gustavo Dudamel

It is impossible to explain the power of music and what it creates in you because it is very subjective. Even if a song has a sad lyric, for some people it can be inspiring.

I grew up listening to The Doors and what amazed me about this group was of course their connection and the lyrics, but also the rhythm was unique. That was John's creation. Then, when I had the chance to see one of Jim's poetry books, that really made me see another dimension.

For me, it's not that I'm sitting in front of a score and studying what Beethoven, Bach, Mozart or Stravinsky told me. There is something behind the notes that goes far beyond the technical side and that is what conquers me. That is what helps me to survive. The Spanish poet Federico García Lorca wrote a lot about the concept of '*el duende*'. It's this idea of experiencing a heightened state of emotion in reaction to a musical piece or performance. It comes from somewhere within you, affecting you physically, and it is universal, having nothing to do with educational background or requiring a special talent. That uncontrollable response to great artists and their work is not part of some unique formula, it is because they possess *duende*. It's magic.

I did a gala concert and invited John to play and, of course, we did 'L.A. Woman'. It was a remarkable experience and it felt like I was working with the soul of The Doors. Even though it was only John there, I felt like the whole band were present. The beauty of a live performance is the energy that is there in the audience. In that moment you feel you could almost touch that energy. It's the creation of a real, spiritual, energetic universe.

I believe the mission of musicians, whether classical, pop or rock, is to destroy borders, the walls that we sometimes put up around us. Mozart was the popular music of his time and Beethoven was a rock star. He was loved and people went crazy for him. When Stravinsky premiered *The Rite of Spring* in 1913, people started fighting, there was blood. Then you have The Doors, who will go on to become the Mozart, Beethoven and Stravinsky of their time.

ACKNOWLEDGEMENTS

Special thanks to:

The Doors: Jim Morrison, Ray Manzarek, John Densmore and Robby Krieger

Worldwide Management: Jeffrey Jampol and Kenny Nemes for JAM, Inc.

David Dutkowski, archivist for The Doors

Bruce Botnick, Anne Morrison, Tristin Dillon, David Brake, Max Michaels, Gary Greenberg, Alyssa Greenberg, Chris Lohr, Frank Lisciandro, George Rodriguez and Paul Ferrara

A big thank you to Krist Novoselic and Gustavo Dudamel

David Ponak at Rhino Records

Primary Wave

The family of Jim Morrison for use of the Jim Morrison archive

All at Genesis Publications, especially Catherine Roylance, Nick Roylance, Rona Elliot, Katy Baker and Megan Lily Large

Everyone that contributed their thoughts and memories to this book.

Morrison Hotel, Los Angeles, CA, 1971

STUDIO RELEASES

THE DOORS
RELEASED: 4 JANUARY 1967
STUDIO: SUNSET SOUND RECORDERS

LABEL: Elektra
PRODUCER: Paul A. Rothchild
ENGINEER: Bruce Botnick
RECORDED: August–September 1966
LENGTH: 43:34
REISSUES: 40th Anniversary Edition, 50th Anniversary Edition

SIDE A:
1. BREAK ON THROUGH (TO THE OTHER SIDE)
2. SOUL KITCHEN
3. THE CRYSTAL SHIP
4. TWENTIETH CENTURY FOX
5. ALABAMA SONG (WHISKY BAR)
6. LIGHT MY FIRE

SIDE B:
7. BACK DOOR MAN
8. I LOOKED AT YOU
9. END OF THE NIGHT
10. TAKE IT AS IT COMES
11. THE END

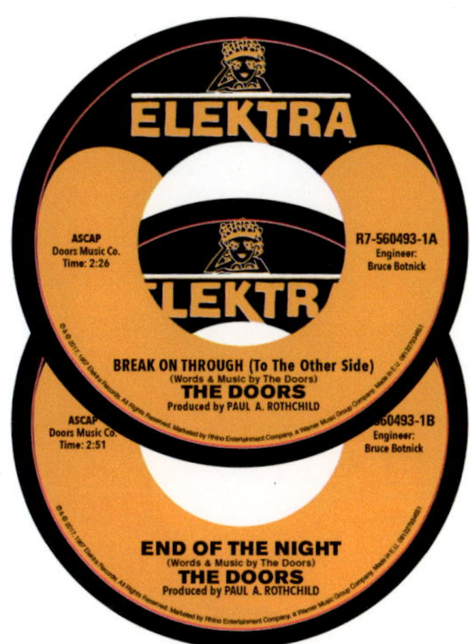

BREAK ON THROUGH (TO THE OTHER SIDE) / END OF THE NIGHT
1 JANUARY 1967

LIGHT MY FIRE / THE CRYSTAL SHIP
24 APRIL 1967

PEOPLE ARE STRANGE / UNHAPPY GIRL
4 SEPTEMBER 1967

LOVE ME TWO TIMES / MOONLIGHT DRIVE
NOVEMBER 1967

STRANGE DAYS
RELEASED: 25 SEPTEMBER 1967
STUDIO: SUNSET SOUND RECORDERS

LABEL: Elektra
PRODUCER: Paul A. Rothchild
ENGINEER: Bruce Botnick
RECORDED: February–August 1967
LENGTH: 34:49
REISSUES: 40th Anniversary Edition, 50th Anniversary Edition

SIDE A:
1. STRANGE DAYS
2. YOU'RE LOST LITTLE GIRL
3. LOVE ME TWO TIMES
4. UNHAPPY GIRL
5. HORSE LATITUDES
6. MOONLIGHT DRIVE

SIDE B:
7. PEOPLE ARE STRANGE
8. MY EYES HAVE SEEN YOU
9. I CAN'T SEE YOUR FACE IN MY MIND
10. WHEN THE MUSIC'S OVER

WAITING FOR THE SUN
RELEASED: 3 JULY 1968
STUDIO: SUNSET SOUND RECORDERS & TTG STUDIOS

LABEL: Elektra
PRODUCER: Paul A. Rothchild
ENGINEER: Bruce Botnick
RECORDED: November 1967–May 1968
LENGTH: 32:49
REISSUES: 40th Anniversary Edition, 50th Anniversary Edition

SIDE A:
1. HELLO, I LOVE YOU
2. LOVE STREET
3. NOT TO TOUCH THE EARTH
4. SUMMER'S ALMOST GONE
5. WINTERTIME LOVE
6. THE UNKNOWN SOLDIER

SIDE B:
7. SPANISH CARAVAN
8. MY WILD LOVE
9. WE COULD BE SO GOOD TOGETHER
10. YES, THE RIVER KNOWS
11. FIVE TO ONE

THE UNKNOWN SOLDIER /
WE COULD BE SO GOOD TOGETHER
MARCH 1968

HELLO, I LOVE YOU / LOVE STREET
11 JUNE 1968

TOUCH ME / WILD CHILD
DECEMBER 1968

WISHFUL SINFUL /
WHO SCARED YOU
MARCH 1969

THE SOFT PARADE
RELEASED: 18 JULY 1969
STUDIO: ELEKTRA SOUND STUDIOS

LABEL: Elektra
PRODUCER: Paul A. Rothchild
ENGINEER: Bruce Botnick
RECORDED: July 1968–May 1969
LENGTH: 33:39
REISSUES: 40th Anniversary Edition, 50th Anniversary Edition

SIDE A:
1. TELL ALL THE PEOPLE
2. TOUCH ME
3. SHAMAN'S BLUES
4. DO IT
5. EASY RIDE

SIDE B:
6. WILD CHILD
7. RUNNIN' BLUE
8. WISHFUL SINFUL
9. THE SOFT PARADE

MORRISON HOTEL
RELEASED: 9 FEBRUARY 1970
STUDIO: ELEKTRA SOUND STUDIOS

LABEL: Elektra
PRODUCER: Paul A. Rothchild
ENGINEER: Bruce Botnick
RECORDED: 19 August 1966 ('Indian Summer') & November 1969 –January 1970
LENGTH: 37:05
REISSUES: 40th Anniversary Edition, 50th Anniversary Edition

SIDE A: HARD ROCK CAFE
1. ROADHOUSE BLUES
2. WAITING FOR THE SUN
3. YOU MAKE ME REAL
4. PEACE FROG
5. BLUE SUNDAY
6. SHIP OF FOOLS

SIDE B: MORRISON HOTEL
7. LAND HO!
8. THE SPY
9. QUEEN OF THE HIGHWAY
10. INDIAN SUMMER
11. MAGGIE M'GILL

TELL ALL THE PEOPLE / EASY RIDE
JUNE 1969

RUNNIN' BLUE / DO IT
AUGUST 1969

YOU MAKE ME REAL / ROADHOUSE BLUES
MARCH 1970

LOVE HER MADLY / (YOU NEED MEAT) DON'T GO NO FURTHER
MARCH 1971

THE DOORS
OTHER VOICES

L.A.WOMAN
RELEASED: 19 APRIL 1971
STUDIO: DOORS WORKSHOP

LABEL: Elektra
PRODUCER: The Doors, Bruce Botnick
ENGINEER: Bruce Botnick
RECORDED: December 1970–January 1971
LENGTH: 48:25
REISSUES: 40th Anniversary Edition, 50th Anniversary Edition

SIDE A:
1. THE CHANGELING
2. LOVE HER MADLY
3. BEEN DOWN SO LONG
4. CARS HISS BY MY WINDOW
5. L.A. WOMAN

SIDE B:
6. L'AMERICA
7. HYACINTH HOUSE
8. CRAWLING KING SNAKE
9. THE WASP (TEXAS RADIO AND THE BIG BEAT)
10. RIDERS ON THE STORM

OTHER VOICES
RELEASED: 18 OCTOBER 1971
STUDIO: DOORS WORKSHOP

LABEL: Elektra
PRODUCER: The Doors, Bruce Botnick
ENGINEER: Bruce Botnick
RECORDED: 1970–1971
LENGTH: 39:42
REISSUES: 2015 CD & vinyl reissue (with *Full Circle*)

SIDE A:
1. IN THE EYE OF THE SUN
2. VARIETY IS THE SPICE OF LIFE
3. SHIPS W/ SAILS
4. TIGHTROPE RIDE

SIDE B:
5. DOWN ON THE FARM
6. I'M HORNY, I'M STONED
7. WANDERING MUSICIAN
8. HANG ON TO YOUR LIFE

RIDERS ON THE STORM / THE CHANGELING
JUNE 1971

TIGHTROPE RIDE / VARIETY IS THE SPICE OF LIFE
OCTOBER 1971

SHIPS W/ SAILS / IN THE EYE OF THE SUN
MAY 1972

GET UP AND DANCE / TREETRUNK
JULY 1972

AN AMERICAN PRAYER
JIM MORRISON
MUSIC BY
THE DOORS

FULL CIRCLE
RELEASED: 15 AUGUST 1972
STUDIO: A&M

LABEL: Elektra
PRODUCER: The Doors
ENGINEER: Henry Lewy
RECORDED: Spring 1972
LENGTH: 40:05
REISSUES: 2015 CD & vinyl reissue (with *Other Voices*)

SIDE A:
1. GET UP AND DANCE
2. 4 BILLION SOULS
3. VERDILAC
4. HARDWOOD FLOOR
5. GOOD ROCKIN'

SIDE B:
6. THE MOSQUITO
7. THE PIANO BIRD
8. IT SLIPPED MY MIND
9. THE PEKING KING AND THE NEW YORK QUEEN

AN AMERICAN PRAYER
RELEASED: 17 NOVEMBER 1978
STUDIO: ELEKTRA SOUND STUDIOS & VILLAGE RECORDERS (POETRY) / HOLLYWOOD SOUND RECORDERS (MUSIC)

LABEL: Elektra/Asylum
PRODUCER: John Haeny, Ray Manzarek, Robby Krieger, John Densmore and Frank Lisciandro
ENGINEER: Henry Lewy
RECORDED: March 1969, December 1970 & 1978
LENGTH: 38:40
REISSUES: 1995 CD reissue

SIDE A:
1. AWAKE: 'GHOST SONG', 'DAWN'S HIGHWAY', 'NEWBORN AWAKENING'
2. TO COME OF AGE: 'BLACK POLISHED CHROME', 'LATINO CHROME', 'ANGELS AND SAILORS', 'STONED IMMACULATE'
3. THE POET'S DREAMS: 'THE MOVIE', 'CURSES, INVOCATIONS'

SIDE B:
4. WORLD ON FIRE: 'AMERICAN NIGHT', 'ROADHOUSE BLUES', 'LAMENT', 'THE HITCHHIKER'
5. AN AMERICAN PRAYER: 'HOUR FOR MAGIC', 'FREEDOM EXISTS', 'A FEAST OF FRIENDS'

THE MOSQUITO / IT SLIPPED MY MIND
AUGUST 1972

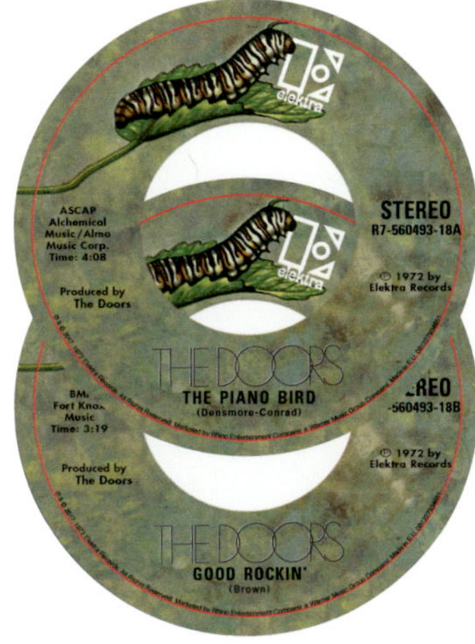

THE PIANO BIRD / GOOD ROCKIN'
FEBRUARY 1973

ROADHOUSE BLUES (LIVE) / ALBINONI: ADAGIO
1978

GLORIA (LIVE) / MOONLIGHT DRIVE (INC. HORSE LATITUDES) (LIVE)
1983

OTHER RELEASES

LIVE ALBUMS
ABSOLUTELY LIVE (1970)
ALIVE, SHE CRIED (1983)
LIVE AT THE HOLLYWOOD BOWL (1987)
IN CONCERT (1991)

ARCHIVE ALBUMS
THE BRIGHT MIDNIGHT SAMPLER (2000)
LIVE IN DETROIT (2000)
BRIGHT MIDNIGHT: LIVE IN AMERICA (2001)
LIVE IN HOLLYWOOD: HIGHLIGHTS FROM THE AQUARIUS THEATRE PERFORMANCES (2001)
LIVE AT THE AQUARIUS THEATRE: THE FIRST PERFORMANCE (2001)
LIVE AT THE AQUARIUS THEATRE: THE SECOND PERFORMANCE (2001)
NO ONE HERE GETS OUT ALIVE (2001)
THE LOST INTERVIEW TAPES FEATURING JIM MORRISON VOL. 1 (2001)
THE LOST INTERVIEW TAPES FEATURING JIM MORRISON VOL. 2 (2002)
BACKSTAGE AND DANGEROUS: THE PRIVATE REHEARSAL (2002)
LIVE IN HOLLYWOOD (2002)
BOOT YER BUTT! THE DOORS BOOTLEGS (2003)
LIVE IN PHILADELPHIA '70 (2005)
SET THE NIGHT ON FIRE: THE DOORS BRIGHT MIDNIGHT ARCHIVES CONCERTS (2006)
LIVE IN BOSTON (2007)
LIVE IN PITTSBURGH 1970 (2008)
LIVE AT THE MATRIX 1967 (2008)
LIVE IN NEW YORK (2009)
LIVE IN VANCOUVER 1970 (2010)
LIVE AT THE BOWL '68 (2012)
STRANGE NIGHTS OF STONE: THE DOORS BRIGHT MIDNIGHT ARCHIVES CONCERTS VOL. II (2013)
LONDON FOG 1966 (2016)
LIVE AT THE ISLE OF WIGHT FESTIVAL 1970 (2018)
LIVE AT THE MATRIX 1967: THE ORIGINAL MASTERS (2023)
LIVE IN BAKERSFIELD: AUGUST 21, 1970 (2023)
LIVE AT KONSERTHUSET, STOCKHOLM, SEPTEMBER 20, 1968 (2024)

COMPILATION ALBUMS
13 (1970)
WEIRD SCENES INSIDE THE GOLD MINE (1972)
THE BEST OF THE DOORS (1973)
STAR COLLECTION (1975)
STAR COLLECTION 2 (1975)
GREATEST HITS (1980)
THE DOORS CLASSICS (1985)
THE BEST OF THE DOORS (1985)
GREATEST HITS (ENHANCED CD 1996) (1996)
ESSENTIAL RARITIES (1999)
THE BEST OF THE DOORS (2000)
THE VERY BEST OF THE DOORS (2001)
LEGACY: THE ABSOLUTE BEST (2003)
THE VERY BEST OF THE DOORS (2007)
SCATTERED SUN (2007)
THE FUTURE STARTS HERE: THE ESSENTIAL DOORS HITS (2008)
THE PLATINUM COLLECTION (2008)
L.A.WOMAN: THE WORKSHOP SESSIONS (2012)
BEHIND CLOSED DOORS: THE RARITIES (2013)
CURATED BY RSD (2014)
THE SINGLES (2017)

POST-DOORS
BUTTS BAND – BUTTS BAND (1973)
RAY MANZAREK – THE GOLDEN SCARAB (1974)
RAY MANZAREK – THE WHOLE THING STARTED WITH ROCK & ROLL NOW IT'S OUT OF CONTROL (1974)
BUTTS BAND – HEAR AND NOW (1975)
NITE CITY – NITE CITY (1977)
ROBBY KRIEGER – ROBBIE KRIEGER & FRIENDS (1977)
NITE CITY – GOLDEN DAYS DIAMOND NIGHTS (1978)
ROBBY KRIEGER – VERSIONS (1982)
RAY MANZAREK – CARMINA BURANA (1983)
ROBBY KRIEGER – ROBBY KRIEGER (1985)
ROBBY KRIEGER – NO HABLA (1989)
ROBBY KRIEGER – DOOR JAMS (1989)
RAY MANZAREK AND MICHAEL McCLURE – LOVE LION (1993)
RAY MANZAREK – THE DOORS, MYTH AND REALITY: THE SPOKEN WORD HISTORY (1996)
DARRYL READ AND RAY MANZAREK – FRESHLY DUG (1999)
ROBBY KRIEGER – CINEMATIX (2000)
RAY MANZAREK AND MICHAEL McCLURE – THERE'S A WORD (2001)
RAY MANZAREK – LOVE HER MADLY (2006)
RAY MANZAREK AND BAL – ATONAL HEAD (2006)
DARRYL READ AND RAY MANZAREK – BLEEDING PARADISE (2007)
RAY MANZAREK AND ROY ROGERS – BALLADS BEFORE THE RAIN (2008)
ROBBY KRIEGER – SINGULARITY (2010)
RAY MANZAREK AND ROY ROGERS – TRANSLUCENT BLUES (2011)
RAY MANZAREK AND MICHAEL McCLURE – THE PIANO POEMS (2012)
RAY MANZAREK AND ROY ROGERS – TWISTED TALES (2013)
ROBBY KRIEGER – THE RITUAL BEGINS AT SUNDOWN (2020)
ROBBY KRIEGER – ROBBY KRIEGER & THE SOUL SAVAGES (2024)

FILM
LOVE THY CUSTOMER (FEATURING THE MUSIC OF THE DOORS) (1966)
BREAK ON THROUGH (1967)
THE UNKNOWN SOLDIER (1968)
FEAST OF FRIENDS (1968)
TRIBUTE TO JIM MORRISON (1981)
DANCE ON FIRE (1985)
LIVE AT THE HOLLYWOOD BOWL (1987)
LIVE IN EUROPE (1988)
THE SOFT PARADE: A RETROSPECTIVE (1991)
THE BEST OF THE DOORS (1997)
THE DOORS ARE OPEN (1998)
THE DOORS COLLECTION (1999)
STORYTELLERS (2001)
NO ONE HERE GETS OUT ALIVE (2001)
SOUNDSTAGE PERFORMANCES (2002)
LIVE IN EUROPE (2004)
CLASSIC ALBUMS: THE DOORS (2008)
WHEN YOU'RE STRANGE (2010)
MR. MOJO RISIN': THE STORY OF L.A.WOMAN (2011)
LIVE AT THE BOWL '68 (2012)
R-EVOLUTION (2013)
FEAST OF FRIENDS (2014)
LIVE AT THE ISLE OF WIGHT FESTIVAL 1970 (2018)
BREAK ON THRU, CELEBRATION OF RAY MANZAREK AND THE DOORS (2018)

TV APPEARANCES

BOSS CITY
RECORDED FEBRUARY 1967
AIR DATE 18 FEBRUARY 1967
LOCATION KHJ-TV STUDIOS, 5515 MELROSE AVENUE, HOLLYWOOD, CA

KTLA'S SHEBANG
RECORDED 25 FEBRUARY 1967
AIR DATE UNKNOWN
LOCATION KTLA STUDIOS, 5800 SUNSET BOULEVARD, LOS ANGELES, CA

CLAY COLE'S DISKOTEK
RECORDED MARCH 1967
AIR DATE 1 APRIL 1967
LOCATION WPIX STUDIOS, 220 E. 42ND STREET, NEW YORK, NY

BOSS CITY
RECORDED MAY 1967
AIR DATE 20 MAY 1967
LOCATION KHJ-TV STUDIOS, 5515 MELROSE AVENUE, HOLLYWOOD, CA

CLAY COLE'S DISKOTEK
RECORDED 13 JUNE 1967
AIR DATE 24 JUNE 1967
LOCATION WPIX STUDIOS, 220 E. 42ND STREET, NEW YORK, NY

DISC-O-TEEN
RECORDED 15 JUNE 1967
AIR DATE 15 JUNE 1967
LOCATION MOSQUE THEATRE, 1020 BROAD STREET, NEWARK, NJ

AMERICAN BANDSTAND
RECORDED 12 JULY 1967
AIR DATE 22 JULY 1967
LOCATION KABC STUDIOS, 4151 PROSPECT AVENUE, LOS ANGELES, CA

MALIBU U
RECORDED AUGUST 1967
AIR DATE 25 AUGUST 1967
LOCATION LEO CARRILLO STATE BEACH, 9000 BUILDING, HOLLYWOOD, CA

THE ROCK SCENE – LIKE IT IS!
RECORDED 8 AUGUST 1967
AIR DATE 16 OCTOBER 1967
LOCATION CBC STUDIO 7, 263 MUTUAL STREET, TORONTO, CA

MURRAY THE K IN NEW YORK
RECORDED SEPTEMBER 1967
AIR DATE 22 SEPTEMBER 1967
LOCATION NEW YORK, NY

THE ED SULLIVAN SHOW
RECORDED 17 SEPTEMBER 1967
AIR DATE 17 SEPTEMBER 1967
LOCATION CBS STUDIO 50/ED SULLIVAN THEATRE, NEW YORK, NY

BRUCE MARROW'S MUSIC POWER
RECORDED 29 SEPTEMBER 1967
AIR DATE 8 NOVEMBER 1967
LOCATION UNIVERSITY OF DENVER, CO

THE JONATHAN WINTERS SHOW
RECORDED 4 DECEMBER 1967
AIR DATE 27 DECEMBER 1967
LOCATION STAGE 43, CBS TELEVISION CITY, LOS ANGELES, CA

THE WAY IT IS
RECORDED 20 APRIL 1968
AIR DATE 26 MAY 1968
LOCATION CBC STUDIOS, TORONTO, CANADA

HY LIT SHOW
RECORDED AUGUST 1968
AIR DATE AUGUST 1968
LOCATION WKBS STUDIOS, 3201 S. 26TH STREET, PHILADELPHIA, PA

TOP OF THE POPS
RECORDED 5 SEPTEMBER 1968
AIR DATE 5 SEPTEMBER 1968
LOCATION LIME GROVE STUDIOS, LONDON, UK

THE DOORS ARE OPEN
RECORDED 3–7 SEPTEMBER 1968
AIR DATE 17 DECEMBER 1968
LOCATION LONDON, UK

4-3-2-1 HOT AND SWEET
RECORDED 13 SEPTEMBER 1968
AIR DATE 14 SEPTEMBER 1968
LOCATION RÖMERBERG, FRANKFURT, GERMANY

BEAT-CLUB
RECORDED 14 SEPTEMBER 1968
AIR DATE 25 JANUARY 1969
LOCATION KONGRESSHALLE, FRANKFURT, GERMNAY

DANISH TELEVISION
RECORDED 18 SEPTEMBER 1968
AIR DATE 30 OCTOBER 1968
LOCATION GLADSAXE-BYEN STUDIOS, COPENHAGEN, DENMARK

THE SMOTHERS BROTHERS COMEDY HOUR
RECORDED 6 DECEMBER 1968
AIR DATE 15 DECEMBER 1968
LOCATION STAGE 33, CBS TELEVISION CITY, LOS ANGELES, CA

CRITIQUE
RECORDED 28_29 APRIL 1969
AIR DATE 25 JUNE 1969
LOCATION NEW YORK, NY

GTK (GET TO KNOW)
RECORDED NOVEMBER 1970
AIR DATE DECEMBER 1970
LOCATION THE DOORS WORKSHOP, LOS ANGELES, CA

POP HOT
RECORDED 30 APRIL 1972
AIR DATE 16 SEPTEMBER 1972
LOCATION PAVILLON MONTREUX, MONTREUX, SWITZERLAND

BEAT-CLUB
RECORDED 3 MARCH 1972
AIR DATE 27 MAY 1972
LOCATION RADIO BREMEN STUDIO 3, BREMEN, DENMARK

OLD GREY WHISTLE TEST
RECORDED 9 MAY 1972
AIR DATE 9 MAY 1972
LOCATION PRES. B. STUDIO, BBC TELEVISION CENTRE, LONDON, UK

THE DICK CAVETT SHOW
RECORDED 24 AUGUST 1972
AIR DATE 25 AUGUST 1972
LOCATION ABC STUDIOS, 58TH STREET, NEW YORK, NY

TOUR HISTORY

1965
14 OCTOBER
PIONEER CLUB,
HARBOR CRUISE
SAN DIEGO, CA, US

NOVEMBER
HUGHES AIRCRAFT
UNION DANCE
LOS ANGELES, CA, US

18 DECEMBER
ROYCE HALL
AUDITORIUM, UCLA
WESTWOOD, CA, US

31 DECEMBER
PRIVATE SHOW
LOS ANGELES, CA, US

1966
JANUARY
MOONFIRE RANCH
TOPANGA, CA, US

FEBRUARY
VALLEY TEEN CENTER
VAN NUYS, CA, US

MARCH–MAY
LONDON FOG (HOUSE
BAND)
WEST HOLLYWOOD, CA, US

23 APRIL
WILL ROGERS STATE PARK
LOS ANGELES, CA, US

6–7 MAY
WARNER PLAYHOUSE
WEST HOLLYWOOD, CA, US

EARLY/MID MAY
WHISKY A GO GO
WEST HOLLYWOOD, CA, US

12–14 MAY
BRAVE NEW WORLD
LOS ANGELES, CA, US

13–14 MAY
WARNER PLAYHOUSE
WEST HOLLYWOOD, CA, US

15 MAY
STARLIGHT BALLROOM
OXNARD, CA, US

19 MAY
BETTY'S MUSIC
VENICE, CA, US

23 MAY–21 AUGUST
WHISKY A GO GO (HOUSE
BAND)
WEST HOLLYWOOD, CA, US

30 MAY
HULLABALOO
HOLLYWOOD, CA, US

JUNE
PANDORA'S BOX
WEST HOLLYWOOD, CA, US

21 JULY
ROSE BOWL
PASADENA, CA, US

28 JULY
STARLIGHT BALLROOM
OXNARD, CA, US

JULY
EARL WARREN
SHOWGROUNDS
SANTA BARBARA, CA, US

29_31 JULY
FIFTH ESTATE
TEMPE, AZ, US

5 AUGUST
STARLIGHT BALLROOM
OXNARD, CA, US

6 AUGUST
EARL WARREN
SHOWGROUNDS
SANTA BARBARA, CA, US

SEPTEMBER
CINNAMON CINDER
STUDIO CITY, CA, US

SEPTEMBER
BIDO LITO'S
HOLLYWOOD, CA, US

24 OCTOBER
ONDINE
NEW YORK, NY, US

1–27 NOVEMBER
ONDINE
NEW YORK, NY, US

9–10 DECEMBER
SEA WITCH
WEST HOLLYWOOD, CA, US

16–17 DECEMBER
SEA WITCH
WEST HOLLYWOOD, CA, US

31 DECEMBER
CASA DORINDA
MONTECITO, CA, US

1967
6–8 JANUARY
FILLMORE AUDITORIUM
SAN FRANCISCO, CA, US

13–15 JANUARY
FILLMORE AUDITORIUM
SAN FRANCISCO, CA, US

31 JANUARY-2 FEBRUARY
GAZZARRI'S
WEST HOLLYWOOD, CA, US

10 FEBRUARY
MODESTO SKATE ARENA
MODESTO, CA, US

14–15 FEBRUARY
WHISKY A GO GO
SAN FRANCISCO, CA, US

21 FEBRUARY
GAZZARRI'S
WEST HOLLYWOOD, CA, US

22 FEBRUARY
VALLEY MUSIC THEATRE
WOODLAND HILLS, CA, US

23–28 FEBRUARY
GAZZARRI'S
WEST HOLLYWOOD, CA, US

25 FEBRUARY
GREEK THEATRE,
GRIFFITH PARK
BURBANK, CA, US

25 FEBRUARY
HULLABALOO
HOLLYWOOD, CA, US

2 MARCH
GAZZARRI'S
WEST HOLLYWOOD, CA, US

3-4 MARCH
AVALON BALLROOM
SAN FRANCISCO, CA, US

7–11 MARCH
THE MATRIX
SAN FRANCISCO, CA, US

13 MARCH–2 APRIL
ONDINE
NEW YORK, NY, US

7 APRIL
AMERICAN LEGION HALL
MERCED, CA, US

8 APRIL
TURLOCK FAIRGROUNDS
TURLOCK, CA, US

9 APRIL
CHEETAH
SANTA MONICA, CA, US

14–5 APRIL
AVALON BALLROOM
SAN FRANCISCO, CA, US

21–23 APRIL
KALEIDOSCOPE AT CIRO'S
WEST HOLLYWOOD, CA, US

28 APRIL
MONROVIA HIGH SCHOOL
MONROVIA, CA, US

29 APRIL
EARL WARREN
SHOWGROUNDS
SANTA BARBARA, CA, US

7 MAY
VALLEY MUSIC THEATRE
WOODLAND HILLS, CA, US

12–13 MAY
AVALON BALLROOM
SAN FRANCISCO, CA, US

14 MAY
CHEETAH
SANTA MONICA, CA, US

16–21 MAY
WHISKY A GO GO
WEST HOLLYWOOD, CA, US

20 MAY
BIRMINGHAM STADIUM
VAN NUYS, CA, US

26 MAY
CRESCENTA VALLEY HIGH
SCHOOL
LA CRESCENTA, CA, US

27 MAY
DARBY PARK
RECREATION CENTER
INGLEWOOD, CA, US

27 MAY
EARL WARREN
SHOWGROUNDS
SANTA BARBARA, CA, US

3–4 JUNE
AVALON BALLROOM
SAN FRANCISCO, CA, US

8 JUNE
AMERICAN LEGION HALL
MERCED, CA, US

9 JUNE
FILLMORE AUDITORIUM
SAN FRANCISCO, CA, US

10 JUNE
FANTASY FAIR & MAGIC
MOUNTAIN MUSIC FESTIVAL
MILL VALLEY, CA, US

10 JUNE
FILLMORE AUDITORIUM
SAN FRANCISCO, CA, US

11 JUNE
VILLAGE THEATRE
NEW YORK, NY, US

12–15 JUNE
SCENE
NEW YORK, NY, US

16–17 JUNE
ACTION HOUSE
ISLAND PARK, NY, US

18 JUNE
TOWN HALL
PHILADELPHIA, PA, US

19 JUNE–1 JULY
SCENE
NEW YORK, NY, US

3 JULY
SANTA MONICA
CIVIC AUDITORIUM
SANTA MONICA, CA, US

4 JULY
KAISER DOME
SAN BERNARDINO, CA, US

5 JULY
LOWELL HIGH SCHOOL
WHITTIER, CA, US

6 JULY
SELLAND ARENA, FRESNO
CONVENTION CENTER
FRESNO, CA, US

8 JULY
BALBOA STADIUM
SAN DIEGO, CA, US

13 JULY
CIVIC AUDITORIUM
OAKLAND, CA, US

14 JULY
CALIFORNIA STATE
FAIR GRANDSTAND
SACRAMENTO, CA, US

15 JULY
FANTASY FAIRE & MAGIC MUSIC FESTIVAL
NORTHRIDGE, CA, US

15 JULY
ANAHEIM CONVENTION CENTER ARENA
ANAHEIM, CA, US

20 JULY
VICTORIA MEMORIAL ARENA
VICTORIA, BC, CANADA

21–22 JULY
DANTE'S INFERNO
VANCOUVER, BC, CANADA

23–24 JULY
EAGLES AUDITORIUM
SEATTLE, WA, US

26 JULY
PORTLAND MASONIC TEMPLE
PORTLAND, OR, US

27 JULY
SALEM ARMORY AUDITORIUM
SALEM, OR, US

28–30 JULY
FILLMORE AUDITORIUM
SAN FRANCISCO, CA, US

5 AUGUST
EARL WARREN SHOWGROUNDS
SANTA BARBARA, CA, US

10–11 AUGUST
CROSSTOWN BUS
BRIGHTON, MA, US

12 AUGUST
FOREST HILLS TENNIS STADIUM
FOREST HILLS, NY, US

15 AUGUST
COMMODORE BALLROOM
LOWELL, MA, US

18 AUGUST
ANNAPOLIS NATIONAL GUARD ARMORY
ANNAPOLIS, MD, US

18 AUGUST
ALEXANDRIA ROLLER RINK ARENA
ALEXANDRIA, VA, US

19 AUGUST
HAMPTON BEACH CASINO
HAMPTON BEACH, NH, US

25 AUGUST
LAS VEGAS CONVENTION CENTER
LAS VEGAS, NV, US

27 AUGUST
CHEETAH
SANTA MONICA, CA, US

2 SEPTEMBER
ASBURY PARK CONVENTION HALL
ASBURY PARK, NJ, US

3–4 SEPTEMBER
WILL ROGERS EXHIBIT BUILDING
FORT WORTH, TX, US

8 SEPTEMBER
LAGOON PATIO GARDENS
FARMINGTON, UT, US

9 SEPTEMBER
VILLAGE THEATRE
NEW YORK, NY, US

11 SEPTEMBER
OSWEGO LEE HALL, STATE UNIVERSITY OF NY
OSWEGO, NY, US

13 SEPTEMBER
CANTON HIGH SCHOOL
CANTON, IL, US

14 SEPTEMBER
MUSICARNIVAL
WARRENSVILLE HEIGHTS, OH, US

21 SEPTEMBER
STAPLES HIGH SCHOOL
WESTPORT, CT, US

22 SEPTEMBER
MEEHAN AUDITORIUM, BROWN UNIVERSITY
PROVIDENCE, RI, US

23 SEPTEMBER
STONY BROOK UNIVERSITY
STONY BROOK, NY, US

24 SEPTEMBER
OAKDALE MUSIC FAIR
WALLINGFORD, CT, US

27 SEPTEMBER
KRNT THEATER
DES MOINES, IA, US

29 SEPTEMBER
UNIVERSITY OF DENVER
DENVER, CO, US

30 SEPTEMBER
THE FAMILY DOG
DENVER, CO, US

6 OCTOBER
EAGLES NEST GYMNASIUM, CALIFORNIA STATE COLLEGE
LOS ANGELES, CA, US

7 OCTOBER
HI CORBETT FIELD
TUCSON, AZ, US

8 OCTOBER
TULSA ASSEMBLY CENTER
TULSA, OK, US

11 OCTOBER
DANBURY HIGH SCHOOL
DANBURY, CT, US

12 OCTOBER
SURF
HULL, MA, US

13 OCTOBER
LYRIC THEATRE
BALTIMORE, MD, US

14 OCTOBER
WEBER CHAPEL AUDITORIUM, SUSQUEHANNA UNIVERSITY
SELINSGROVE, PA, US

15 OCTOBER
BERKELEY COMMUNITY THEATRE
BERKELEY, CA, US

20 OCTOBER
INTRAMURAL SPORTS BUILDING, UNIVERSITY OF MICHIGAN
ANN ARBOR, MI, US

21 OCTOBER
BROADMOOR HOTEL BALLROOM
COLORADO SPRINGS, CO, US

27 OCTOBER
CALIFORNIA POLYTECHNIC STATE UNIVERSITY
SAN LUIS OBISPO, CA, US

28 OCTOBER
ROBERTSON GYM, UNIVERSITY OF CALIFORNIA
GOLETA, CA, US

3 NOVEMBER
CONTINENTAL BALLROOM
SANTA CLARA, CA, US

4 NOVEMBER
COMMUNITY CONCOURSE GOLDEN HALL
SAN DIEGO, CA, US

10 NOVEMBER
EAGLES AUDITORIUM
SEATTLE, WA, US

11 NOVEMBER
GILL COLISEUM, OREGON STATE UNIVERSITY
CORVALLIS, OR, US

16 NOVEMBER
FILLMORE AUDITORIUM
SAN FRANCISCO, CA, US

17–18 NOVEMBER
WINTERLAND
SAN FRANCISCO, CA, US

24 NOVEMBER
HUNTER COLLEGE
NEW YORK, NY, US

25 NOVEMBER
INTERNATIONAL BALLROOM, HILTON HOTEL
WASHINGTON DC, US

26 NOVEMBER
BUSHNELL MEMORIAL AUDITORIUM
HARTFORD, CT, US

1 DECEMBER
CAL STATE MEN'S GYM
LONG BEACH, CA, US

2 DECEMBER
PORTLAND MEMORIAL COLISEUM
PORTLAND, OR, US

8 DECEMBER
HOUSTON FIELD HOUSE, RENSSELAER POLYTECHNIC INSTITUTE
TROY, NY, US

9 DECEMBER
NEW HAVEN ARENA
NEW HAVEN, CT, US

15 DECEMBER
SACRAMENTO MEMORIAL AUDITORIUM
SACRAMENTO, CA, US

16 DECEMBER
SWING AUDITORIUM
SAN BERNARDINO, CA, US

22–23 DECEMBER
SHRINE EXPOSITION HALL
LOS ANGELES, CA, US

26–28 DECEMBER
WINTERLAND
SAN FRANCISCO, CA, US

29–31 DECEMBER
FAMILY DOG
DENVER, CO, US

1968

19–20 JANUARY
CAROUSEL THEATRE
WEST COVINA, CA, US

10 FEBRUARY
BERKELEY COMMUNITY THEATRE
BERKELEY, CA, US

17 FEBRUARY
ARIZONA VETERANS MEMORIAL COLISEUM
PHOENIX, AZ, US

15 MARCH
COLGATE UNIVERSITY
HAMILTON, NY, US

16 MARCH
EASTMAN THEATRE
ROCHESTER, NY, US

17 MARCH
BACK BAY THEATRE
BOSTON, MA, US

22–23 MARCH
FILLMORE EAST
NEW YORK, NY, US

29 MARCH
KALEIDOSCOPE
HOLLYWOOD, CA, US

11 APRIL
KALEIDOSCOPE
HOLLYWOOD, CA, US

13 APRIL
SONOMA COUNTY FAIRGROUNDS
SANTA ROSA, CA, US

19 APRIL
WESTBURY MUSIC FAIR
WESTBURY, NY, US

20 APRIL
CNE COLISEUM
TORONTO, ON, CAN

10 MAY
CHICAGO COLISEUM
CHICAGO, IL, US

11 MAY
COBO ARENA
DETROIT, MI, US

19 MAY
SANTA CLARA
COUNTY FAIRGROUNDS
SAN JOSE, CA, US

24 MAY
HI CORBETT FIELD
TUCSON, AZ, US

25 MAY
LAGOON PATIO GARDENS
FARMINGTON, UT, US

7 JUNE
FRESNO DISTRICT
FAIRGROUND
FRESNO, CA, US

8 JUNE
BAKERSFIELD CIVIC
AUDITORIUM
BAKERSFIELD, CA, US

15 JUNE
SACRAMENTO MEMORIAL
AUDITORIUM
SACRAMENTO, CA, US

28 JUNE
LA PLAYA STADIUM
SANTA BARBARA, CA, US

29 JUNE
COMMUNITY CONCOURSE
GOLDEN HALL
SAN DIEGO, CA, US

30 JUNE
BRUCE BOTNICK'S
WEDDING
LOS ANGELES, CA, US

5 JULY
HOLLYWOOD BOWL
HOLLYWOOD, CA, US

6 JULY
KALEIDOSCOPE
HOLLYWOOD, CA, US

9 JULY
DALLAS MEMORIAL
AUDITORIUM
DALLAS, TX, US

10 JULY
SAM HOUSTON COLISEUM
HOUSTON, TX, US

12 JULY
SEATTLE CENTER ARENA
SEATTLE, WA, US

13 JULY
PACIFIC COLISEUM
VANCOUVER, BC, CANADA

20 JULY
HONOLULU INTERNATIONAL
CENTER ARENA
HONOLULU, HI, US

1 AUGUST
JOHN F. KENNEDY STADIUM
BRIDGEPORT, CT, US

2 AUGUST
SINGER BOWL
FLUSHING, NY, US

3 AUGUST
CLEVELAND PUBLIC
AUDITORIUM
CLEVELAND, OH, US

4 AUGUST
ARENA
PHILADELPHIA, PA, US

30 AUGUST
MERRIWEATHER
POST PAVILION
COLUMBIA, MD, US

31 AUGUST
ASBURY PARK
CONVENTION HALL
ASBURY PARK, NJ, US

1 SEPTEMBER
SARATOGA PERFORMING
ARTS CENTER
SARATOGA SPRINGS, NY, US

6–7 SEPTEMBER
ROUNDHOUSE
LONDON, UK

14 SEPTEMBER
KONGRESSHALLE
FRANKFURT, GERMANY

15 SEPTEMBER
CONCERTGEBOUW
AMSTERDAM,
NETHERLANDS

17 SEPTEMBER
FALKONER CENTRET
COPENHAGEN, DENMARK

20 SEPTEMBER
KONSERTHUSET
STOCKHOLM, SWEDEN

31 OCTOBER
FREEDOM HALL
LOUISVILLE, KY, US

1 NOVEMBER
MILWAUKEE ARENA
MILWAUKEE, WI, US

2 NOVEMBER
VETERANS MEMORIAL
AUDITORIUM
COLUMBUS, OH, US

3 NOVEMBER
CHICAGO MUSEUM
CHICAGO, IL, US

7 NOVEMBER
ARIZONA VETERANS
MEMORIAL COLISEUM
PHOENIX, AZ, US

8 NOVEMBER
DANE COUNTY
MEMORIAL COLISEUM
MADISON, WI

9 NOVEMBER
KIEL AUDITORIUM
CONVENTION HALL
ST LOUIS, MO, US

10 NOVEMBER
MINNEAPOLIS
AUDITORIUM
MINNEAPOLIS, MN, US

14 DECEMBER
THE FORUM
INGLEWOOD, CA, US

1969

24 JANUARY
MADISON SQUARE GARDEN
NEW YORK, NY, US

1 MARCH
DINNER KEY AUDITORIUM
MIAMI, FL, US

14 JUNE
AUDITORIUM THEATRE
CHICAGO, IL, US

15 JUNE
MINNEAPOLIS
AUDITORIUM
MINNEAPOLIS, MN, US

27-30 JUNE
THE FORUM
MEXICO CITY, MEXICO

21 JULY
AQUARIUS THEATRE
HOLLYWOOD, CA, US

25 JULY
COW PALACE
DALY CITY, CA, US

26 JULY
HAYWARD FIELD
EUGENE, OR, US

27 JULY
GOLD CREEK PARK
WOODINVILLE, WA, US

13 SEPTEMBER
VARSITY STADIUM
TORONTO, ON, CANADA

14 SEPTEMBER
MONTREAL FORUM
MONTREAL, QC, CANADA

19 SEPTEMBER
PHILADELPHIA ARENA
PHILADELPHIA, PA, US

20 SEPTEMBER
PITTSBURGH CIVIC ARENA
PITTSBURGH, PA, US

4 OCTOBER
ICE PALACE
LAS VEGAS, NV, US

1970

17–18 JANUARY
FELT FORUM
NEW YORK, NY, US

5–6 FEBRUARY
WINTERLAND
SAN FRANCISCO, CA, US

7 FEBRUARY
LONG BEACH ARENA
LONG BEACH, CA, US

13–14 FEBRUARY
ALLEN THEATRE
CLEVELAND, OH, US

15 FEBRUARY
AUDITORIUM THEATRE
CHICAGO, IL, US

10 APRIL
BOSTON ARENA
BOSTON, MA, US

12 APRIL
UNIVERSITY OF DENVER
DENVER, CO, US

18 APRIL
HONOLULU INTERNATIONAL
CENTER
HONOLULU, HI, US

1 MAY
SPECTRUM
PHILADELPHIA, PA, US

2 MAY
PITTSBURGH CIVIC ARENA
PITTSBURGH, PA, US

8 MAY
COBO ARENA
DETROIT, MI, US

10 MAY
BALTIMORE CIVIC CENTER
BALTIMORE, MD, US

5 JUNE
SEATTLE CENTER COLISEUM
SEATTLE, WA, US

6 JUNE
PACIFIC COLISEUM
VANCOUVER, BC, CANADA

21 AUGUST
BAKERSFIELD
CIVIC AUDITORIUM
BAKERSFIELD, CA, US

22 AUGUST
SAN DIEGO SPORTS ARENA
SAN DIEGO, CA, US

30 AUGUST
ISLE OF WIGHT FESTIVAL
ISLE OF WIGHT, UK

11 DECEMBER
STATE FAIR MUSIC HALL
DALLAS, TX, US

12 DECEMBER
A WAREHOUSE
NEW ORLEANS, LA, US

1971

12 NOVEMBER
PERSHING MUNICIPAL
AUDITORIUM
LINCOLN, NE, US

13 NOVEMBER
AUGSBURG COLLEGE
MINNEAPOLIS, MN, US

14 NOVEMBER
ST LAWRENCE HALL
TORONTO, ON, CANADA

18 NOVEMBER
PEACE BRIDGE
EXHIBITION CENTER
BUFFALO, NY, US

20 NOVEMBER
EASTOWN THEATRE
DETROIT, MI, US

22 NOVEMBER
BOSTON MUSIC HALL
BOSTON, MA, US

23 NOVEMBER
CARNEGIE HALL
NEW YORK, NY, US

24 NOVEMBER
IRVINE AUDITORIUM
PHILADELPHIA, PA, US

26 NOVEMBER 1971
HOLLYWOOD PALLADIUM
HOLLYWOOD, CA, US

2 DECEMBER
BERKELEY COMMUNITY THEATRE
BERKELEY, CA, US

1972

7 JANUARY
AERIAL TRAMWAY LODGE
PALM SPRINGS, CA, US

2 MARCH
DOME AUDITORIUM, C.W. POST COLLEGE
GREENVALE, NY, US

3 MARCH
PAINTERS MILL MUSIC FAIR
OWINGS MILLS, MD, US

4 MARCH
COLLEGE OF WILLIAM AND MARY HALL
WILLIAMSBURG, VA, US

5 MARCH
COUNTY HALL
CHARLESTON, SC, US

8 MARCH
CAROLINA COLISEUM
COLUMBIA, SC, US

10 MARCH
PIRATES WORLD
DANIA, FL, US

11 MARCH
DOAK CAMPBELL STADIUM, FLORIDA STATE UNIVERSITY
TALLAHASSEE, FL, US

12 MARCH
FORT HOMER W. HESTERLY ARMORY
TAMPA, FL, US

8 APRIL
RATCLIFFE STADIUM, FRESNO CITY COLLEGE
FRESNO, CA, US

27 APRIL
FALKONER CENTRET
COPENHAGEN, DENMARK

28 APRIL
CIRCUS KRONE BAU
MUNICH, GERMANY

29 APRIL
JAHRHUNDERTHALLE
FRANKFURT, GERMANY

30 APRIL
PAVILLON MONTREUX
MONTREUX, SWITZERLAND

1 MAY
PARIS OLYMPIA
PARIS, FRANCE

5 MAY
SALLE DE LA MADELEINE
BRUSSELS, BELGIUM

6 MAY
DE DOELEN
ROTTERDAM, NETHERLANDS

7 MAY
THEATER CARRE
AMSTERDAM, NL

10 MAY
NEWCASTLE CITY HALL
NEWCASTLE, UK

11 MAY
KINETIC CIRCUS
BIRMINGHAM, UK

12 MAY
GREAT HALL, IMPERIAL COLLEGE
LONDON, UK

13 MAY
UNIVERSITY OF READING
READING, UK

14 MAY
GUILDFORD CIVIC HALL
GUILDFORD, UK

21 JULY
ARAGON BALLROOM
CHICAGO, IL, US

22 JULY
TYNDALL ARMORY
INDIANAPOLIS, IN, US

23 JULY
SUMMERFEST AMPHITHEATER
MILWAUKEE, WI, US

13 AUGUST
BALBOA STADIUM
SAN DIEGO, CA, US

16 AUGUST
BOSTON COMMON
BOSTON, MA, US

18 AUGUST
DILLON STADIUM
HARTFORD, CT, US

19 AUGUST
PALACE THEATRE
PROVIDENCE, RI, US

20 AUGUST
DAR CONSTITUTION HALL
WASHINGTON, DC, US

21 AUGUST
WOLLMAN RINK, CENTRAL PARK
NEW YORK, NY, US

23 AUGUST
RITZ THEATRE
STATEN ISLAND, NY, US

24 AUGUST
NORFOLK CITY HALL
NORFOLK, VA, US

27 AUGUST
COUNTY MUSIC HALL
MEMPHIS, TN, US

1 SEPTEMBER
MAJESTIC THEATRE
DALLAS, TX, US

2 SEPTEMBER
MUNICIPAL AUDITORIUM
NEW ORLEANS, LA, US

3 SEPTEMBER
MICHIGAN PALACE
DETROIT, MI, US

4 SEPTEMBER
CHANDLER RACEWAY PARK
CHANDLER, IN, US

10 SEPTEMBER
HOLLYWOOD BOWL
HOLLYWOOD, CA, US

CONTRIBUTORS

BRUCE BOTNICK *is an engineer and producer. With a calm, supportive demeanour and superb technical skills, Botnick engineered the first five Doors studio albums. It was these qualities that made him a perfect fit to take over as producer for the band's last album with Jim Morrison,* L.A.Woman. *His idea to record at The Doors' office and rehearsal space, where the band was more comfortable than in the studio, helped create the conditions for one of their finest albums.*

Botnick also produced Other Voices, *the first Doors album after Jim Morrison's death, and (with Paul Rothchild) remastered the extended 1995 rerelease of Jim Morrison's spoken word album* An American Prayer.

ALICE COOPER *is a pioneer in theatrical heavy metal/hard rock. Drawing from horror movies, vaudeville and garage rock, Cooper and his band of the same name created a stage show that featured electric chairs, guillotines, fake blood, boa constrictors, tacky make-up and outrageous outfits. Cooper's stage shows, both in the band and later as a solo artist, have rattled cages for generations.*

Cooper became friends with the The Doors and particularly Jim when both bands were just starting out, and attended some of their recording sessions, including the take of 'The End' that is featured on the band's first album.

HENRY DILTZ *is one of rock and roll's most beloved and respected photographers. Since the mid-Sixties, his iconic images have appeared in* Rolling Stone, Life, People, *the* Los Angeles Times *and the* New York Times, *and have graced more than 200 album covers, including The Doors'* Morrison Hotel.

GUSTAVO DUDAMEL *is a violinist and conductor and currently the music director of the Simón Bolívar Symphony Orchestra and the Los Angeles Philharmonic. A fan of The Doors' music since he was young, Dudamel became friends with John Densmore after the pair met backstage following an LA Philharmonic concert. In 2019, Densmore was invited on stage to play 'L.A. Woman' with the LA Philharmonic.*

DAVID DUTKOWSKI *is the official archivist for The Doors, Robby Krieger, and the Ray Manzarek Estate. After being hired by Danny Sugerman in the Nineties, David has been continually working with The Doors as historian, caretaker of the band's audio/film and photo archives, and has assisted on all Doors projects. David is also the creator of The Doors' official mobile app, The Doors.ai.*

PERRY FARRELL *is a singer, songwriter and philanthropist, and has revolutionised alternative music, underground culture and modern festivals. The ground-breaking alt-rock band Jane's Addiction was Farrell's creative fusion of Seventies psychedelia, metal, punk and proto-grunge; it established the band at the vanguard of what he called 'the alternative nation'. In the wake of the first Jane's Addiction hiatus, he went on to form the equally influential quartet Porno for Pyros.*

PAUL FERRARA *is a photographer who first met Jim Morrison and Ray Manzarek while at UCLA film school. In 1968, The Doors hired Ferrara to photograph the band and create their first official concert programme. He then went on to work with the band shooting footage for their film* Feast of Friends, *and later Jim's unreleased film* HWY. *Ferrara was also a musician, and The Doors (minus Jim Morrison) contributed to his songs 'One More Drink' and 'Hopi'.*

DAVID FRICKE *is a music journalist and the host of* The Writer's Block *on SiriusXM Radio. He was a senior editor and writer for* Rolling Stone *for more than three decades; was the American correspondent for the British weekly* Melody Maker *in the Eighties and Nineties; and has written for Britain's* MOJO *since the magazine's inception in 1993. He is a four-time winner of the ASCAP-Deems Taylor Award for excellence in music journalism and is a Grammy-nominated writer of album liner notes, contributing to releases by artists such as The Velvet Underground, The Byrds, Metallica, Paul McCartney and The Rolling Stones, while his extensive writing on The Doors includes essays featured in the 50th anniversary editions of the band's studio albums.*

BILL GRAHAM *was one of the most influential concert promoters in history. In the early Sixties, Graham moved to San Francisco where he founded the Fillmore and helped launch the careers of Janis Joplin, Otis Redding, Jefferson Airplane, The Doors, Cream, The Grateful Dead and more. He later opened the Fillmore East in New York, which also became a key venue for rock bands to play.*

RONNIE HARAN *is an actor, photographer, band manager and talent scout. It was she who first invited The Doors to play at the iconic Hollywood venue the Whisky a Go Go. There, as the house band, The Doors worked on perfecting their set and created a whole host of moments that have found their place in music history, including performing with Van Morrison and developing their epic song 'The End'.*

JAC HOLZMAN *is recognised as one of the key figures in the creation of the modern recording industry, having launched Elektra Records in 1950 while still at college. Artists that he signed to the label include Love, The Doors, The Stooges, The Paul Butterfield Blues Band, Queen, Bread, Theodore Bikel, Carly Simon and Harry Chapin. He discovered folk singer Judy Collins, and Jackson Browne's first recordings took place in the experimental studio Holzman greenlighted. In addition to Elektra, he founded the classical label Nonesuch Records. When Elektra and Nonesuch became part of the Warner Music Group, Holzman remained involved and he continues to work with Rhino Records, another Warner label, on their catalogue rereleases.*

PAUL KANTNER *was an American musician who co-founded the psychedelic rock band Jefferson Airplane. They had hit singles 'White Rabbit' and 'Somebody to Love', from the album* Surrealistic Pillow. *The band co-headlined with The Doors in Europe in September 1968. Many legendary artists opened for the Airplane, including Grateful Dead, Santana, The Doors, Jimi Hendrix, Creedence Clearwater Revival, The Who, Janis Joplin and Steve Miller. Jefferson Airplane was inducted into the Rock and Roll Hall of Fame in 1996. Kantner continued as a member of Jefferson Starship, Jefferson Airplane's successor band, until his death in 2016.*

JIM KERR *is the lead singer of the rock band Simple Minds. They have become one of the most successful bands ever to come from the UK, selling over 60 million records worldwide, having number one singles on both sides of the Atlantic, and number one albums the world over, including five in the UK.*

As a teenager, Kerr was deeply affected by The Doors' music after hearing it on the radio aged 11, and was determined and inspired to find out about other Californian counter-cultural icons. The Doors also helped inspire him to form his own band as an outlet for his artistic expression.

FRANK LISCIANDRO *is a filmmaker, writer and photographer. He studied filmmaking at UCLA and it was there that he became friends with Ray Manzarek and got to know Jim Morrison. His published books include* A Feast of Friends *(1991),* Jim Morrison: An Hour for Magic *(1993), and* Friends Gathered Together *(2014), a book of interviews with Morrison's friends.*

Lisciandro selected and co-edited Jim Morrison's writings for the collections Wilderness *(1989) and* The American Night *(1991). Beginning in 2010, he also collected, collated, edited and created a complete manuscript of Morrison's writings, published in 2021 as* The Collected Works of Jim Morrison *and in the Genesis publication* A Guide to the Labyrinth *(2022).*

VAN MORRISON *is a prolific singer-songwriter, with a career spanning seven decades. Morrison rose to prominence in the mid-Sixties as the lead singer of the Belfast R&B band Them, whose song 'Gloria' went on to become a garage rock staple and was covered by The Doors. Morrison has gone on to have a hugely successful solo career with hits including 'Brown Eyed Girl', 'Domino' and 'Blue Money'. Morrison continues to work on new material today.*

KRIST NOVOSELIC *is an American musician and political activist, best known as the bassist of the rock band Nirvana. Nirvana achieved massive success, earning multiple gold and platinum awards and touring the world at sold-out shows.*

After Nirvana disbanded following the death of its frontman, Kurt Cobain, in 1994, Novoselic formed Sweet 75 in 1995 and Eyes Adrift in 2002, releasing one album with each band. From 2006 to 2009, he played in the punk rock band Flipper, and in 2011 he contributed bass and accordion to the Foo Fighters song 'I Should Have Known'. He has been playing bass and accordion in the band Giants in the Trees since 2017. Novoselic identifies himself as part of the second generation of Doors fans, having discovered their music as a teenager in the late Seventies.

NILE RODGERS *is a songwriter, composer, producer, arranger, guitarist and co-founder of the disco band Chic. Rodgers pioneered a musical language that generated chart-topping hits like 'Le Freak', the biggest selling single in the history of Atlantic Records, 'I Want Your Love' and 'Good Times'.*

Rodgers cites The Doors song 'The End' as a significant influence for him, as it introduced him to psychedelia.

PAUL ROTHCHILD *was a producer at Elektra Records who was at the heart of The Doors' career, producing all of their albums before Jim Morrison's death apart from* L.A.Woman. *Unlike other producers of the time, whose word was the final authority in the studio, Rothchild worked alongside the band and took on board their suggestions. He was, however, also a perfectionist; his insistence on multiple takes eventually became a source of tension between him and the band. By* L.A.Woman, *Rothchild decided it would be best if he left The Doors to produce themselves.*

KATE SIMON *is a photographer whose work has documented the artists, poets and musicians in New York City during the Seventies and Eighties.*

Simon's work as a photojournalist brought her to England, where she first saw reggae musician Bob Marley. From taking live shots of the Exodus tour in 1977 and the Kaya *album cover, to recording candid and personal moments offstage, Simon had unique access to Bob Marley and the Wailers up until Marley's death in 1981. Simon's photographs of Bob Marley and the wider Jamaican scene are published in her book* Rebel Music *(Genesis Publications, 2004).*

It was while Simon was studying in Paris that she met Jim Morrison who helped her finish a term paper on Eugene O'Neill.

NANCY SINATRA *is an American singer and actress who forged a successful music career separate from that of her famous father, singer and actor Frank Sinatra. She cemented her status as a recording artist in her own right with her number one hit 'These Boots Are Made for Walkin'' in 1966, which became her signature song. In 1969, Sinatra covered The Doors' hit song 'Light My Fire'.*

SLASH *is lead guitarist of the hard rock band Guns N' Roses. He joined the band in 1985 and earned international acclaim for riffs on songs such as 'Sweet Child o' Mine'. Slash went on to form a series of bands during Guns N' Roses' latent periods, including Slash's Snakepit and a blues cover band called Slash's Blues Ball. In 2003, he formed Velvet Revolver, which was widely heralded as a successful comeback. Slash has also released two solo albums,* Slash *(2010) and* Orgy of the Damned *(2024).*

As a young child visiting Los Angeles, Slash remembers the impact of The Doors and 'Light My Fire', marking a pivotal moment in his life in music.

GRACE SLICK *has reigned over rock and roll for three decades in three bands: the legendary Jefferson Airplane, Jefferson Starship, and finally Starship. In 1968, at the height of the acid-laced psychedelic era, the Airplane shared the bill on a European tour with The Doors, a series of concerts that generated many outrageous tales of excess.*

Slick has also enjoyed a successful solo career, been recognised with multiple gold and platinum records, and created a handful of Top 40 hits. Her songwriting credits include rock classics 'Somebody to Love', 'White Rabbit' and 'Nothing's Gonna Stop Us Now'. For many, Grace Slick is the definitive female rock star.

PATTI SMITH *is an American singer, songwriter, poet, painter, author and photographer whose 1975 debut album* Horses *was one of the founding works of the New York punk rock movement. Smith has fused rock and poetry in her work. After seeing The Doors live in 1967, Smith was greatly influenced by the poetry and performance of Jim Morrison.*

VINCE TREANOR *was The Doors' tour manager from 1967 until the group disbanded. Working the stage at every concert, he built, maintained and repaired the band's equipment and sound system and was an older and essential member of their team.*

Treanor was offered the job of tour manager after he had helped The Doors' business manager, Bill Siddons, move and load the band's stage equipment after the infamous New Haven gig where Jim Morrison was maced by police and then arrested on stage. From then onwards, Treanor was on hand to witness Morrison's most renowned and controversial performances, such as the fateful Dinner Key Auditorium show in Miami.

MARK VOLMAN *is an American vocalist, guitarist and songwriter, best known as a founding member of the Sixties rock band The Turtles, and, along with his bandmate and friend Howard Kaylan, was a member of the Seventies rock duo Flo & Eddie, where he used the pseudonym Flo (short for The Phlorescent Leech). Volman also became a stand-out figure upon joining Frank Zappa's band, The Mothers of Invention. Volman became familiar with The Doors when The Turtles and The Doors regularly played on the same bill at the Whisky a Go Go.*

CREDITS

All reasonable effort has been made to identify and contact the copyright holders of the photographs and artwork in this publication. Any omissions are inadvertent.

A special thank you to Logan Janzen at MildEquator.com

PHOTOGRAPHY AND EPHEMERA

Photos © Alamy
Associated Press/Alamy Stock Photo
Pages 51, 315 (bottom right)
booksR/Alamy Stock Photo
Page 24 (right)
Glasshouse Images/Alamy Stock Photo
Page 318 (bottom right)
Globe Photos/ZUMA Wire
Page 181
Pictorial Press Ltd/Alamy Stock Photo
Page 202 (bottom left)
TCD/Prod.DB/Alamy Stock Photo
Page 318 (top left)
Universal Images Group North America LLC/Alamy Stock Photo
Page 303
Bill Waterson/Alamy Stock Photo
Page 123 (top left)

Photos © Gene Anthony/Wolfgang's Vault
Page 113

Photos © Edgar Bernstein
Pages 226 (middle), 228

Photos © David Burnett/Contact Press Images
Page 192

Photos © Jim Coke
Pages 116 (bottom left), 117 (top right)

Photos by Tom Copi © Doors Property, LLC
Pages 262, 263

Photos © John Densmore
Pages 15 (top left), 324

Photos © Henry Diltz
Pages 8, 28 (top), 30 (top right), 171 (bottom), 172, 173, 175, 177 (top), 215, 243, 246, 248, 249, 251 (top), 252 (top), 253 (top), 254, 255, 256, 257, 322

Photos © Doors Property, LLC / Courtesy of David Dutkowski
Pages 146 (left), 147

Photos © David Dutkowski
Pages 86, 87 (top), 154 (bottom left), 155 (left), 156 (bottom), 176, 177 (bottom), 196 (bottom)

Courtesy of David Dutkowski
Pages 12 (top left), 13 (middle bottom), 14 (top left), 16, 17 (bottom right, top left), 19 (middle left), 20 (bottom left, top right), 21, 22, 23 (top middle), 25, 26, 29 (bottom right), 31 (right), 42 (top right), 43 (top right), 44 (top left), 46 (left), 72, 92 (bottom right), 103, 104 (bottom right), 107 (right), 121 (bottom left), 132 (bottom right), 146 (right), 154 (top left, middle), 155 (bottom right), 156 (top left), 159 (bottom right), 209 (top left), 211 (bottom right), 213, 221 (top left), 230 (bottom right), 231, 250 (top), 252 (bottom left), 258 (top left), 261 (bottom left and right), 264, 265, 280, 281, 290 (bottom right), 302 (left), 305, 307 (left, bottom right), 339

Photos © Elektra Records
Page 109 (top)

Photos © Charles Everest, Cameronlife Photo Library
Page 268

Photos by Paul Ferrara © Doors Property, LLC
Pages 6, 7, 126, 127, 128 (top), 129, 130, 131, 132, 133, 134, 135, 136, 137, 139, 141, 142, 143, 144, 145, 148, 149, 150, 154 (top), 155 (top right), 157, 158, 159, 160, 161, 166, 167, 168, 169, 170, 182, 183, 208, 209 (top left, top right, bottom left), 216, 217, 221 (bottom), 223, 298

Photos © Janice Tallulah Fortier
Page 111

Photos © James Fortune/Rock and Roll Gallery
Pages 97 (top right), 98, 100 (top left, top right), 101 (right), 102, 104, 105, 321

Photos © Robert Freeman
Pages 24 (left), 27

Photos © Claude Gassian
Page 301

Photos © Getty Images
Bettmann/Getty Images
Pages 45 (top), 245 (top left)
CBS via Getty Images
Pages 118, 220 (top)
Kevin Cummins/Getty Images
Page 242 (top right)
Jasper Dailey/Michael Ochs Archives/Getty Images
Page 85
Elektra Records/Michael Ochs Archives/Getty Images
Page 325
Express Newspapers/Getty Images
Page 184
Charlie Gillett/Redferns
Page 323 (top left)
Keystone/Getty Images
Page 300 (left)
Earl Leaf/Michael Ochs Archives/Getty Images
Page 48 (top)
Elaine Mayes/Getty Images
Page 112 (middle)
Fred W. McDarrah/MUUS Collection via Getty Images
Pages 162 (bottom left), 164
Michael Montfort/Michael Ochs Archive/Getty Images
Pages 200, 201
Michael Ochs Archives/Getty Images
Page 63
Don Paulsen/Michael Ochs Archives/Getty Images
Pages 67 (top), 94
Jan Persson/Redferns
Pages 197, 203 (top), 205 (top), 206 (top)
Jack Rosen/Getty Images
Pages 110, 114, 115
Paul Ryan/Michael Ochs Archives/Getty Images
Page 165 (right)
Jack Smith/NY Daily News via Getty Images
Page 66 (bottom right)
Edmund Teske/Michael Ochs Archives/Getty Images
Pages 236 (left), 261 (top), 315, 316 (top)
TPLP/Getty Images
Page 307 (right)
Universal Archive/Universal Images Group via Getty Images
Page 314 (bottom right)
University of Southern California/Getty Images
Page 23 (bottom)
Santi Visalli/Getty Images
Page 66 (top right)
Chris Walter/WireImage
Page 185

Photos © Alyssa Greenberg
Pages 2, 14 (right), 15 (top right, bottom right), 17 (top right, middle right), 19 (top right, middle right), 206 (bottom left), 207 (bottom right), 260, 277, 286, 287 (top, bottom left), 288

Photos © Gary Greenberg
Page 319

Photos © Robert Haimer
Pages 304, 306, 308 (top), 309, 310, 311, 312, 313, 314 (top), 326

Photos © Bill Harvey
Pages 31 (left), 34, 35, 36, 37, 38 (top), 40, 41

Photos © Heritage Auctions / HA.com
Page 117

Photos by Jerry Hopkins © Doors Property, LLC
Pages 238 (top), 239, 240, 241, 274, 275 (top), 282 (top), 287 (middle), 289, 291

Photos by Kurt Ingham © Doors Property, LLC
Page 244

Photos © Art Kane
Page 124

Photos by Bobby Klein © Doors Property, LLC
Pages 4, 29 (top right), 39, 62, 74, 75 (top), 76, 78, 79, 80 (bottom), 81, 82, 83, 88 (top), 89, 95, 108, 116 (top), 119 (left), 120 (top left, top right)

Photos © Allan Koss
Pages 237 (top), 247 (top)

Photos © Robby Krieger
Page 13 (middle left)

Photos © David E. LeVine
Page 230 (top)

Photos © Frank Lisciandro
Pages 232, 233, 234, 272, 273, 276 (top), 278, 279, 284, 285

Photos © Chris Lohr
Pages 12 (top right, bottom), 13 (right), 69, 96, 97 (bottom left), 138, 140, 234 (bottom right), 235, 282 (bottom), 283

Photos © Los Angeles Public Library Photo Collection
Page 207 (top left)

Photos © Ray Manzarek
Page 29 (middle left)

Photos © Paul McCartney/Photographer: Linda McCartney. Under exclusive licence to MPL Archive LLP
Page 65

Courtesy of Mild Equator/Logan Janzen
With additional credit to Stev Bauske, Bruno Ceriotti, Ron Fritts, Simone Giuseppin, Roger Holzberg, Rainer Moddemann, Andreas B. Østeraas, Alfred Ruppert, Chris Simondet, Mark Smigel
Pages 13 (top left), 14 (bottom left), 17 (bottom right), 18 (bottom right), 23 (middle left), 29 (top right), 50, 66 (middle, bottom left), 68, 88 (bottom right), 99 (left), 101 (left), 112 (bottom left), 132 (middle), 149 (bottom right), 152 (top left), 162 (middle left), 165 (left), 171 (top), 174, 181 (top right), 187 (left), 190 (top left), 192 (top left), 199 (middle right), 203 (bottom right), 218 (top right), 219 (bottom right), 221 (top right), 226 (top left, bottom middle, bottom right), 229, 230 (top left), 236 (top right), 237 (middle right), 238 (bottom), 242 (middle right), 259 (top), 263 (left), 267 (top right), 270, 271 (bottom right), 294 (bottom right)

Photos © Thomas Monaster
Pages 67 (bottom left), 218 (bottom), 219 (right)

Photos by Michael Monfort © Doors Property, LLC
Pages 198, 199

Photos and writings © The George Morrison Family Partnership, L.P. and the Courson Family Enterprises, LLC
Pages 5, 18 (bottom left, top right, top left, middle left), 19 (bottom left, top left), 20 (middle right), 23 (top right, bottom right), 24 (bottom right), 28 (bottom right), 38 (bottom), 44 (middle left), 77 (top), 91 (bottom), 92 (left), 106, 107 (left), 109 (bottom), 115 (left), 120 (middle left, bottom left), 122, 123, 147, 151 (bottom right), 171 (middle), 175 (middle left), 184 (top left), 207 (top right), 214, 218 (bottom right), 220 (bottom left), 226 (middle right), 237 (bottom right), 241 (top right), 245 (top right), 248 (top right), 253 (bottom right), 266, 269, 276 (bottom left), 290 (top right), 291 (bottom left), 292 (top right), 293 (top right), 296 (bottom), 299 (bottom), 302 (top right), 316 (bottom), 317, 323 (bottom right)

Photos © Victor Moscoso
Pages 80 (top right), 89 (bottom left)

Photos by Nettie Peña © Doors Property, LLC
Pages 42 (left), 43 (left), 44 (bottom), 45 (bottom), 46 (right), 47

Photos by Barry Plummer © Doors Property, LLC
Pages 186, 267 (middle)

Photos © Rhino Entertainment Company
Page 43 (bottom right)

Photos © George Rodriguez
Page 52, 53, 55, 56, 57, 60

Photos © Ed Ruscha, courtesy of the artist and Gagosian
Page 32

Photos by Ethan Russell © Doors Property, LLC
Pages 187 (right), 188, 189, 190, 191, 193, 194, 195, 196 (top)

Photos © Klaus Schnitzer
Pages 87 (bottom), 204, 205 (bottom)

Photos © Shutterstock
Yale Joel/The LIFE Picture Collection/Shutterstock
Pages 152, 153, 162 (right), 163
VanoVasaio/Shutterstock
Page 300 (right)

Photos © Joe Sia/Wolfgang's Vault
Page 258

Photos by Gloria Stavers © Doors Property, LLC
Pages 90, 91 (top), 93, 121 (top), 297, 320

Photos © Guy Webster
Pages 33, 70, 71, 73

Photos © Gilles Yepremian
Pages 293 (top), 295 (top)

CONTRIBUTORS' TEXT

New interviews have been conducted with John Densmore, Robby Krieger and many of the contributors exclusively for this book. These have been supplemented with archive quotes from the following sources.

John Densmore
Riders on the Storm: My Life with Jim Morrison and The Doors, 1990; *Guardian*, 2002, 2018; Hall of Fame Series: Interview with John Densmore of The Doors, 2012; 'The Doors: Robby Krieger and John Densmore', *Broken Record with Rick Rubin, Malcom Gladwell, Bruce Headlam and Justin Richmond*, July 2022; *San Jose Rocks Podcast*, November 2022; *The Vinyl Guide Interview – For Record Collectors & Music Nerds,* January 2024; Raymanzarek.com; *No One Here Gets Out Alive*, 2001; *Doorstown: Jim Morrison and The Doors*, 2013; @JohnDensmore via X; *The Doors: Mr Mojo Risin': The Story of L.A. Woman*, 2012; Liner notes from *Other Voices/Full Circle,* 2015; *The Doors: Unhinged*, 2023; *When You're Strange*, 2009; *Musician*, 1991; *Classic Rock*, 2014

Robby Krieger
Interview with Jeff Alulis, *Live Talks Los Angeles*, 2021; *Guardian*, 2018; *Set the Night on Fire: Living, Dying and Playing Guitar with The Doors*, 2021; *No One Here Gets Out Alive*, 2001; *Jonesy's Jukebox*; *California Dreaming*; Interview with Matt Pinfield, 2022; 'The Doors: Robby Krieger and John Densmore', *Broken Record with Rick Rubin, Malcom Gladwell, Bruce Headlam and Justin Richmond*, July 2022; Interview with Joe Smith, *Off the Record*, March 1986; Reddit Q&A; *Follow the Music: The Life and High Times of Elektra Records*, 1998; Raymanzarek.com; 'Song Stories: Robby Krieger on the Origin of The Doors' "Peace Frog" & "Light My Fire", *Reverb*, June 2016; Interview with Musician's Hall of Fame & Museum, April 2020; *Classic Rock*, May 2014, August 2020; Liner notes from *Other Voices/Full Circle,* 2015

Ray Manzarek
Light My Fire: My Life with The Doors, 1998; *In the Studio with Redbeard*; *No One Here Gets Out Alive*, 2001; Rock and Roll Hall of Fame induction speech, 1993; 'Ray Manzarek Interview', *Pop Star Conversations*; 'The Guard Scene', WMCA Radio, 1967; *Follow the Music: The Life and High Times of Elektra Records*, 1998; Raymanzarek.com; Interview at State University of New York at Oswego, 1967; *The Doors: Box Set*, 1997; *The Doors: Mr Mojo Risin': The Story of L.A. Woman*, 2012; *The Tapes Archive*, 1998; Interview with Jeff Katz, 1973; Interview with Susan Marie, 2010

Jim Morrison
No One Here Gets Out Alive, 2001; *Circus*, 13 October 1970; Interview at State University of New York at Oswego, 1967; *Creem*, 1969; Interview with Canadian Broadcasting Corporation, 1970; *The Ultimate Collected Spoken Words 1967–1970*; *Hit Parader*, September 1967; *Los Angeles Free Press*, 1968; *Rave*, December 1968; *Rolling Stone*, 26 July 1969; *Rolling Stone*, 30 March 1970; *Doorstown: Jim Morrison and The Doors*, 2013; Interview with Geoffrey Cannon, 1968; Interview with Bob Chorush, 1970; *When You're Strange*, 2009; *Toronto Star*, 13 September 1969

Joan Didion
The White Album, 1979

Paul Ferrara
Flash of Eden, 2007

Perry Farrell
The Story of 'Break On Through' by The Doors, 2009

David Fricke
Liner notes from *Other Voices/Full Circle*, 2015

Bill Graham
No One Here Gets Out Alive, 2001

Jac Holzman
Thedoors.com; Liner notes from *Other Voices/Full Circle*; *Follow the Music: The Life and High Times of Elektra Records*, 1998; *A Guide to the Labyrinth*, 2022

Paul Kantner
The Doors: Live in Europe 1968, 1990

Paul Rothchild
Interview recorded at Englewood, NJ, March 1967; *BAM*, July 1981

Grace Slick
The Doors: Live in Europe 1968, 1990

Patti Smith
Just Kids, 2010

Vince Treanor
Jim Morrison: Friends Gathered Together, 2013; *Follow the Music: The Life and High Times of Elektra Records*, 1998; *Vince Treanor: Behind The Doors*, 2022; Recordmecca.com

Contextual words sourced from TheDoors.ai and written by David Dutkowski (pages 29, 46, 75, 122, 155, 156, 178, 224, 234, 238, 242, 301, 312, 313)

INDEX

CREATED BY GENESIS PUBLICATIONS

A SAFE PLACE
10/15/3/13
DOORS
MORRISON
HOTEL
SESSIONS
OUT TAKES
#1
BONDED ARCHIVES
12977828
DOO-
889
BEKINS
ACCOUNT #
BEKINS #
TAPE #
1310
the DOORS
ORIGINAL
DO NOT USE
STRANGE DAYS
DOORS
WEDNESDAY
15 JAN 69
9
DOO-
894
BEKINS
ACCOUNT #
BEKINS #

DOORS

I
ROCK
IS
DEAD

BONDED SERVICES
8047532

BM 69.39

A SAFE PLACE
3/22/3/9
PUP SOUND
381946

The DOORS
ORIGINAL
DO NOT USE